Praise for *Medical*

'So here we have our Butch and S
with heads full of stray cats and gentle giants, imaginative ruinours
surging up from hidden volcanoes, new lands glistening with life
in a Roger Dean dawn. For all those boys in RAF greatcoats with
stacks of LPs tucked under their arms waiting for MAN to come
on; all those girls who insisted you come with them to see King
Crimson at the Rainbow in 1973 and to their spiritual descendants,
wherever and whoever they may be'   Spider Stacey

'Not sure how two heads discussing weirdo music became the
feelgood music book of the year, but if the legendary Nurse With
Wound List blew your mind, Steve and Kavus's navigation of the
freak zone will warm your heart'   David Keenan

'*Medical Grade Music* is an extraordinary, vital trip to the heart
of the underground. Funny, deeply human and often surreal, it's
one of the most original and entertaining music books I've ever
read - but it's also one of the most touching'   Harry Sword

'Amiable, unusual and occasionally impenetrable . . . [Davis and
Torabi] recall their intertwining musical passions with self-effacing
wit and no small measure of detail'   *Mirror*

'Theirs is one of the great unlikely bromances, and their enthusiasm
for the music that they champion, as fans, curators and creators
fizz off the page with the kind of dilated, white knuckle spirit of
adventure that created it in the first place. This is a trip into a par-
allel musical universe and a great primer in the kind of ambitious
music that the more conservative punk/pop/rock narratives tend
to dismiss. More than this though, it's a roadmap on how to follow
your dreams (and trips) to their illogical conclusions and a paean
to friendship, and a rollicking read'   *Louder Than War*

'An enjoyable "pot-pourri of excess, poor behaviour and unfortunate lifestyle decisions"'   *Choice*

Steve Davis is a six-time World Snooker Champion, BBC snooker 'pundit' and well-known enthusiast for out-there music.

Kavus Torabi is a member of Gong, Cardiacs and many other underground psychedelic bands.

They met many years ago and forged a friendship through a shared love of cult experimental music. They became DJs – both on the live circuit and on their monthly 'Fire Shuffle' show on NTS – and they are now The Utopia Strong, a band with a celebrated album release and many gigs behind them. This is their story.

MEDICAL GRADE MUSIC

STEVE DAVIS
& KAVUS TORABI

(with the assistance of Ben Thompson)

WHITE
RABBIT

First published in Great Britain in 2021 by White Rabbit
This paperback edition published in 2022 by White Rabbit
an imprint of The Orion Publishing Group Ltd
Carmelite House, 50 Victoria Embankment
London EC4Y 0DZ

An Hachette UK Company

1 3 5 7 9 10 8 6 4 2

Image credits: p.1 Above © Georgina Torabi; p.2 Below © Paul Mingo; p.3 Above
© Cardiacs; p.3 Below © Kenneth Bray; p.4 Left © Martin Argles/*Guardian*;
p.4 Below © Martyn Goodacre; p.5 Above © Sam Shepherd; p.5 Left © Ashley Jones;
p.5 Right © Katie Davies; p.6 Above © Sean Pitching; p.7 Below © Stephen Heliczer;
p.8 Above © Simon B. Knights; p.8 Below © Katie Davies

ISBN (Mass Market Paperback) 978 1 4746 1951 6
ISBN (eBook) 978 1 4746 1950 9
ISBN (Audio) 978 1 4746 2184 7

Typeset by carrdesignstudio.com
Printed and bound in Great Britain by Clays Ltd, Elcograf, S.p.A.

MIX
Paper from
responsible sources
FSC® C104740

www.whiterabbitbooks.co.uk
www.orionbooks.co.uk

Contents

Introductions

Steve:

When we started working on this book, in the winter of 2017-18, Kavus Torabi and I were hosting our weekly radio show on Brentwood and Billericay's community station, Phoenix FM, and were soon to start a monthly one on the higher-profile NTS platform. The plan was to put together a learned (or at least, as learned as possible) primer of the kind of music we played on the radio and on our increasingly frequent DJ outings into the heady world of music venues and festivals.

We would select fifty-two artists who we regarded as essential – a few household names for balance but mostly left-field acts that we loved from the more obscure end of the spectrum – and argue our way to a consensus as to which recording represented the best 'way in' to their oeuvre. As well as baptising the uninitiated in the life-giving waters of Albert Marcoeur and Univers Zero, we hoped to make a general case for music that, while it might be perceived as 'difficult' or even – in some cases – unlistenable, could bring a huge amount of joy to those willing to make the effort to get to know it properly.

Our vision was that the victims who bought this book and the idea behind it would spend a week listening to each artist while devouring these pages and thus totally blow a whole year of their lives in the process. As if anyone has ever done anything so stupid. (I admit, I recently did a condensed version of that with Graham Bennett's book *Soft Machine: Out-Bloody-Rageous*, but that was only a two-week period!) Perhaps if our book had been published in March 2020, we might have had a few takers in this format.

We set about this task with the evangelical zeal of Victorian missionaries. At last, this was our chance to show the world why it was wrong not to regard the music of Henry Cow as one of the essential building blocks of human civilisation. We would have a lot of fun arguing the relative merits of different albums by Gentle Giant. And if we could open the ears of just a few readers to such previously esoteric delights then our efforts would have been fully rewarded.

That sense of a new world opening up inside our heads was a feeling music had given us many times over the years, and the more we wrote about the artists and records we loved, the more we noticed the human hinterland surrounding these moments of epiphany. From my teenage trips up to London to see Magma in the early seventies with my schoolfriend and musical 'influencer' Neil Rogers, to Kavus' induction into the magical realm of Voivod at the hands of a friend's sarcastic stepdad in the suburban waste-land of Plymouth fifteen years later, could these happy accidents of musical satori be separated from the places we had them in and the people we had them with? Quite possibly not.

Even as the ground shifted beneath our feet in terms of the structure and subject matter of the book, something yet more momentous was happening in our lives away from the laptop. Let's just say our plan for a rigorously researched and encyclopaedic guide to alternative music was overtaken by events. (No, not the fucking virus! Earlier than that.) Suddenly, our radio shows and DJ appearances had an unexpected rival for our attention as we found ourselves becoming two thirds (with Coil and Current 93's Mike York completing the team) of what we can now modestly assert is Britain's number one harmonium/guitar/bagpipes and modular synth power trio, The Utopia Strong.

For Kavus - a touring musician of many years' standing and at the time an integral member of the ongoing collective that is Gong - joining one more band was hardly the stuff of his wildest fantasies. However, for myself - an ex-professional snooker player in my early sixties with no musical training whatsoever and an occasional day job as a TV pundit - making an album and going out on the road playing live electronic music represented about

3

as sharp a turn in the road of life as could possibly be imagined.

We've had a lot of fun refining the brief of this book to reflect our entirely unexpected new reality - flipping the script to let the music tell its own story. We can only hope that the much less stratified and more personal volume you hold in your hand bears witness to the wonderfully unexpected places to which our obsessions have taken us. In the end, we went with the title *Medical Grade Music*. Why? Because we feel the music we listen to and are now physically involved in together is the good gear. Medical Grade Music is the stuff that separates the heads from the haircuts. Our self-titled debut album had already had the inscription printed on the back cover and it felt like this book was a continuation of that unfolding story. And besides, Mike York coined the phrase and we'd already had badges made and given them out at Glastonbury in 2019.

It's the story of our lives in alternative music, and as absurd and specific as many of the details of this story are, I hope there are things in here that will strike a chord with any reader who has ever obsessed over arcane points of rock lore. *We* are the type of people who would buy this book, but for the fact we already know what's inside. I'll probably buy it anyway! For Kavus and me, our DJ partnership was the way in to a creative adventure neither of us could possibly have anticipated, and I hope you'll enjoy joining us on a trip back down that yellow brick road.

Kavus:

In November 1980, on the cusp of turning nine, I watched Top of the Pops *to see Stray Cats performing 'Runaway Boys' and right there I knew what I wanted to do when I grew up. It was like the world went into 3D. Whatever Brian Setzer was, that's what I wanted to be, and it never changed.*

Having this epiphany so early in life was a godsend and if there was ever an element of choice, I don't remember making it. From that day on I've always known where I was going. I put up my sails on the sea of consequence, pointed the prow of the ship towards that wondrous liquid architecture of music and let the winds steer me where they would. With no real design, the journey brought me a deluge of beautiful friendships, ludicrous adventures and incredible memories that I'll carry to the grave. Strangest of all, it led me to six-time world snooker champion Steve Davis.

While this book charts my meteoric ascent from anonymity to obscurity, encompassing our love of music in a single volume posed Steve and me different challenges. For him, there's obviously a huge element of his personal history - the thing he is most known for - which has nothing to do with music, and therefore could be safely left out. Somehow I've managed to sustain my status as a marginal figure in the dark recesses for nigh on thirty years without straying much outside the Venn diagram marked 'music'. As a result, there's been a large amount of editing involved in my half. There are three whole chapters about my Plymouth metal band - Die Laughing - of whom I'm well aware only a tiny percentage of this book's readership will have heard, but relatively little about my time in Cardiacs, Knifeworld or Guapo.

My life has been spent among fellow artists, doing this because they have no choice - a welcoming community that has provided me with a network of support, encouragement and kindness for three decades. The price for following your muse and doing everything on your own terms is almost always to live in relative poverty, but that's been a price well worth paying. Not least because, for me, music has always drawn a larger circle around any arbitrary differences of age, gender, race, sexuality, class or background. It's much more important than that. It's the most important thing there is.

Chapter 1
Magma

Steve

The start of the swinging seventies didn't swing as much as was advertised, at least not for a shy, lanky, ginger-haired 14-year-old schoolboy living in a council flat in Abbey Wood, South-East London. I was just about to discover snooker at a holiday camp in Kent and my career path was, in hindsight, mapped out for me. It was obvious I was destined to become a multiple world champion of put-ball-in-hole-with-pointed-stick. I'd cried when I lost to some old fucker who kept snookering me in the semi-finals of the holiday camp event and who then further rubbed it in by announcing 'that's the name of the game!' I was a very young teenager for my age. Maybe we all were back then. Today's kids seem to be far more switched on than we seemed to be – but then again, as memories go, generally, mine is shit. My dad beat him in the final, though.

I do know that once I'd entered secondary school, my earliest dream job spec of becoming a professional footballer had evaporated owing to sheer lack of talent, combined with even less ability to grow muscles at the same rate as my peers. The closest thing I had to a hobby was playing Subbuteo. Could that primitive but exhilarating 'flick to kick' entertainment really be called a hobby? Especially when it was played on a living room floor at a mate's house and our only spectator was a Great Dane. At various intervals this canine behemoth would leave the terraces, lollop across the pitch and cut short some of our best painted strikers' careers. Occasionally, he'd smash his cock and bollocks into our faces when our guard was down, possibly distracted by a discussion about whether the crouching goalkeeper was better than the diving one. Some things you don't forget.

With a dog's genitals the biggest thing on our cultural horizon at that point, we were ideally placed to be introduced to the UK's latest musical craze, progressive rock. I'm not sure my musical interests would have taken exactly the same path had I not been fortunate enough to be thrown together with a musically like-minded soul, but Neil Rogers was my best mate at school and we were relatively inseparable. As the seventies unfolded, the musical landscape was taking on an interesting new shape and Roger Dean was in charge of mapping it out. While Subbuteo remained a constant in the early seventies, our mutual interest became music.

The first five pieces of vinyl I can remember buying were Neil Young's 'Heart of Gold', Argent's 'Hold Your Head Up' and *In Deep*, Man's *Back into the Future* and Gentle Giant's *In a Glass House*. I think the progression is clear for all to see.

I was a coin collector as a boy. I had all the old pennies from 1890-something up until the (then) present day (other than the holy grail 1933 rarity). But what can you do with coins, other than spend or look at them? Stamps are the same. OK, I grant you that you can lick them, but from a collecting aspect, apparently that gum stuff is the valuable bit. It's obvious, at least to me, that records are the best thing to collect in the world. There might be more financially beneficial collectors' markets available, like antiques or fine wine, but then you're back to just looking at them or trying to resist drinking them - and it turns out that the empty-bottle market is far less buoyant than Gordon Sumner first thought.

Like most musical nonconformists from that era, I was probably pointed in the right direction of these enchanting new musical vistas by John Peel, but it could also have been Alan 'Fluff' Freeman - an unheralded champion of the obscure at the time. Exactly how I managed to afford these records is also uncertain, as I don't recall having any disposable income and my mother can't recall ever dipping into her purse to fund my newly acquired addiction.

On reflection, the necessary modest upturn in my financial fortunes probably occurred at the age of sixteen, when I followed Neil Rogers into the world of Saturday jobs. The butchery department of F.J. Wallis supermarket in Woolwich was the job on offer – twenty-eight pence an hour for ten hours at the weekend. In fact, it was shortly after getting that job that I visited the local record shop to buy the Neil Young album, *Harvest* – £2 was the asking price. That was three quarters of my pay packet! So I bought the single instead for something like forty pence.

It was once I'd made my big money, pre-Bosman transfer to Makro's Charlton cash and carry as a barrow boy at £1 an hour, that weekends started to take on a new shape. I was loaded. A concert in central London was no longer out of the question. The journey started at Abbey Wood station with its wonderful memory of the adjoining railway crossing, sadly a thing of the past, although I wonder how many there are still around the country.

I'd love to say that Abbey Wood's location on the train line somewhere between London and Canterbury might have played a small part in helping me to access the wonderful pastoral jazz rock sounds of the Canterbury scene. Unfortunately, to claim that you could hear the sound of Caravan's *In the Land of Grey and Pink* if you put your head down to the ground by the railway tracks would be a total exaggeration, as the need to change at Gillingham might have introduced too much resistance to the signal flow. But it did feel like I was in the right part of the country for the changing musical times.

Back then, platform shoes, Oxford bags and Ben Shermans were the height of fashion, but the jury was still out on the Afghan coat. Having more or less nailed my musical colours to the mast by frequenting increasing numbers of left-field gigs, it became apparent that even though I wasn't a hippie and wouldn't have known what to do with a bong or block of hash had I been gifted some, musically my yellow brick road was starting to morph into what Gong fans know as the Oily Way.

So I followed Neil Rogers' lead in his sartorial as well as his musical experimentation and we each invested in a reeking coat of many colours. It was only a number of years later that I discovered that the Afghan coat wasn't actually made from the hide of the

Afghan hound. It's interesting to consider the uproar that would have ensued were dogs - as opposed to sheep - bred to produce Afghan coats, regardless of the sheep's delight at having their load shared by man's best friend.

Our cutting-edge garments were great at a concert at the Marquee in Soho but not so acceptable in the queue for the fish and chip shop in Abbey Wood where once, while waiting for a takeaway for our train journey (pickled onions in proper malt vinegar, not that see-through crap) I remember being accosted by a woman who ripped into us and called us 'queers'. It's crazy to think that had this statement had any validity, it would have been several more years before we'd have been free to indulge in such activities without fear of legal stricture. As it was, her vitriolic torrent of abuse came as quite a shock. Thankfully, the UK is a far more tolerant society these days . . . !

In terms of its impact on the rest of my life, this minor incident would be dwarfed by having to deal with the consequences of another growing source of nationwide outrage. This new-fangled prog rock was the devil's music as far as parents were concerned and listening was banished to the bedroom. Radio Caroline had been bad enough during the sixties, but this was a new low. What parents couldn't avoid, though, was girls' hair growing on boys' heads. Fathers in particular were struggling to come to terms with this unmanly fashion statement. Neil's parents were particularly length-sensitive, I seem to recall. For me, having ginger hair was a curse regardless, but long hair seemed the lesser of the two evils compared to the skinhead look, which attracted not only parental disdain, but also risked unwanted attention from the Old Bill.

Our cutting-edge musical tastes also ensured that while not quite banned from using the turntable in the Abbey Wood Comprehensive school sixth form common room, my access to it was certainly unfairly restricted, as was Neil's. Not many 16-year-olds were into Captain Beefheart, Hatfield and the North, and the even more left-field Henry Cow. The vast majority of our schoolmates preferred boogieing to Steve Harley & Cockney Rebel to joining our earnest

11

attempts to decipher the latest Frank Zappa, NEU! or Third Ear Band release. So the experience of having our minds properly blown by live music in a large crowd of like-minded people was one we were definitely ready to explore. But on the night of that exciting eventuality, it was the last thing we were expecting.

The seismic impact that the December 1973 release of Magma's third album *Mëkanïk Dëstruktïẁ Kömmandöh* (their first on A&M Records) would have on my musical consciousness took a little while to become apparent. The album was initially championed by Steve Lake from *Melody Maker* and because of its major label association (and maybe sixties impresario Giorgio Gomelsky's involvement), it got plenty of press here in the UK. One of my inner circle of friends bought the album and was smitten but my initial response wasn't so positive.

I'll always have a soft spot for the then Waddington's board game Risk. Not because the game is any good – if I remember rightly, it was actually quite boring – but such was the rock 'n' roll lifestyle I lived back then that a bunch of us going round to a mate's house for some dice-determined world domination would often be my best option for a night's worth of entertainment. The riskiest thing that happened that night was my mate's decision to put *Mëkanïk Dëstruktïẁ Kömmandöh* on his turntable.

At the time I thought it was impenetrable and was far more interested in trying to invade Poland, so a few months later, when Magma were advertised to play at the Camden Roundhouse, it wasn't even them I was intending to see.

Regardless of the villainesque role that Richard Branson plays now, back then, Virgin Records were our heroes. The success of Mike Oldfield's *Tubular Bells* meant that every other label was championing prog rock and Canterbury jazz rock was cool. Well, they were in my circle of (maybe three at most) teenage South-East London prog-heads. Robert Wyatt was soon to join the Virgin crew and create the masterpiece *Rock Bottom*, but we were well ahead of the curve having discovered his involvement prior to this with free-form legends Soft Machine. Their second and third albums (*Volume Two* and *Third*) were fixtures on our turntables and while *Fourth* and *Fifth* didn't get as much of our attention, *Six* captured our collective imagination, albeit Wyatt had long gone by then.

Bassist Hugh Hopper's reaction to *Six* seemed to have been less favourable than ours as he left the band immediately after this recording. In 1973, he put out his first solo album, *1984*. Hugh was notoriously as bad at maths as George Orwell, but as loyal Softs disciples, we had no option but to acquire it. We were duly smitten by Hugh's 'fuzz bass' - although in truth, at the time I didn't have a clue what that meant.

At this point we would have happily followed Hugh to the ends of my schoolmate's dining table. Luckily, Hugh had just joined Canterbury jazz rockers Isotope as their bassist and they had a gig at the Camden Roundhouse. Isotope were supporting Magma, and the plan was to watch them and then slope off before the headliners, to find a publican who wasn't too bothered about underage drinking and then be certain of catching the last train home. Now, I'm not sure if Robert Burns would have been into Magma - as a patriotic Scot, I suppose he'd have preferred Marillion - but his poetic reference to 'the best laid plans of mice and men' was definitely relevant here. Curiosity got the better of us concerning Magma and as this bunch of black-clad weirdos, sporting strange medallions, descended on the Roundhouse, our evening went all 'agley' (as Rabbie would have said) and we sat, jaws dropped, while they totally rewired our brains.

The spectacle of Klaus Blasquiz in full demonstrative vocal flow was truly mesmerising. I remember staring open-mouthed when one of Jannick Top's bass strings snapped and his hands just continued as a blur - because the show must go on. And then there was the leader of the pack - Magma's shamanic drummer Christian Vander, with steam from his body rising up into the dome of the Roundhouse. He was an animalistic presence - a magnetic visionary, holding court behind the drums. The whole night is etched in my mind in a spiritual way and we left the Roundhouse in disbelief at what we'd witnessed, Isotope a distant memory. I haven't got a clue how we got home. It didn't matter how long they'd played for, I'd have stayed there forever - and in a way, I have.

Chapter 2

Stray Cats

Kavus

My mum was a nurse from Hull who moved to Iran, where she met my dad, a doctor, in a village called Ghorveh. I was born in Tehran in December 1971. My dad took our names from the Shahnameh, *the Persian book of ancient kings from the pre-Islamic Zoroastrian era. I often wondered why I'd never heard of another Kavus. Years later, my wife, Dawn, read the* Shahnameh, *looking for a similarly alluring Persian name for our expected offspring (having an unusual name never did me any harm, I reasoned). Reading the chapter on Kai (King) Kavus, it transpired he was a vainglorious failure. A self-obsessed egotist who frittered his rulership on folly. O cruel destiny, must you chide me so?*

My first language was Farsi, not that I can remember any of it now. The three of us moved to the UK to live with my mum's parents in Hull in 1973. The plan, initially, was for my dad to qualify as a geriatrician over here, then return and set up a life for us there, but an increasingly volatile Iran and the events that culminated in the Islamic revolution of 1979 meant that by the time he qualified, there was no way we were returning.

Throughout the mid-seventies, we moved regularly around the north of England to wherever there was available work, from one hospital accommodation to another. I can trace my complete absence of both patriotism and sense of belonging to a specific place to having never settled anywhere for any length of time until I was eight years old – something for which I'm considerably grateful. I can feel at home anywhere, really.

Before arriving in Plymouth 1977, I had lived in Hull, York, Nuneaton and Sheffield. We finally got our own house in Charlton Road behind the army barracks in Crownhill, Plymouth in 1978 and were joined by my cousin from Iran, Arash, in 1979. His dad had died and his mum moved to America, so our Iranian grandparents brought him up, but following the revolution it was decided that life might be better for him with us. Arash was a couple of years older than me. It was a strange dynamic – sort of like having another brother. As far back as I can remember, I loved music, but until the age of eight my exposure had been largely limited to TV themes and hymns. My favourites were 'O Come, All Ye Faithful' – particularly the descant part in the last verse, which still makes me go all funny – and the music from American cop show CHiPs. I loved the latter so much that I invented a form of musical notation and 'scored' it onto a piece of card (the sort used to stiffen a school shirt), which I kept under my pillow in case I ever forgot how it went. I would make up theme songs for my toys and always got choked up on the instrumental refrain for a plastic Fisher Price pilot I had christened 'Professor Pear'.

Soon after we settled in Charlton Road, we acquired a piano. I never took to lessons but would use it to make up my own tunes and can still remember how to play my first 'composition', 'Highway Hotel'. I don't ever actually play it, of course, because it's rubbish.

Back in Iran, the Torabi side of my family was status-obsessed, a common Persian trait, and from my understanding, to be a musician was considered a low, shameful job, ranking somewhere between prostitute and dustman. Certainly this was my dad's viewpoint and one he'd express regularly over the decades to come. Although my mum came from a family of keen amateur musicians, the gift had either eluded her or she chose to ignore it. They owned four LPs between them (The Best of John Williams, The Very Merry Macs, The Best of Johnny Mathis and Arthur Lyman's Taboo) and in all the time I was growing up, I never heard them play a single one.

No one I knew listened to pop music. It was the boring bit that punctuated cartoons on Saturday morning television and in our house, showing off was considered a heinous vice and these frivolous pop stars the worst practitioners.

How suddenly that changed, like an act of subterfuge, as if pop were using whatever nefarious means it could to infiltrate the Torabi defences. To get us out of the house and keep us busy during the summer holidays of 1980, my mum insisted we participate in a scheme with the local *library. I was a keen reader, but this sounded like a drag. The library issued a weekly worksheet with questions and projects to keep children occupied. Most of the topics were the usual Devonian fare (Sir Francis Drake, the Plymouth Dockyard, the destruction of the city centre during the Blitz), but one particular week, the sheet turned its attention to pop music, asking questions such as 'Who were The Fab Four?', 'Who was the King of Rock?' and 'Which TV programme on Thursday night is unmissable to the pop fan?'*

While we could get the first two answers, the third question required us to consult the TV listing in the Plymouth Evening Herald. *There it was, at 7.30 p.m. on BBC One, right after* Tomorrow's World. *We'd never heard of* Top of the Pops *before, but our interest was piqued and that week, we decided to tune in. For both Arash and me, it was instant love. We tuned in the following week, then the next.* Top of the Pops *became our focal point. While the first couple of months gave us a good flavour of what pop had to offer, I was ill-prepared for the events of that November.*

Following Tommy Vance's introduction, the camera swung over to a trio of skinny outlaws all dressed in black with wild hair. Leather-jacketed Lee Rocker on the right slapped an upright bass while Slim Jim Phantom stood up at a drum set that consisted merely of a kick drum, snare and ride cymbal. What was this stripped-down synergy? In between them, with an impossibly high peroxide quiff, holding a big Gretsch guitar, was a male Marilyn Monroe. Still a boy at twenty-two, thin, pale and tattooed, he was disarmingly beautiful. Having lived a mere nine years on the earth at the time, I didn't know what my exact feelings towards Brian Setzer were and still don't, but I knew in a flash what I wanted to be when I grew up, and it was no longer a spy.

The look, the sound, the attitude – everything about Stray Cats seemed arch, deliberate and correct. From that moment, the world I had grown up in seemed slow, staid and stale – I wanted out of whatever it was that I was in. I wanted to live like them, be like them. And when I found out the circumstances behind their arrogant, dangerous-looking brand of cool – how they'd had to move to England and squat in Brixton before getting the recognition they were initially denied in the USA – I wanted to dress in black, sing and play the guitar, and live in a hovel in London. Boy, did I ever get my wish.

'Runaway Boys' was a swinging stomp built around a descending guitar riff. Its tale of a dissatisfied underage youth spoke to me directly. What was it about them that affected me so much? They didn't look or sound like anything else around at that time and, having no prior knowledge of the history of rock, I was unaware that their style was a throwback to an earlier era. Stray Cats made the most important, vital music I had ever heard. They gave my life meaning and for the next year and a half were all I could think about.

The excitement of discovering that theirs was a job that grown-ups could have was quite the revelation. After Stray Cats, I no longer experienced music as an observer – once I'd heard 'Runaway Boys', all I ever wanted to do was to be a musician and be in a band. In retrospect, I feel fortunate to have found my thing at such an early age: pop music would be the passport that got me out of my dreary existence.

The early eighties was a fantastic era for music and I'm grateful to have stepped aboard the pop train at the dawn of this radiant decade. At that time, Top of the Pops was dominated by exciting and vibrant British bands, the charts were full of Madness, Bow Wow Wow, The Beat, Haircut 100, XTC, Altered Images and The Specials, and this was also the dawn of synth pop – The Human League, Depeche Mode: I loved them all. The USA hardly seemed to get a look-in and when it did, the music – Stray Cats excepted – seemed corny, slick and boring in its blue-jeaned earnestness. I had no idea who Rick Springfield, Kim Carnes, Chicago and Bruce Springsteen were aimed at, but I knew it wasn't me.

From 1980 onwards, I have always had a means of remembering exactly what I was doing at any arbitrary point in my history simply by recalling what music was being released or, more recently, what music I was releasing. My listening from month to month, year to year, has acted as a far less embarrassing alternative to keeping a diary.

In line with my all-engulfing obsession, my Action Men Paul and Steve (gtr/vox and bass/vox respectively) had formed a band with Evel Knievel on drums, his fucked arm predating Def Leppard's Rick Allen. I made instruments out of cereal packets, while their military vehicle had become a tour bus. The tours generally consisted of two venues: one under Arash's bed, the other under mine.

Each Sunday I'd set the band up on the mantlepiece of our shared bedroom and listen to the top forty rundown on Plymouth Sound, our local radio station, while imagining Paul, Steve and Evel Knievel performing the songs. I moved on from that station fairly quickly – a few short years later, they'd regularly play a jingle that boasted 'Plymouth Sound! No Rap!'

The first album of my own was Stray Cats' sensational self-titled debut, which I bought from Plymouth's WHSmith with my Christmas money. My second purchase was in November the following year, when their rapid-fire follow-up – Gonna Ball – was released and I involuntarily had my first mystical experience.

On first listen, I was shocked by a supernatural occurrence during the guitar solo of 'Little Miss Prissy'. Brian Setzer did something for about three seconds that had such a profound effect on me. For whatever reason the strange, blurry lick against the backbeat temporarily reversed the structure of existence, altered the rules of life. Perhaps the room changed dimensions or maybe a portal opened. I can't describe what came over me, but something was fundamentally modified during those brief seconds. I dashed over to my little jumble sale record player, the stylus modified with a one-pence piece Sellotaped to it, lifted the needle and popped it back a few grooves. There it was again.

I repeated this action many times. While it no longer triggers the same reason-questioning response, that part of the song still makes my pulse race. This brief glimpse of eternity lit up a circuit which I struggled to rationalise (it didn't have this effect on anyone else I played it to), but was the beginning of a greater understanding about the power and importance of music – the moment I realised, 'Oh, so it can do that'.

The Mad Bats (Mk 1) came about owing to the twin obsessions of Arash and me. His favourite band was Madness and we wanted to combine the two. Mad Cats sounded too generic to our refined ears, what with The Polecats being a thing.

The initial Mad Bats duo consisted of Arash on guitar/vocals and me on drums/vocals. Because Arash had been given a cheap three-quarter-

length nylon-stringed Spanish guitar, this meant it was his instrument, so instead I fashioned a snare out of a biscuit tin filled with dried beans wrapped in cling film and a bass drum made from a gypsum render tub. Played with cricket stumps, it was one hell of a kit.

The Mad Bats (Mk 1) played strictly original music. The formidable Torabi/Torabi songwriting team – I was nine, Arash was eleven – amassed two songs: 'Rockin' Alley' ('Rockin', rockin' alley, ride a Raleigh') and 'Regret' ('Regret yeah, yeah, regret your life. Regret yeah, yeah, Re-ger-et').

Despite the unquestionable quality of my chosen instrument, it was a disappointment to discover that the drums weren't for me. I just couldn't make my limbs reproduce what was in my head. What I would have given to be a drummer. To this day still, but even during the days of The Mad Bats (Mk 1) I knew that I would never be Slim Jim Phantom.

Once I'd borrowed Arash's guitar (later christened 'The Bear'), I set about writing tunes. My mum attempted to show me some basic C, G and D chords from her brief foray into the guitar in her early twenties, but I wasn't sure that this was the kind of musical foundation I required. She would announce, almost with pride, that she'd missed out on the great social upheaval of the late sixties. Given how little she understood of rock 'n' roll, I assumed these 'square' chords would be unhelpful. Instead, I barred my entire index finger across the neck and moved it up and down chromatically in a fashion that I was convinced sounded like rockabilly. My first composition, 'Discordant Wasp', was a great success in that respect.

We split the band shortly afterwards, but I couldn't bear the idea of wasting such a good name, so I formed The Mad Bats (Mk 2) with my schoolfriends Tim Morsley (keys) and Paul Tresise (drums). On guitar and vocals, I assumed the position of frontman and designed a band logo – the M and B fashioned to resemble a treble and bass clef.

The Mad Bats (Mk 2) were a far more focused affair. We were managed by my friend Matt Tiller, who used to pay us five pence each per rehearsal, giving me unrealistic expectations of the manager's role later on. We rehearsed in the school music room during first break as often as we were allowed. The drum kit this time involved two tiny bongos, played with plastic mallets, and a hand cymbal that Matt, in his role as manager, held for Paul in lieu of a stand.

Paul Tresise was a natural and while Tim Morsley took a more free-form, improvisational approach to piano, he was a great lyricist, which left me to concentrate on the music. Between the two of us, we cooked up quite a catalogue. The topical number, 'Rhodesia' ('I went to Rhodesia (x2) On a Laker Sky Train (x2)') , the more personal 'Stop Being So Stubborn' ('Stop being so stubborn or you'll have . . . you'll have to go home') and our theme tune 'Mad Bats' ('We're Mad Bats, we're Mad Bats and we fly in the dead of night (Alright)') were obvious classics and while we never played live, I still have a cassette of one of those rehearsals that I never need to hear again.

Chapter 3

Man

Steve

For me there has always been a special excitement about visiting a record shop. Of course it's the music itself that matters, not the format it arrives in, but my favourite medium - like many people reading this, I assume - is the vinyl LP. The romance and anticipation and then just the sheer therapeutic joy of flicking through racks of albums has never left me, even half a century after I began to do it.

I'm not sure I can fully verbalise the roots of this fascination, but the door to a record shop has always seemed like a gateway to infinite possibilities. It wasn't only the chance of finding a record from your wants list or perhaps stumbling upon a rare record that had been priced up cheaply. Far more importantly, there was also the dream of discovering something that you weren't aware of, either via a recommendation from the vast knowledge a shop owner accumulates, or on almost as many occasions from a like-minded soul flicking through vinyl in the next rack. Even if you don't walk out clutching some polyvinyl chloride under your arm, the process is restorative.

The internet has been an amazing invention, although like many of us, I'm sure, I sometimes pine for the world that preceded it. Artificial intelligence is increasingly infiltrating our lives, probably far quicker than most could have imagined. Governments are spying on their populations and we are sleepwalking down a path that, even within my lifetime, will be a life dominated by algorithms telling us what we're going to be doing tomorrow. But far worse than that is Discogs . . .

Ebay was bad enough, but now we have the definitive guide to record collecting. Why is that a bad thing? Let's face it, Discogs is fantastic. I wish I'd thought of it: a record collector's ultimate resource for checking exactly what issue of any LP, CD, cassette, minidisc, cylinder and even digital file you may own or desire. It's constantly being updated (free of charge . . . for Discogs!) by anyone who logs on. In the words of Sam McPherson, drummer of the rock sensation Dewey Cox, 'it makes even your worst record collecting days amazing . . . it's a nightmare!'

The beauty for the creators of Discogs was that once they reached escape velocity, they were able to blow away every other record-selling site. If you want to let the market decide on a price then obviously eBay is the option, but for the serious collector, then Discogs is the daddy. Part of the fun of collecting is getting the occasional bargain, but the consequence of having everything at your fingertips is that everyone knows the price of everything. And while there are still many items that are not catalogued on Discogs, the monster grows every day.

Of course, nobody begrudges the record shop or record-fair seller making money, but the days of getting a steal have gone, unless you stumble upon someone not paying attention to current prices. Ebay's history of completed items is there for all to peruse, as is Popsike, an independent record-pricing aggregator, for more detailed analysis of trending auction prices.

It were all different when I were a lad. But I didn't care back then. I knew nothing about the collectability of an album – I just wanted to listen to it. My first experiences of the heady thrill of vinyl acquisition took place within the not altogether welcoming portals of Furlongs, the best record shop in Woolwich in the early seventies. To be fair to the exceptionally grumpy proprietor, we were nightmare customers.

With limited funds (the bane of the existence of every would-be rock connoisseur) uppermost in my early teenage mind, it was vital to make every purchase count. Accordingly, my abiding memory of that shop is of us taking records back there because we'd heard the odd pop or a click. Considering the quality of the equipment we played these records on, the poor bastard who owned the shop had every right to be miserable and downtrodden.

It was with justifiable trepidation that we approached this forerunner of Larry David in the hope of a refund. Sometimes he reluctantly agreed with us, but on other occasions, much to our dismay, he refused to exchange our allegedly damaged copy for a pristine one.

The other local retail outlet that got my consumer dollar early on was Twisted Wheel on Plumstead High Street. This was where I'd buy my number-one album of all time, Magma's *Köhntarkösz* and also 'Mekanik Machine' – the Jannick Top-penned growling monster of a 7-inch from the same recording session that never fitted on the album. But as soon as I had funds enough to travel up to the West End, Saturdays would see me making my way to the back of a shoe shop and up the spiral staircase (was it spiral or was I just giddy with excitement?) to the coolest record shop in London – Virgin Records in Oxford Street.

There was a buzz in that place, not entirely unconnected to the presence of a couple of decks you could audition records on. I'm sure many other shops supplied this facility to prospective purchasers back then but, at least in my very limited experience, this was a groundbreaking innovation. And they sold imports! Not so much the Japanese holy grail of pristine virgin vinyl but certainly stuff from the USA, and titles that no other record shops were stocking . . . It was a treasure trove.

But there was bad news brewing for my musical enthusiasms in the shape of a rival force that was starting to compete for my out-of-school-hours leisure time. Snooker was getting its foot well and truly in the door. In my early days of being besotted with the game – in my mid-teens – I was only playing on a full-size table at weekends, tagging along with my father when he went to the local working men's club to pursue his hobby. Midweek nights after school I was resigned to getting my quarter-size Joe Davis snooker table out and balancing it on the kitchen table.

Although it was a small table (six foot by three), it was still far too big for our kitchen space and this meant the top of the table, where you'd spot the black ball, had to butt up against the wall.

I'll leave it to historians of the game to speculate on the impact this had on my technique, but in truth what I was playing at that time wasn't so much snooker as my own version of bar billiards.

Not that I needed any more entertaining, but I'd have my cassette tape player on as background music just to add a bit of extra atmosphere. If you ask someone who their favourite band is and what their top ten albums of all time are, you'll no doubt get an answer. However, there's every chance that their life-listening history will be at odds with those choices. Sadly (or in fact delightfully), the seventies didn't have an iTunes play count to keep a watchful eye over our personal statistics, but back then the record I could never get enough of was *Back into the Future* by the maverick Welsh blues rock band, Man.

This album was the soundtrack of the mid-seventies for me, well, along with a shedload of Magma, Gentle Giant and Canterbury scene albums. My memories of those nightly kitchen practice sessions are inextricably tied up with such Man standards as 'Never Say Nups to Nepalese' and 'Ain't Their Fight' – and these along with their monumental nineteen-minute live version of 'C'mon' were the flavours emanating from our kitchen more often than even my mother's excellent spaghetti bolognese.

If you ask me what exactly it was about the music of Llanelli's rock 'n' roll axe-wielder Deke Leonard and his hirsute cohorts that so appealed to me back then, I'd be hard-pressed to tell you. Maybe it was listening to 'C'mon' and imagining what it would be like to be in the band onstage. Apart from it being a futile desire, I'm not saying I would like to go 'back into my own future', but if you could have multiple futures concurrently then I'd be up for that. Obviously I'd slap the hand of the divine giver and gladly settle for the one life and career I did receive, but of course the grass is always greener. I often wonder what it would have been like to have trodden another path. I'm probably not alone in nominating that of a musician, living a youthful life of unabashed excess and walking on the edge as my first alternative choice.

There was certainly no clue to my yen for the wilder shores of rock experimentation in my other choice of favoured pastime as a teenager.

Although often erroneously lumped in with darts as a 'pub game', in truth, snooker's natural terrain was either the social clubs or the billiard halls. Far from the 'den of iniquity' image that has tended to cling to 'billiard' halls as they were then called, most snooker clubs of that era didn't even have alcohol licences. They tended to be located above Burton Menswear in the high street and the only refreshments available were cups of tea or coffee. In the mid-seventies, snooker and frequenting snooker clubs was seen as a way of wasting one's time instead of whatever wasn't wasting one's time. Ultimately I, on the other hand, was wasting my time only up until the point where I started making a bundle of money from it.

OK, there might have been a little bit of hustling among the hard-core who were trying to get a few quid to keep playing as much as anything else – but when I played with my father at the social club, no gambling ever took place . . . only drinking, but it was social drinking, not the iniquity kind. Anyway, I was underage, so at the weekend I might sneak a couple of lager and limes at best. However, even that got knocked on the head when I started to learn to drive. It took me a while to realise why my father was so keen on me getting a provisional driving licence the moment I turned seventeen. The vast majority of my lessons were return journeys home from the club. Alcohol at home didn't exist like it does today, though – at least not in our house.

My father listened to a fair bit of progressive rock during the seventies, but he was usually asleep in the passenger seat, teaching me to drive at the time. I'm not sure if when you're asleep you can assimilate music, but bombarding people with more esoteric stuff during their shut-eye might be a good way of improving their capacity to appreciate it. Maybe the walls of rejection aren't immediately put up in sleep mode. Either way, my dad's continued resistance to hypnopaedia due to his dislike of the band Egg during his waking hours suggested that the benefits of this strategy were, at best, overrated.

Music was never played in snooker clubs – you weren't even allowed to whistle. Some old clubs still had signs that said 'No whistling, no coin tossing on the table, no spitting' – those were the three golden rules of the snooker club, not that tuberculosis seemed to be that much of an issue in the seventies. Oh! and of course it was a given, just like in all the romantic scenes in old films, that you should have one foot on the floor at all times. But music and snooker? Generally, having feet in two different camps would probably prevent both from being mastered at the same time. There are exceptions. I do know that John Egan, one-time member of the Ozric Tentacles, has a personal best break of 133 and made his first century against the snooker pro Tony Meo. I'm not aware of any other century-makers in the pro musical ranks, though.

Unlike alcohol, singing along to Man was tolerated in my mother's kitchen and that's what I used to do as I practised, little knowing that I was wiring up my mind for a lifetime of listening as well as honing my skills at the hobby that would become my career.

Coming a close second in the kitchen practice session singalong memory-stakes was Caravan's unchivalrously titled fifth album *For Girls Who Grow Plump in the Night*. As a chin-stroking exercise (and one I'd also agree with), the consensus entry point to the Canterbury-based cornucopia that is Caravan's career would be 1971's *In the Land of Grey and Pink*, but my internal play count would definitely favour their later album, which for me was one of the enduring hits of 1973. Many people would disregard Caravan once Richard Sinclair left, but while the band might have become more 'straight' and less psychedelic when Pye Hastings took control, I'd say that *For Girls Who Grow Plump . . .* was my not-so-secret guilty snooker karaoke pleasure.

Chapter 4
Iron Maiden

Kavus

What little heavy metal I'd heard in the early eighties seemed like a bit of a joke, although I quite liked Motörhead's 'Ace of Spades' because the guitars sounded like vacuum cleaners, which we thought was hilarious. I'd ask Arash, 'Hey, wanna hear the new Motörhead single?' while driving the upright Hoover repeatedly into the skirting, shouting, 'The ace is played! The ace is played!' Aside from that, our exposure had been limited to AC/DC's 'Let's Get It Up', which I thought sounded old and plodding, Saxon ('And the Bands Played On') and Gillan ('New Orleans'), neither of whom could be taken seriously, owing to them having members who were either balding or sported moustaches. Or both.

Then, on a Thursday evening in February 1982, a metamorphosis occurred which, four decades on, has yet failed to reverse. A bewitchment so powerful it dramatically reshaped me. How could I have known? That cursed evening when the die was cast, an eldritch spell worked its way inwards, razing all in its path. A hex so forceful it proclaimed itself by relegating Stray Cats from prime mentors to mere irrelevance. Then it really set to germinating.

I was in a dark, hateful mood - an open invitation to the Prince of Darkness right there - having been forbidden from watching Top of the Pops. Whatever the minor infraction on my part was that led to such drastic disciplinary action on that cold, fateful night of revelation has long since been forgotten.

O feeble chastisement! You know Apollyon not.

Arash watched the weekly chart show, a little guiltily, from the adjoining sitting room while I sat seething at the dining room table, pretending to examine the tediously inconsequential maths (my weakest subject) homework my mum had set me.

Beware! For when Mephistopheles comes knocking, he cares not for sums.

Deftly angling the glass door of the sideboard, I realised I could see the reflection of the television in the next room. A satanic reversal, HE only appears in the mirror.

'And now let's look at the charts . . .'

It was Tommy Vance. Again.

'Adam and the Ants with "Deutscher Girls" is new in at number twenty and at nineteen here at Top of the Pops, *we invite you to run for the hills with the sound of Iron Maiden . . .'*

They were showing the video.

I had heard of Iron Maiden. Some of the Scout leaders at Cubs liked them. I knew they were heavy metal. They probably had moustaches.

These five self-assured, slim, long-haired young men in tight PVC trousers didn't look like Gillan. The spectacle was disturbing yet exhilarating: the fast edits, maniacally grinning zombie face, the funny-shaped guitars and shrieking vocals, the relentlessly unhinged sound, breakneck pace and wild, plummeting solo that sounded like the very world was going mad. What infernal wrong was this? Despite having heard pretty much every song to grace the top forty since the summer of 1980, 'Run to the Hills' didn't even really sound like music, at least not as I knew it. I've since watched that video many, many times (although never since reflected in the door of a sideboard) trying to piece together exactly how I felt that night.

The unsettling memory of that glimpse into something truly unholy wouldn't leave me. How could it? Over the following fortnight, my thoughts kept returning to these sorcerers of the dark arts. I craved further insight into whatever fiendish world they inhabited. Thankfully, 'Run to the Hills' peaking at number seven warranted the video being shown again. Maybe it was the anticipation or that my imagination had already begun to construct a myth around them, but this time it happened, it really fucking happened. The devil had found me and I welcomed him in as a friend.

March twenty-first may well be the first day of spring, but for the Torabi household it was Nowruz, the Iranian new year, a celebration that dates back 7000 years and a highlight of our year, the one custom from the old country that our family upheld. We'd give each other gifts and that year, purchased from Boots, Arash gave me 'Centrefold' by The J. Geils Band, while my younger brother gave me 'Run to the Hills'.

My relationship with 'Centerfold' went no further than a few perfunctory plays; I must have swapped it shortly afterwards because I haven't owned it for years. 'Run to the Hills', however, was vital. It wasn't just the song itself – the B-side, 'Total Eclipse', was monolithic and is still one of my favourite Maiden tunes. Then there was Derek Riggs' seizure-inducing artwork and a photo of the band on the back of the sleeve, wearing leather jackets and drinking beer. Even the inclusion of tour dates read like an enchantment. The diabolical whole was far greater than the sum of its parts. The 7-inch was heavy with a singular charge and it was with this record that the magical imprinting began.

Iron Maiden, from an outsider's perspective, were a Boys Own, sexless and occasionally sexist pantomime rock band with a stupid cartoon monster as their mascot. They were the very antithesis of rock 'n' roll. Whatever I believed at the time, Iron Maiden's music was pretty straightforward – almost every tune used the same three-chord pattern. Band leader, bassist and main songwriter Steve Harris' eagerness to cram in lists of historical facts meant his lyrics often scanned in an awkward way, giving the songs a three-legged feel. When not documenting specific wars or just war in general, they usually took their title from a book or, more often than not, a film, heavy-handedly retelling the story while repeating the title over and over in lieu of a proper chorus.

All this is true, yet none of it matters and herein lies the paradox. Iron Maiden spoke to the outsider, me, like no one else did. Theirs was an inclusive world and being into Iron Maiden felt like being part of something prodigious and exclusive. Grown-ups didn't get them and they were pariahs in the world of pop. Even comparing Iron Maiden to other metal bands was almost pointless; many older metal fans weren't interested. No one just 'quite liked' them – you hated them or they were your favourite band. Iron Maiden insisted you buy into them and their vision, but what a complete vision it was! Like The Residents or Devo, Iron Maiden were a high-concept band. That the nature of the concept was never particularly clear made the whole trip all the more mystical. They existed in their own numinous terrain and to be a fan wasn't just to like a band, it was also to acquiesce to a system of lore, to take on a belief.

There's a purity in the music of Iron Maiden, a soaring, ambitious yearning for something beyond this tawdry existence, this vale of tears. It's utterly heartfelt and glorious. Iron Maiden is the sound of five sincere and honest men putting absolutely everything they have into their songs – a band writing and playing at the limit of their capabilities. There's no tortured genius or delirious visionary, no virtuosos or star players, but somehow, under Steve Harris' tutelage, these primal musical elements, when combined with Derek Riggs' bizarrely chimerical and otherworldly art, created an intoxicating, resonant bewitchment.

Staring at the record sleeves while listening to the albums opened up an incorporeal, dreamlike world, crackling with electricity and strangeness. From the titles, meticulous artwork, Riggs' sigil-like signature, the dominant use of yellow and blue, to the cabalistic names attributed to the production team (Martin 'The Headmaster' Birch) and the cryptic thanks list, every release was a mysterious artefact, something to explore, imbibe. Each one a jigsaw piece, offering further clues to an unfolding realm.

The albums, singles and tour programmes plotted an esoteric narrative, an extending arc. Who exactly was Eddie the Head? One of us? Was he a force for good or evil? Eddie served as our spirit guide, shepherding us through ancient Egypt towards transcendental spheres, into the volatile realms of madness or down to the depths of Hades to witness the very architecture of cruelty itself. From ancient myths to dystopian futures, Eddie was both observer and protagonist.

While unravelling the hidden messages and meanings contained within the artwork, the lyrics spoke of lucid dreams, nightmarish hallucinations, prophecies and sorcery. From the dawn of existence, through the bloody terrors of war, to mania, delusion, bravery and loss, all peppered with biblical quotes, arcane references to Aleister Crowley and H.P. Lovecraft, and charged with an explosive urgency by Bruce Dickinson's impassioned delivery.

Every guitar solo was pregnant with joy, ennui, sadness, heroism and tragedy. Dave Murray's were feminine and fluid, all cascading in swoops and dives, while Adrian Smith's were angular, obtuse and radiant. They were telling you something. Melodic and vital, allusive and elemental, Murray and Smith were like water and glass, and their solos served to illuminate a deeper, more obscure knowledge, a buried significance only hinted at by the lyrics. Great epics like 'Hallowed Be Thy Name', 'To Tame a Land' and 'Rime of the Ancient Mariner' were elaborate tales of tragedy and adventure, punctuated by Murray and Smith's trademark harmony leads. Those folky hooks, moving in thirds, were the pure essence of Iron Maiden, behind which Steve Harris' rattling basslines were married to the dynamic drumming of either Clive Burr or Nicko McBrain, both of whom were brilliant.

The long instrumental passages opened a curtain on fantastic panoramas. Impressionistic melodic sections, opaque words and hidden allusions in the artwork met in a dreamlike no man's land to construct magnificent and intricate architectures. Topped by the instantly recognisable logo, the effect of Iron Maiden was absolute. I was unknowingly projecting onto them all that I wanted from music. The world these five men had created was so much more appealing than the one which I inhabited.

Inevitably, the devastating events of February 1982 meant the writing was on the wall for The Mad Bats (Mk 2), although Tresise and I would continue to work together for a further two years. Nonetheless, towards the end of our tenure, inspired by my newly found love for metal, Tim Morsley and I attempted a far more ambitious concept piece, 'The Disease of Passland'.

Other than my sketching some possible cover art, we never got further than the title. Morsley's heart wasn't in it. He loved pop music and he loved the charts. Every Monday he'd bring his notepad into school, on which he'd meticulously copied the previous evening's chart rundown in elegantly neat handwriting, including misheard titles like 'Soft Cell - Paint in Love'. We'd go through the placings of each single and predict where we thought they'd be the following week. His father, a maths teacher, disliked his infatuation, seeing me as a bad influence.

The school magazine had interviewed all the teachers that year and he'd pointedly listed Stray Cats as his biggest dislike.

Tim really wanted to be a DJ and one of our regular games was Double DJ Show, where we recorded ourselves on cassette announcing singles and engaging in the kind of bland genialities and pleasant bonhomie we'd grown to expect from our disc jockeys. With a fairly limited collection between us, the B-sides got an equal airing: 'And that was Alvin Stardust with "Goose Bumps". We'll be playing that a lot more over the coming weeks.' His approach towards broadcasting was certainly more focused than his piano-playing – at that tender age, he'd already developed a convincing radio voice, so I was really pleased when, decades later, I looked him up and discovered that he was indeed a DJ. I'm glad the Double DJ Show was a dream that both of us ultimately managed to realise.

Chapter 5

Gentle Giant

Steve

As a young sprog I used to love the TV programmes *Pogles' Wood* and *Ivor the Engine*. Was it the possibility of a derailment every week that was the big turn-on, or did I just get sucked in by the brilliant compositions of Vernon Elliott? I recently bought the soundtrack to *The Adventures of Robinson Crusoe* by Robert Mellin and Gian Piero Reverberi. Occasionally, those little earworms from my memories of the TV series dragged it into my subconscious and I found myself whistling some of the themes within the score. I just had to get it!

Fireball XL5, *Thunderbirds*, *Space: 1999*, *Captain Scarlet* and of course *Stingray* also played a big part in showing me how effectively sound and vision could work together. Of course the names of composers like Barry Gray, Johnny Pearson or Keith Mansfield weren't tripping off my tongue at the time, as a bigger issue was how hot Marina was. OK, she did look slightly gormless and bear a striking resemblance to Lady Penelope with a different wig on, but Troy Tempest and I weren't fussed.

On reflection, how little I knew back then. Here was cutting-edge Supermarionation (albeit with strings) complemented by futuristic musical scores (with more strings), because lurking behind those catchy opening themes was a galaxy of invention. These TV and film hired hands were among the best composers of their generation, arguably ahead of their time and therefore by definition 'progressive'.

Alongside hitting balls around the kitchen table to the angular sounds of Man and Caravan, my other abiding soundtrack memory of our Abbey Wood council flat and its musical heritage gives a starring role to Raquel Welch. Without looking her up on Discogs,

I'm not that certain of her recording output, but for me she'll always remain an integral part of the line-up of Gentle Giant . . .

The embarrassment of watching sexually charged material on TV with your parents is one adolescent rite of passage today's self-sufficient teenagers are by and large denied. But for my generation, the considerable impact of a slightly soft porn seventies TV show like *Casanova* had to be mediated awkwardly through the presence of those whose own interaction in this realm had given me life. I do feel slightly cheated that I had to make do with Frank Finlay while today's teenagers get Belladonna, though. Although apparently, if you read the *Daily Mail*, this monumental upgrade isn't as good for them as one might think.

A far less uncomfortable viewing experience but still with an element of *phwoar!* (especially for the Bible Belt of the USA, considering it proved that human beings and dinosaurs were concurrently created) was the classic 1966 film *One Million Years B.C.* Although the original was made in glorious technicolour, colour TV sets couldn't have reached our corner of South-East London by the time I first encountered this cinematic landmark on the small screen, because I saw it in black and white. Just like the millions of people who tuned in to watch snooker's *Pot Black*, which the BBC started airing in 1969 to showcase the new-fangled delights of colour TV; meanwhile, all of us plebs had to decipher a load of grey balls flying about on a grey table.

But a monochrome Ms Welch was still looking incredibly fit as I dropped the needle on the opening track of Gentle Giant's *In a Glass House*. I had intuited that *One Million Years B.C.* probably wouldn't be that rewarding dialogue-wise and so opted to combine the viewing with a first listen, to what would become one of the most treasured records in my collection.

If any film might have been designed as the perfect visual accompaniment to an album, this was it. So while I drooled over Raquel fleeing from a state of the art paper mache Tyrannosaurus rex, I was digging the opening track of the album – called, appropriately enough, 'The Runaway'.

It was track two, 'An Inmate's Lullaby', that truly rearranged my brain, though. It put Gentle Giant into a completely different league from any other prog band of their era. From then on you could stick your Yes and Genesis albums where you never ever saw the sun shine from in Raquel's case – although you'd have plenty of opportunities had it been in Belladonna's. Yes and Genesis just weren't in the same league of sheer out-there inventiveness as Gentle Giant.

In a Glass House isn't the portal I'd recommend to those wanting to get to know the band's music, but it was certainly my way in and it led me to investigate their four previous albums. I loved them all, and my affinity for Gentle Giant confirmed the clear blue water between my tastes and the vast majority of the rest of my school year.

The hierarchy of who got to choose what was played on our sixth form common room turntable is now shrouded in the mists of time but was no doubt decided by popular consensus. Yes' 'Roundabout' sticks in my mind alongside Alice Cooper, Rod Stewart and David Bowie as having been on heavy rotation to general acclaim. I do remember putting on Gentle Giant and it getting the thumbs down from everyone except my inner circle. Magma's *MDK* was obviously out of the question for the 'normies', but in that regard the Abbey Wood school clientele probably wasn't that different from any other one around the UK.

In defence of my cloth-eared schoolmates, there's an element of additional complexity in Gentle Giant's music that might turn some people off. But funnily enough, even though this band have been a slow burn, they're so much more appreciated worldwide now than they've ever been.

They probably got a bad rap, inasmuch as the tracks often flew off on tangents – OK, admittedly that was a prog trend, but maybe the Shulman brothers et al. went too far off the flight path for most. For me, though, that was a great trip. Sure, some people might think their music was occasionally twee, but some of it was totally out there and, in retrospect, if you put them up against any other prog artists (Canterbury bands excepted), they just piss all over them (a technical term I've learned since becoming a musician).

Even as someone who didn't play any kind of musical instrument, I could still get a feel for what Gentle Giant were doing with changes in time signature and how that defined their music. I used to love working that out. It's like when people become switched on to the complex end of classical music. They might not have a technical understanding of what's going on, but they can still sit in their living room and basically conduct it - following it to the nth degree - because the magic of the piece has become totally accessible to them. The same sentiments would also apply to Cardiacs.

I saw Gentle Giant in late 1975 at the New London Theatre, and witnessed Derek Shulman strutting around the stage in his overalls, holding court. They were all brilliant musicians. What I found fascinating about them was the way they managed to tie all the different pieces of their music up and bring it back to the riff again. Is 'the breakdown' the right musical term for that? I don't think it's 'the bridge'. Either way, what I think of as the bridgy breakdowns in their music are fucking weird sometimes and there's something delightful about how clever they've been to get things back on course. If you've never experienced Gentle Giant, then seek out the video footage of them recorded by the German TV station ZDF and prepare to be amazed.

The first time I saw Guapo was about twenty years ago at the Spitz in East London, after Kavus had joined. There was a band on before them called Misty's Big Adventure whose drummer - Sam - was Kerry Minnear's son. I know that because he came up to me in the crowd and said, 'Apparently you like Gentle Giant - I'm Kerry Minnear's son,' which I still consider to be one of my favourite icebreakers of all time. I remember being a bit pissed on the night, but hopefully Sam relayed my message back to his dad that he was a total fucking genius. At the time of writing, I've still not met any of the band themselves. There was once talk of me presenting Derek Shulman with an award at an event for services to prog music (and possibly boiler suits), but this eventuality never transpired. It would have been lovely, because there are certain people in your life you just want to thank for all the enjoyment they've given you. I suppose this book is as good a place as any.

In terms of my recommended way in to Gentle Giant, well, that's a tough one. With some bands it's obvious which album is the way in, but with Gentle Giant I feel it's more of a challenge. You could suggest *Octopus* or arguably *Free Hand*, but those would be totally different things.

When you know an artist inside out, you're trying to untangle your own emotional investment from making the right choice in order to suck people into their whole body of work. The pressure is massive! For instance, just as for me *In a Glass House* will always conjure up images of Raquel Welch getting her kit off, I can't ever hear the song 'Playing the Game' without remembering having to walk home from school in my plimsolls after having my *The Power and the Glory* album - along with my shoes (which were far less important) - stolen from the PE lockers.

And while you're on YouTube, check out the video of The Muppets singing 'Edge of Twilight' from the *Acquiring the Taste* album. That song is totally psychedelic and if anybody needed proof that Gentle Giant were leagues ahead of their prog contemporaries, then listen no further. As for the video, it's a bloody masterpiece. The section with the hens playing the piano is inspired.

The Gentle Giant album I can't get away from, though, goes completely against what I've said about trying to set aside your personal viewpoint for an awareness of the common good. If I'd managed to do that, I'd probably have recommended *The Power and the Glory*. OK, I'm recommending *The Power and the Glory*. But on another day, and I know it's a controversial choice, then possibly *Three Friends*. Oh, fuck it!

Right, *Three Friends* isn't the album the cognoscenti tend to rave about - in fact, it's considered one of Gentle Giant's weaker earlier offerings - but teenage boys (as anyone who has ever dealt with one will generally agree) tend to be quite basic, literal-minded creatures. And for me and my two prog mates – Neil Rogers, who you've heard about, and the other one who owned Risk and was soon to introduce us to the action-packed gambling world of Escalado – the title track of the *Three Friends* album was written specifically for us. The future paths of our lives seemed to stretch out in front of us in that song. The lyrics charted the career paths of three schoolfriends and these offered us a choice of possible destinies as either the Artist, the Businessman or the Labourer, and we spent many happy hours (or it could have been minutes) debating which of us was more likely to go in which direction.

Although our school adhered to the seventies streaming system, none of us were in the class where they'd give out raffia to keep the kids entertained, but both Neil and the Waddington's rep ended up being considerably more boffin-like than me in terms of their exam results and later career directions. So at the time I couldn't really protest when I was allotted the Labourer, even accounting for that lack of muscular tissue clinging to my skeleton. As long as you're happy on the planet, it doesn't matter one iota what you do, but I was pleasantly surprised when at the age of twenty-one I turned professional at snooker and thus officially became 'the Artist', and then astonished forty years later when I doubled down and became a musical one, too!

Chapter 6

The Smiths

Kavus

'Electric guitar'. I still love the sound of those two words. An electric guitar seemed like pure abandonment, the tool to free me from a tedious existence where nothing ever happened and kept not happening forever. Machine heads, humbucker, whammy bar, scratch plate, truss rod, toggle switch, fretboard – even the terminology sparkled with an occult charge. Like a tarot deck or Ouija board, the electric guitar was a necromantic artefact and I knew that once I eventually had one, the devil would have a direct line of communication between his fiery home and the Torabi household. Passing a music shop in Cattedown, near the city centre, I begged my mum to take me in so I could look at these nefarious articles close up. As I stared from one to the other hung about the walls, the owner approached and, sensing my interest, asked my mum if I'd like to see the recording studio in the back.

A recording studio? In Plymouth? Recording studios were somewhere else, not here in Cattedown, surely?

He led my mum and me along the back corridor into a cramped control room that housed a small mixing desk, a reel-to-reel tape machine, a tangled mayhem of wires and cables, and a polystyrene coffee cup full of what looked like cigarette ends. Noticing my eyes almost popping out of my head, an affable long-haired man gave me a quick rundown of what all the equipment did. I had so many questions, but excitement and nerves rendered me speechless. Agog, I tried to take in this fantastical world before my mum unexpectedly announced that we had to leave and abruptly ushered me out.

She was tight-lipped and bristling on the journey home. While attempting to rationalise what I'd just witnessed, something about that brief vision of paradise had clearly troubled her. I blurted out that 'I would love to record there one day.'

This was the trigger she finally needed to explode. 'Over my dead body!' she screamed. 'I'll never bloody let you in there! They'll put drugs in your tea and turn you into an addict.'

At the age of ten, I didn't think the music industry could get any more exciting.

Clearly, I still had much to learn.

A few months later, I passed my eleven-plus exam and, as a reward, my dad took me to Tottles Music Shop in Honicknowle, where he purchased a Satellite electric guitar with a missing tremolo arm for £40. It was a rubbish guitar, which I think I must have known even then, but although it would be a further four years before I got my first amp, I didn't care. It was a real electric guitar and it was mine.

Transitioning from 'The Bear' to this little Strat-shaped oddity only increased my fascination with writing music. Since getting my metal ears, my playing had become more disciplined in that instead of moving my fingers arbitrarily up and down the fretboard in an attempt to recreate the wildly fluid playing of Brian Setzer, I'd started to grasp the concept of 'The Riff', my first foray into which was a, thankfully long-forgotten, instrumental called 'Earthquake'. To this day, many of my songs still start with a non-plugged-in electric guitar on my lap.

While there was never any doubt in my mind, my parents still saw this fascination with becoming a rock star as a phase I was going through. Like being a stuntman had been a few years earlier. For a while it was tolerated but not encouraged – my brother and I were going to grow up to be professionals. Coming from relatively meagre beginnings, as she did, Mum wanted us to have the kind of opportunities that had been denied to her. Because she and Dad wanted to give us the best possible start in life, having had such an interrupted education thus far with all the moving around we'd done, they decided to send us to the local public school.

At the time I thought that our household might have more pressing spending priorities, such as getting central heating installed in the house. Although these practical objections were waved aside, I was right to be sceptical about the economic value of a private education, because it turned out to be a complete waste of their money – something that I'm sure still upsets them.

So it was that in September 1983, four months after the release of Iron Maiden's Piece of Mind, *I set out on what would become the most miserable five years of my life. Plymouth College, an all-boys' school with a strong military leaning, was a traditional and strict establishment, granite grey with compulsory school on Saturday morning. The imposing vampiric head teachers wore gowns while some of the staff were ex-forces and took a similar approach to discipline. Being a private school, Plymouth College didn't have to conform to the more progressive changes the eighties were ushering in, notably doing away with corporal punishment. Pupils were beaten regularly, having been first ordered to the porter's office to fetch the cane before being humiliatingly thrashed in front of the class. It was bad enough being a day boy or, as the boarders dubbed us, 'gay boys', but as one of the very few 'foreign' kids, for the first couple of years I found myself on the blunt end of racism from both pupils and teachers alike, often asked why I didn't go back to my own country. Wherever that was.*

As the perennial 'last to be picked for games' boy, I was lucky to form a small coterie of like-minded misfits – for whose companionship and support I'm grateful to this day. We found each other and our friendship saw me through the darkest times. Despite being in different classes, we'd meet up during breaks and spend long summers roaming the suburbs or at each other's houses. We're still friends now.

While I wasn't an outwardly rebellious child, I set out my stall from day one – whatever the school was for, that's what I was against – and devoted myself to cultivating the air of a sixties dropout, a persona that was completely out of step with the rugby-playing, military-leaning school regimen.

By the second year my nickname had progressed from 'Paki Crap' to 'Fucking Hippy'. Now, the insult was on my terms. The only thing these philistines knew about hippies was Neil from The Young Ones *and I deliberately aped his vernacular, peppering my talk with 'oh man', 'groovy' and 'far out' . . . much as I still do today. I became the only vegetarian in the school and grew my hair about as long as was* permitted – just touching the collar. I looked awful but at least I didn't look like them.

One particular PE lesson began with the teacher – a former Met Police officer cunt called Mr Bentley whose oft-repeated catchphrase was 'Pain is a figment of the overactive imagination' –instructing us to take our shirts off as we entered the gymnasium. Looking at his stopwatch, he announced, 'For the next five minutes, I'd like you all to slap each other as hard as you can.' I looked around the class – surely this was a joke. He happily blew his whistle. It wasn't. It transpired games like this were a common occurrence.

'It's good,' he explained over the smacking and screaming, 'because the more you get slapped, the more you want to slap someone else.' But I didn't play. I gritted my teeth and stood my ground. I received but didn't give and endured the agonising five minutes until I was red raw. But I had won. I hadn't become one of them. Fuck that school and fuck everything it stood for. I learned that if you're going to be different, you'll get rocks thrown at you. Learn to love getting rocks thrown at you.

Although rock music generally had to be left at the gate, I'd wear an Iron Maiden T-shirt under my school shirt – even in the sweltering heat – as an act of passive rebellion and would often bring my guitar in and practise during break times. Being the only guitarist I knew, I was yet to have The Distortion Pedal Epiphany and the sound of my ineptly played Satellite plugged directly into the school amp was less than inspiring. I attempted a short-lived ensemble, Earthquake, with Paul Tresise, but it wasn't until the third year that I finally managed to put together a full band to play my songs.

Before school broke up for the summer holidays in 1984, Iron Maiden announced they were to play at Cornwall Coliseum in St Austell on 22 September as part of their 'World Slavery Tour'. I was only twelve years old, but there was no conceivable way I wasn't going to be at that concert. I was expecting a battle, knowing how much my parents disliked my obsessive interest in music but, improbably, they agreed to let me go, provided I could find a responsible adult to take me.

It didn't take long to convince my friend Chris Bertram to work on his metal-loving stepdad, Nigel, who was going anyway, and a week *later we both had tickets. We were actually going to see the real Iron Maiden at an actual real gig! This was hands down the most exciting thing that had ever happened to me.*

A newsletter from the Iron Maiden fan club insisted it was going to be loud, so Chris arranged a few training sessions in Nigel's tiny music room. With our heads between his impressively powerful hi-fi speakers, he ratcheted the amp up to an ear-splitting volume as we attempted to acclimatise ourselves. Who hadn't heard of 'the guy who put his head in the speaker' at a Motörhead gig only to emerge with 'blood pouring out of his ears'?

Released on 3 September 1984, Powerslave *was Iron Maiden's fifth album. I bought it on the day it came out, from a tiny record shop in Blandford Forum in Dorset, where my dad was working as locum for a couple of weeks while the rest of the family took a holiday. Throughout our stay, I studied the majestic Egyptian-themed artwork, lyrics and sleeve notes intensely; although, owing to there being no record player at the house where we were staying, it would be a further week or so before I finally heard this glorious sun-baked masterpiece. After returning home to Plymouth, I played it immediately and thought it was the best thing they'd ever done.*

While in its past Plymouth had boasted gigs by Jimi Hendrix and the debut performance of Emerson Lake & Palmer, by the early eighties there were few suitable venues and, at my tender age, none that would allow my entry. Cornwall Coliseum was located in St Austell, about an hour's drive from Plymouth. It was a 3400-capacity rock venue with a balcony that had in recent months hosted Black Sabbath, UFO and Whitesnake – all of whom my older friend John Clarke had seen, much to my envy. Bearing in mind the shape of England, the only concession that touring bands would usually make to the south-west was a show in Bristol.

Such was my excitement and trepidation, I had three anxiety dreams about the gig in the preceding weeks. One about missing it, another in which they were so loud that I went deaf and, finally, one where the band I was watching wasn't even really Iron Maiden. I arrived at school on Monday, 22 September with my jeans, trainers and denim jacket – covered with Iron Maiden patches and badges – concealed inside my school bag.

To get to Cornwall, you had to drive through Plymouth. To think that, at some point during the previous twelve hours, Iron-actual-fucking-Maiden and the real Adrian Smith would have passed within a two-mile radius of us seemed implausible. Yet there, in my blazer pocket, with that day's date clearly printed on it, was my ticket. We had games that afternoon and, conspiratorially, Chris and I talked in breathless wonder. What were they doing right now? Were they soundchecking? Did they even do their own soundcheck? Perhaps they'd stopped off and were walking around Plymouth town centre. What if they'd walked past our school?

We walked back to Chris' place after school, changed and had dinner before a couple of Nigel's amiable metaller pals turned up, at which point the five of us squashed into the car and headed over the River Tamar into Cornwall. We were subjected to NWOBHM (that's the New Wave of British Heavy Metal, for the benefit of squares) also-rans Persian Risk and Tokyo Blade on the tinny car stereo for the journey there. This would be the only time I heard either.

Turning off the main road into the enormous car park revealed a huge utilitarian sixties structure. A large sign above the entrance read 'TONIGHT IRON MAIDEN' in flashing lights – confirmation that they hadn't cancelled or died on the way there. This was really happening.

We joined the be-denimed queue. Clearly the youngest in attendance, Chris and I entered the hangar-like hall in time to see the support band, Waysted, featuring Pete Way from UFO, take the stage. 'Let's get fucking Waysted!' announced frontman Fin Muir, in the way only a man who would go on to sing The Office theme could. It was nowhere near as loud as I'd expected. I routinely checked my ears for blood but, disappointingly, nothing.

Following Waysted's departure, the atmosphere immediately became more charged. After an agonising wait, amid the orgiastic clamour, Churchill's not especially Egyptian 'We will fight them on the beaches' speech burst out of the PA, struggling to be heard above the mighty roar of the crowd. The stage remained empty as the atmospheric twin guitar *intro to 'Aces High' began. I was nervous as all hell and I loved it. The huge cloth obscuring the stage dropped and the lights came on - these weren't the illuminations afforded to Waysted - revealing a huge painted backdrop of a seated Eddie monument.*

And then the gates of hell were unbolted.

The soothsayers had arrived and they were wearing Spandex.

It was really them. I was a slight, bespectacled and gangly pre-pubescent and struggled to see much over the large friendly and excitable adult crowd. Once we'd acclimatised - this was unlike anything life had prepared me for - Nigel asked if we'd like to get closer to the front, so we pushed our way through the beery surging and swaying mass until we were within ten metres of the stage. The view was much improved but still wasn't good enough for me so, without asking if it was OK, I shoved further into the throng.

Closer to the barrier, things were much livelier and I was in danger of getting crushed until I heard a man's voice behind me, over the galloping bedlam, shouting 'Hey, steady! There's a kid here!' Those immediately around me backed off a little, creating some space, and I looked around to see a cheery, grizzly bear-sized grebo lean down as he shouted in my ear 'Do you wanna get on my shoulders?' I nodded and he lifted me above his head and sat me down. I could see everything - the full remarkable spectacle of Iron Maiden in their prime. I looked from the stage to the sea of nodding heads as my new friend held on to my legs and advanced forwards until I found myself in direct eye contact with Dave Murray.

He looked up, met my gaze, smiled right at me and waved.

At me.

Dave Murray smiled at me.

Nothing else mattered.

I tapped my new friend on the shoulder and he let me down. I was almost crying as I thanked him and retreated back to where Chris and Nigel were. 'Did you see me?' I asked.

The difference in atmosphere couldn't have been more pointed when I returned to the Cornwall Coliseum two years later to watch The Smiths touring The Queen Is Dead *on 17 October 1986. The Smiths were a* polarising band. I'd been on the fence about them since 'This Charming Man'. I didn't dislike them, but it took the release of 'The Boy with the Thorn in His Side' for the coin to drop fully. Once I'd crossed the line, I truly heard The Smiths in all their greatness - one of the major British pop groups of the eighties. For me it's a triptych of XTC, Madness and The Smiths - Swindon, London and Manchester - and probably no coincidence that my three favourite pop bass players are Colin Moulding, Mark Bedford and Andy Rourke. 'The Headmaster Ritual', from Meat Is Murder, is perhaps my favourite of theirs, with a curious quality of sounding neither minor nor major. No other song describes the hellish half-decade I spent at that oppressive private boys' school better, either.

A common criticism of The Smiths was that Morrissey's melodic choices were limited, that he always sang the same tune. This was to a large extent true but, to my ears, that missed the point. With so much movement and interplay between Johnny Marr's sparkly cascading parts and Andy Rourke's baroque basslines, Morrissey's simple melodies and terrific lyrics cut a straight path through the middle for the instrumentalists to weave around. See also Roth-era Van Halen. As a singer, Morrissey really came into his own as a solo artist, though.

I was fourteen and a late developer - still gangly, bespectacled and barely into my adolescence. I got down the front to guarantee my prime position in time for the interminably dreary support, Raymonde. Once they'd finished, I held my ground until the intro tape of Prokofiev's 'March of the Capulets' (from Romeo and Juliet) played for far longer than was necessary. Eventually, backlit, Mike Joyce appeared behind the kit and began the tribal pounding of the toms in an extended opening of 'The Queen is Dead'.

The place went nuts and quickly descended into a shoving orgy of kicks and elbows, completely at odds with what I'd interpreted as their core message, as 3000 fans desperately tried to prove that they were more into The Smiths than the next man. And yes, it was a mainly male crowd. Surrounded by a combative and threatening pack, there were no friendly shoulder-rides on offer and I was forced back. 'Morrissey! I love you but I hate you also!' declared the wanker next to me, flinging his arms into the air as the iconic singer took the stage and knocking my glasses to the ground into the bargain. 'If anyone throws anything, please feel free to pummel them,' announced Morrissey after the third song.

Iron Maiden, whose lyrics detailed war, apocalypse, murder and devil-worship, were followed by a joyous audience united in their love of the music – a spirited but affable congregation. The Smiths, a band that glorified the disaffected outsider and promoted vegetarianism, peace and love, attracted an audience of aggressive narcissistic pricks.

I watched the remainder of the gig from the back of the hall.

Chapter 7

more Magma

Steve

The oft-heard statement that punk killed prog is of course total bollocks. What actually killed prog was snooker. In 1979, so many people tuned in to watch Terry Griffiths beat Dennis Taylor at the Crucible Theatre that record sales slumped badly. This gave Derek Shulman no option but to seek out John Bongiovi's mum and get her to sign on the dotted line by convincing her that all the shit she'd had to endure over the years might be exactly what PolyGram Records and a whole bunch of musical morons had been waiting for.

By 1977, I was so busy pursuing my new pointed-stick-wielding dream that I had no real time for music in my life. As I became more professionally minded, I was too focused on what I was doing to want the distraction of being part of the brotherhood of Man while I was practising. I'd drastically reduced my whistling, too, and was still yet to get both feet off the floor.

I'd continued to support Magma and Gentle Giant with their recent releases *Attahk* and *The Missing Piece* respectively, but as far as any other bands were concerned, I'd flown the prog nest. I was on a snooker mission and that job spec guided me into very different musical territory. Because once I started to achieve a few of my goals in the sport, my working hours became more refined to just the winter months, with the summers relatively free. My capacity to enjoy music during those months did begin to return, but it came back in an altered state.

Helped no end by the intermittent balmy summer evenings, chilling out to London-based pirate radio stations like Horizon and JFM, I fast became a soul boy. Mole Jazz record shop in Kings Cross was my initial bricks-and-mortar gateway from British jazz rock to American jazz funk. They stocked both. The staff were obviously knowledgeable and pounced quickly on my claims of modest familiarity with Herbie Hancock's *Thrust*, Chick Corea's *Hymn of the Seventh Galaxy* and Weather Report's *Tale Spinnin'* and probed further. Once I'd got over my surprise that some of these jazz fusion-style bands also made music with people actually singing, I was ready to explore.

One Dee Dee Bridgewater album later and I was a changed man. For my sins, I demoted John Peel to the subs bench and turned my attention to the Robbie Vincent radio show for my weekly music fix (he had me at 'Patrice Rushen'). It was Mr Vincent who played the one particular mid-eighties tune that finally pushed me over the edge into the abyss of serious soul music record collecting. I don't know whether to thank him or hold him accountable.

Oscar Perry's 'Merry-Go-Round' was the 7-inch single and because I couldn't buy it in my local soul music record shop, the legendary JiFS Records in Chadwell Heath, I got in touch with Robbie and he directed me down the extraordinary rabbit hole of the mail-order soul outlets. In the blink of an ear I was addicted to the thrill of chasing obscure soul 45s - collecting huge amounts of rare and great performances, while my old staple diet of jazz rock couldn't get a look-in. I'd fully jumped ship.

At the height of my soul obsession I was in regular touch with another big music influencer in my life. Rod Dearlove is a committed soul music fan and has an encyclopaedic knowledge of the genre. In seeking out the more obscure soul 45s, I stumbled upon his excellent fanzine, *Voices From The Shadows*. I became a subscriber and he took me on an amazing journey into the musical backwaters of the USA. Eventually, we joined forces and made the magazine a glossier affair. It was still pre-internet, so we took it one step further by setting up a company selling 'independent' soul to the hungry collector. We bought a couple of job lots of 45s from record distributors in the USA who were dumping vinyl in favour of CDs and ended up with a barn full of around 200,000 American soul singles.

Even though I've intimated that I regretted my blinkered approach in the past, these were great times. Rod would discover new indie 45s and 12-inch singles. We'd ship them over then put out a regular mail-order list and wait for the phone to ring. His taste was immaculate. Rod was and is a great writer and the fanzine became an inspirational source of information for soul fans. If he ever wrote a book on the subject it would be essential reading.

Our greatest coup was securing the release of the track 'After All' - of which we were the sole distributor - by the legendary soul singer and writer Sam Dees. Our greatest claim to fame, though, was getting a namecheck in Nick Hornby's much-loved novel *High Fidelity*. We didn't make the cut for the film, but we are there in black and white, Chapter 24, page 128.

Prior to Rod Dearlove, my jazz, funk and soul music years were, as mentioned, inextricably linked to Robbie Vincent and this connection went worldwide. On a mid-eighties snooker trip to São Paulo in Brazil, I went in search of local jazz-flavoured music and discovered the Som da Gente label. I found some wonderful artists on this imprint - probably their most famous being Hermeto Pascoal (check out his 'Live in Montreux' 1979 performance online) and bought them in units of ten each. The record shop owner thought I was mad. We were flying first class (someone else was paying - my favourite way to fly), but even with the large weight allowance, I still hit my limit.

Luckily, I was flying with my manager and great friend Barry Hearn and I somehow convinced him to carry seventy albums as hand luggage. Looking back, I regard this as one of the greatest achievements of my career - getting Barry, who has spent his life convincing other people to settle on a deal, which was most probably in Barry's favour, to carry a ton of obscure Brazilian jazz fusion over the Atlantic Ocean.

I was smitten with one album in particular, Grupo Medusa's *Ferrovias*, and I sent a copy, along with a couple of others, to Robbie Vincent as a sort of thank you for all the great music he'd put me on to. Robbie concurred with my judgement, played a track on his show and back-announced it, giving not only me a namecheck, but also a tongue-in-cheek thanks to my hod-carrying lackey, Barry Hearn. This exchange led to one of my formative DJ experiences, filling in for Robbie on one of his Radio London shows. A proud moment indeed.

The soul music stage of my musical journey was an exciting one, almost to the extent of it being a bit of a blur now. I met loads of great characters on the scene, attended a few soul weekenders and became addicted to the thrill of seeking out obscure and rare releases, but if I had my time over again, I'm not sure I'd repeat it. I think I'd rather have continued on the path that I'd started out on in my teens – imagine how far into Steve Reich's back catalogue I could have got!

It's not that I've lost my regard for soul music – a lot of it is inspirational, heart-wrenching stuff, albeit with what now seems like an incredibly narrow subject matter. In a nutshell, it's mostly about who the singer wants to shag or that the person they're shagging is shagging someone else. But now I've belatedly returned to the musical motherlode of my adolescence, I often feel like I'm playing catch-up for the years I missed and struggling to find the right balance between listening to new releases and old albums. Then again, maybe that's where some of my sense of urgency comes from. Because however much post-punk or experimental electronic music I listen to now, I'm never going to catch up with everything I missed while I was on my shag-fest. To think of how many times during the nineties, when playing snooker in Sheffield, I walked past the Warp Records shop on Division Street without going in . . . well, a crying shame is what it is. If only to have experienced the buzz of Autechre first time round.

More recently, I recall explaining to Rod Dearlove that I'd practically stopped listening to soul music. I thought he'd be disappointed at my confession. On the contrary, he surmised that when people reached a 'certain age', they often return to the music of their teenage years. But I definitely think the idea of making up for lost time is just as much a motivating factor in my relentless quest for new sounds to explore than any nostalgic impulse. After all, it was called progressive rock for a reason, even if the vast majority of new stuff that now claims that title is about as progressive as an episode of *It Ain't Half Hot Mum*.

Either way, it took me all of the eighties and a fair portion of the nineties to get back to my roots.

The first sign of the green shoots of that return came when I was at a loose end one afternoon in London and for old times' sake visited the Virgin Records shop on Oxford Street. It was 1987. The shop had morphed and grown into a super-duper megastore. By then, my main interest wasn't so much the obscure Canterbury scene or jazz rock releases that used to draw me in there as the mad world of the collectable 7-inch soul single. Not Northern soul, just soul. It's an important distinction.

Having dipped more than just my toe into the UK soul scene, in my experience, Northern soul hasn't got as much to do with soul as you'd think. OK, admittedly on a Venn diagram the circles will have a large overlap, but to my mind the mentality of the fan is fundamentally different. In a nutshell, Northern soul tends to be assessed according to its danceability factor above all else, whereas plain old soul (with a small 's') is everything about the vocal performance. They're a different beast and they attract a different clientele. The level of commitment is consistent, though.

We've all seen fights outside pubs, but I had the good fortune to witness record fair carnage one Saturday morning at a big London event. The doors opened and the ever-hopeful early risers were eager to jostle for position for the bargains. It was packed, but I was able to get stuck into a box of soul albums while two other guys started flicking through a neighbouring box from either end. The flicking was frantic, but I wasn't finding anything of interest in my box, so I was effectively occupying space in a holding pattern until another box became free, when all of a sudden, the two guys next door discovered a rare soul LP by obscure female artist Alex Brown.

They both had a hand on it. If it had been a teddy bear fair, there may well have been stuffing everywhere. Then, luckily, they just started arguing about whose hand had touched the holy grail first and before either of them had even checked the condition of the record, they were on the floor having a full-on fight. You wouldn't expect record collectors to manage much more than the infamous *Inbetweeners* movie holiday ruckus, but these two were hardcore. Security was called and they were escorted out well before either of them could land the decisive blow and claim the prize. When the fuss had died down, I calmly paid a tenner for a record I subsequently sold for £400 a decade later . . . you never have the last laugh with vinyl, though. The current asking price on Discogs is two grand!

Soul music has the maddest prices attached (even for average-quality performances) than probably any other genre of music. The best day of my record collecting life was the one in the late nineties when, on a day off during a snooker event in Croydon, I discovered a Univers Zero LP lurking in the pop section of one of the most well-known record shops in South London at that time, Beanos. The day before I'd been listening to a Daniel Denis solo record and here I was, elated to find a first edition of his band's fourth album, *Uzed*, on the Cryonic label crying out for a home. Even though I'd started to leave my soul days behind me at this point, I'd always check out the soul stock for rarities. I walked up the stairs and started flicking through the three boxes of soul 45s, all priced at fifty pence. Among them were some surprisingly rare records. I pulled out about thirty and went to the counter to pay, mentioning that I was surprised to find so many I wanted. The guy behind the counter said, 'We had a collection in yesterday - there's loads more out the back.'

A couple of hours later I handed over £800 for one thousand, six hundred 45s. Stupidly, I should have bought the lot, but I still did a relatively good job of hoovering up the big titles. I took a punt on a number of items - well, at fifty pence it would have been rude not to - and a month later I put three of these 'unknown' (to me) funk records on eBay and they sold for £790! I reckon fifteen hundred and ninety-seven records for ten quid is a pretty good haul.

At the height of the Northern soul all-nighters of the seventies, things were even crazier. Competition on the scene was so cut-throat that so-called fans of the artist and their music started the infamous 'cover-up' abomination. DJs were so desperate to be the only one with a rare track (something that could stand them in good stead for future bookings) that not only did the prices of these rare and, in some cases, near one-off sixties soul 45s smash through the financial roof, but in order to acquire status, some DJs also sought out nefarious rules of engagement. It went something like this. A DJ travels to the USA in search of unknown sixties Northern soul-style dance tracks, on obscure indie labels that are probably already as 'rare as hen's teeth'. He (it was only ever a 'he') finds a suitable one, brings it back and covers the labels up with brown paper. He DJs with this track and the punters do the 'backdrop' all night long and a star is born, but it's not the artist, it's the DJ. Once the DJ had elevated this track to 'holy grail' level, they'd sell it for a king's ransom to the highest-bidding starry-eyed collector who would then proudly show it off to his mates. This cycle would continue over and over.

In a normal scenario – without the record being 'covered up' – even though the artist wouldn't see the immediate financial benefit of a ten-year-old record selling for well over its original price, there would have been the possibility of an invite to the UK for live gigs. This would set up a possible UK reissue and a lot more exposure, which on occasion did reignite the odd dormant career. In the 'cover-up' instance, the DJ was hoping nobody would discover the identity of the record or artist. This was immoral enough, but things got a whole lot worse. The records usually got given a fictitious artist and title name. Instead of the DJ eventually spilling the beans on the real identity, they sometimes decided to try to profit from this skullduggery. The record would be bootlegged under its fictitious name and sold at their gigs, while the original artist was no doubt grafting away in his or her day job to make ends meet. Rant over.

Anyway, back to the Virgin Megastore. On this particular occasion, there wasn't a great deal to interest me soul-wise, so I hopped over to the 'M's in the rock section. This is something I've always found myself doing – searching for Magma records I already own. If I find one, I rescue it from the evil shop owner, like some knight in shining armour. I don't like to see their albums sadly lying there in the racks looking as if nobody likes them. I don't do this with any other artist, which is how I know that 1. Magma are my favourite band, and 2. You don't get to be a multiple world champion at something without being slightly unhinged.

Flicking through a few Charly reissues of the band's mid-seventies albums (never buy a Charly reissue, as Magma saw no money from those; only buy releases from Magma's Seventh Records online outlet) I stumbled upon a new Magma release – or rather, 'Christian Vander presents Offering'. Considering neither O nor V look remotely like the letter M, all credit to the Branson employee who took it upon themselves to fly in the face of any previously known filing system, because without this wonky-minded Virgin cataloguer, a sliding-doors moment would have certainly been missed. I took the album home and stuck it on and once again, I was transfixed by the brilliance of Christian Vander's compositions. It was a different, softer listening experience overall, but it still had the hallmark of that Magma/Vander sound and the magic was still there.

I'm not sure what possessed me – maybe a rush of the same kind of initial enthusiasm for the band that I'd felt in my teenage years – but I started to think, wouldn't it be good to see them performing this stuff live. The stupidest but also most magnificent idea then formulated in my brain – I wasn't exactly struggling for a few quid at the time (actually, I was fucking minted, as this was pre the marriage and divorce chapters), so why didn't I just bring them to London.

They hadn't played in the UK since 1975 and I had no idea about promoting events, but between Magma and a few of their long-time friends in the UK, we somehow put it all together. Considering I was one of the highest-profile sporting personalities in the UK at the time, getting publicity was a piece of piss. Of course, I had to meet my heroes - an unnerving experience that I'd recommend to everyone, if only for the fact that if someone is subsequently for any reason overawed in your presence, you'll have far more empathy for their plight.

When I meet people who are huge snooker fans and consequently vulnerable to imbuing our encounter with more significance than it possibly ought to have, I generally tend to feel a certain amount of responsibility to try to relax them. I didn't get the impression Magma's Christian Vander was feeling that pressure, though.

He wasn't rude - in fact, he was very polite - but he does have a strange energy and for possibly the only time in my life, I was overawed. I guess it was strange from his point of view, too, because I don't suppose snooker had played a big part in his life up to that point and now this guy he'd never heard of (even though we lived less than 250 miles apart) was putting on these gigs that were getting a kind of tabloid publicity he certainly wasn't expecting.

The first time I met him was at the press conference a week before the gigs I promoted in London in 1988. It generated a shedload of interest with even London TV news crews in attendance. Christian Vander didn't speak much English - or at least he didn't speak much English on that occasion - and after we'd posed for a few photos together, I kind of kept my distance and chatted more with Stella Vander.

I got the impression Christian was wondering what the fuck was going on and he wasn't the only one. The hardcore Magma cognoscenti in the UK were also probably scratching their heads because technically they weren't even Magma gigs. Offering was Christian Vander's spiritual jazz homage to his idol, John Coltrane. To me, it sounded enough like Magma for me to think it was Magma and when I booked them, they politely didn't inform me of my mistake, so even though it said Magma on all the posters, the offering they offered up was Offering. Oh, with the exception of performing

'Zëss', which is a tour de force that has only recently been committed to disc, with its colours firmly nailed to the Magma mast.

It's probably the first and only time their music has been misrepresented in that way. But I'm glad to say that it was still just as possessed - in some ways even more so.

I put on three consecutive nights at the Bloomsbury Theatre and charged £6 a ticket. I had no idea how many people were going to turn up, but as it turned out, every night was full. I sat there in the theatre watching as the doors opened and the fans rolled in. The first person who caught my eye was a guy wearing an Afghan coat - so far, so good . . . that could have been me in the seventies. Just behind him was an individual from the opposite end of the catwalk - impeccably dressed in a three-piece suit complete with briefcase and umbrella, who had presumably come straight from the City. It was great to see all these Magma fans coming out of the woodwork, regardless of what they'd been doing for the intervening thirteen years.

The concerts themselves were brilliant and, as stressful as the organisation of it all was, I also have some great memories of that aspect, as well. Basically, I had no idea what I was doing and during the soundcheck on the afternoon of the opening night, Magma/ Offering's tour manager, Georges Besnier, informed me that the house grand piano was rubbish and they needed another one. WTF?!

As blind panics go, I was up there with Corporal Jones. The piano looked lovely and shiny to me! Unbeknown to me, an SOS was put out to Chappell's in London and they did the classiest thing ever - delivered a grand piano free of charge, installed it, tuned it, the lot. In all the hurly-burly and excitement of the actual concerts, I'm not sure I even properly thanked them, so I'd very much like to do that now - better late than never.

Obviously, I was never going to become a full-time concert promoter, but I still set up Interesting Promotions to give those Magma gigs their own place within a few different activities at the time . . . to be honest, mainly to fence off the losses. I did my proverbials on those shows – it's a mark of the novice promoter to sell out every night and still come out massively behind.

When I saw Magma at the Camden Roundhouse all those years before, I know I was in a heady state by the end of the gig, but I was sure there were only five of them in the band. This time – now I was footing the bill – there were twelve. How was I to know they'd proliferated at that rate? The hotel bill alone accounted for the ticket sales!

I believe the producer of the film *Raise the Titanic* was reputed to have said, 'It would've been cheaper to have lowered the Atlantic.' Had the Channel Tunnel been finished, as opposed to the first holes being freshly dug, I could have whizzed over on the Eurostar and watched them in action in Paris a couple of months later for a fraction of the price. A return-fare helicopter would have been cheaper and if the World Wide Web hadn't still been two years away from its inception, then I could have planned a whole Tour de France watching them for less.

It's amazing how easily we forget how much effort was involved in being a music fan in the past. How did we order tickets to gigs in the seventies? Did we just walk up on the night? What if it was sold out!?

How did a Magma fan find out where they were playing in the seventies and eighties? Especially if they couldn't speak French. Not everyone was as clever as I was to think of bringing the band across the Channel, regardless of the maths involved. For all the large dent they left in my wallet, I never regretted putting on those shows – they were worth every penny.

As the nineties moved along, I was still listening to soul music but basically running out of steam as far as being a collector was concerned. I'd no doubt started to see the futility of constantly searching for that elusive rare 45, while completely disregarding the brilliance of a common-as-muck Dramatics albums. I'd got married and had two sons, Greg and Jack, who in their early years, when strapped into car seats, were regularly subjected to a variety of weird and wonderful music. No *Postman Pat*'s greatest hits for them. At the very least, during their trapped-audience years, they did come to appreciate Caravan's 'Golf Girl'. From a musical perspective, I was extremely proud to witness my youngest, Jack, become more than just proficient on the piano and gobsmacked when, last Christmas, he presented me with a USB stick containing a wonderful piano version of our The Utopia Strong track 'Konta Chorus'.

So what was my way back into the world I now inhabit? My personal 'Way In' sign was held aloft by a gentleman I never met and only spoke to once briefly on the phone. His name was Paul Mummery.

First eBay and then Discogs would be game changers for the record collector, but prior to that, if you wanted to seek out a particular record or type of music memorabilia, it was a laborious task. If you couldn't find what you wanted in somebody's mail-order list, the only option was to send a paid - and they weren't giving them away, either - 'wanted' advert to *Record Collector* magazine.

At some point I must have taken a look at the pitiful amount of Magma memorabilia I'd accumulated over the years and decided to seek out more Zeuhl bounty, because I put one of those pricey ads in *Record Collector* and waited excitedly for the magazine to hit the high-street shelves. I didn't get much response, but I did receive encouraging news of the existence of a Zeuhl music fanzine called *Ork Alarm!* (Named after a Jannick Top-penned track from *Köhntarkösz*.)

The genre name 'Zeuhl' - which translates as 'Celestial' - was coined by Magma themselves, rather than by the critics or fans. Early doors, Magma invented a 'singing' language. To my knowledge, it was never fully formed, but it served a purpose inasmuch as I suspect they didn't want to tie themselves to French or, for that matter, any other pre-existing language.

Maybe the exact reasons are lost in time, but suffice to say that this has been mostly a blessing and possibly in only one way a curse. On the one hand, it was an inspired vehicle for the human voice, especially as singing in French would have probably restricted overseas interest severely. But on the other hand, Magma got saddled with the reputation of being a gimmicky sci-fi band that invented a planet – and for some people that was a barrier to taking them seriously.

After subscribing to *Ork Alarm!* and sending off for back issues, I received a treasure trove of articles and information. I was amazed at what had happened to the Zeuhl scene since I'd jumped ship. Yes, I was aware of some of those who had seemingly followed in Magma's footsteps, such as Zao and their amazing 1971 album *Z=7L*, but there were other bands that, had I been in the loop, I'm sure I'd have stumbled upon earlier.

I contacted Paul Mummery, the editor of *Ork Alarm!*, to thank him for enlightening me and he told me that sadly, issue twenty-five was probably going to be the last. This 'sadly' would soon be upgraded to 'tragically', as not long after I discovered that Paul had passed away. A few years went by and the advances in computer software, and uptake of the internet, began to make possible the idea of putting Paul's wonderful publication up online as a tribute to his work. I contacted his father and asked his permission. After kindly agreeing, he then said what a coincidence it was that I'd phoned on that day, as the anniversary of Paul's death had just come round again. He still had a room full of records and memorabilia sitting there and was about to take the whole lot down to the second-hand shop. Unless, of course, I wanted them.

Can you imagine the feelings going through my mind at that moment?

This situation redefined the concept of a 'no-brainer', but it was one that was accompanied by an overbearing sense of responsibility with a poignant cloud hanging over it. OK, it wasn't the rarest or most complete archive of LPs ever, but it was the collection of the man who wrote *the* fanzine. Paul's knowledge – not just of Zeuhl, but also many other associated genres – was second to none and this abundance of music and memorabilia was the accumulation of a lifetime (albeit one sadly cut short) of discovering the styles of music that I so admired.

I gladly took him up on his kind offer. I had to. The thought of this collection going to a second-hand record shop and being broken up was horrifying. Every time I look through his abundance of great and obscure albums, I think of all the shoe leather Paul would have worn through and the enjoyment he must have accrued from tracking them all down and uniting them with the rest of the oeuvre.

I know this might sound stupid, but as far as his collection goes, I'm just their current keeper. There's a regular article in one of the music magazines (*Record Collector* seems the likeliest) where 'celebs' of one sort or another are asked about their record collections and how they plan to dispose of them once they are pushing up roses. The link between mortality and collecting is a strange one. As I get older I wonder what the hell I'm actually doing! For some people, the endless quest for one more vital artefact could be a way of postponing coming to terms with the inevitable. But show other people a meticulously curated collection and their first thought might be: What's going to happen to it all when they die?

It's something best not thought about. I certainly don't think I collect records because it gives me an illusion of immortality. The most plausible idea out there for why people collect stuff is known as the Endowment Effect, which proposes that an individual will value an object higher if they own it. Me? I collect vinyl because I've just got to have it! There's an internet meme I've seen that has Albert Einstein gesturing at a blackboard on which the following formula is displayed: 'Ideal number of records = the number of records you have plus one.' When do you know you have a problem collecting records? When you buy stuff that you don't ever listen to. 'Hello, I'm Steve . . .'

For someone who should be receiving therapy for the condition, it sends a nasty shiver down my spine to think of the thousands of collections that must have been dumped in skips over the years. I know it's a funny thing to view albums as antiques when many of them were pressed up in their thousands, but that's exactly what they are – and if you don't get something in your eye at the prospect of someone's prized collection being reduced to landfill, then you must have a heart of stone. Today, a vinyl album is pressed up in relatively small quantities compared to previous eras. A limited indie release of 250 is commonplace and I reckon the collectors' market will have gone ballistic in twenty years' time.

There were rumours back in the sixties that old 'unsaleable' soul 45s were used as ballast for cargo ships returning across the Atlantic from the USA and that on arrival in the UK they'd dump them. I haven't got a clue if this was the case, but what a cruel story to tell a soul collector. Of course, there are plenty of other reasons why record collections get broken up, divorce being a common one. I bet you could make a few quid at record fairs selling T-shirts bearing the legend 'She got the kids, but I got the 45s.'

When I start thinking it's the grim reaper coming for me every time the doorbell rings, I'll probably feel obligated to do with my collection what Paul's father did with his son's. Seek out a like-minded soul who won't break it up for resale and who will hopefully continue adding to it to the point where it has some small historical value. I can hear Kavus' hands rubbing together as I type! I'm not aware of any kind of museum (akin to the British Library) dedicated to the preservation of recorded sound to which benefactors could bequeath their music collections, but I feel like there ought to be one.

Either way, acquiring Paul's collection was the catalyst that caused my interest in music off the beaten track not just to be reignited, but also to go into overdrive. And if he's looking down at me right now, hopefully he'd give a nod of approval to the part it played in the story you're reading now. There's no one genre of music as such that Paul collected, even though he had a penchant for French artists. It's more that these artists have a common bond through innovation. But like every music fan, it's my judgement as to what I consider is fodder for the accolade 'essential' and, naturally, everyone will have their own yardstick. The important thing is to be open-minded and give everything a fair chance – something I can honestly say I've not done for big chunks of my listening life.

It's a big regret that I spent so many years closing my ears to anything that wasn't my 'genre of the moment', whether it be soul or jazz funk or even Canterbury. Anyway, I've been trying to redress the balance ever since and Kavus has been a big influence in expanding my horizons. The first step in my journey to full rehabilitation was also the next chapter in my 'career' of musical fandom.

In 1996 I was contacted by Paul Golder, an accountant by trade but obviously a frustrated one. He didn't want to settle for the boring life as just a money man – he wanted to walk the tightrope just like my *Spitting Image* puppet had done a decade before. At one stage, Paul was ranked eighth in the UK at Scrabble and he's in the 1994 *Guinness Book of Records* for scoring the most points in twenty-four hours. My kind of guy for sure.

He'd just started a community radio station in Brentwood called Phoenix Radio. Back then you could apply for a month's airtime once every six months. I used to do an irregular soul show for him that ended up being called *The Interesting Soul Show*. Then the Radio Authority (the forerunner of Ofcom) started to open up the airwaves and license a few local commercial FM channels. Paul applied but failed in the bid when a station in Chelmsford got the nod.

Paul carried on plugging away and, in 2002, the Radio Authority also decided to award licences to non-profit-making stations. It was five long years later before Phoenix FM was granted a licence and Paul found himself in control of a full-time community radio station. During that period, my show had morphed into an irregular Zeuhl music-tinged affair and when Paul rang with the news, he asked if I wanted to revert to a weekly soul show or stick with the new 'alternative' style.

I could feel the desperation at the other end of the line. Soul music and 'rare groove' had always been big in Essex. Zeuhl music less so. 'Put me on the Monday night graveyard shift so I don't annoy anybody and I'll go alternative,' I said cheerfully, hearing Paul start to whimper as he put the phone down.

I've generally resisted the temptation to play the music I like to others. Certainly on a one-to-one basis. I think anyone reading this book will know the experience. Watching someone's eyes glaze over gets predictable over time. In the end, you learn to keep the music to yourself. However, I reasoned that if I was to do my radio show at the unfashionable hours of ten until midnight on a Monday, at least people would have *chosen* to tune in as opposed to the band Shub-Niggurath being the cause of an M25 pile-up while I was hosting the drive-time show. So it was that on a dark and very windy Monday night in March 2007, *The Interesting Alternative Show* on the Brentwood and Billericay community radio station Phoenix FM came into being.

Chapter 8
Frank Zappa

Kavus

For pupils entering the third year, Tuesday afternoon at Plymouth College meant two choices: CCF or Dukes. CCF was the 'combined cadet force', army, navy or air force complete with the appropriate uniform. The main thrust of this activity appeared to be marching up and down the playground doing what I imagined was 'drill'. Once a year, a helicopter would land on the school field and some decrepit warmonger would emerge, mumble something about honour and duty, while row upon row of assembled boys saluted and shouted, 'Sah!' It didn't look like my idea of a good time. Alternatively, there was Dukes. Dukes was the Duke of Edinburgh's Award scheme or, as it was dismissively referred to by the CCF boys, 'Commie Skive'.

Along with double art, Commie Skive was a highlight of the school week and aptly named as we stretched the limits of what constituted legitimate activity. It turned out that the few teachers who oversaw Commie Skive were of the same mind as the pupils who took it and basically left us to get on with it with little policing, provided we weren't making trouble. Chris Bertram and I would spend dreamy Tuesday afternoons in a smoky local snooker hall, hopelessly knocking coloured globes across the worn green baize. Snooker wasn't to be my calling and our conversation usually centred around girls and music – Chris usually wanted to talk about girls and I usually wanted to talk about music. Specifically, I wanted to form a proper band.

There were no doubts about Chris' metal credentials, what with Nigel being his stepdad. Chris was very taken with Judas Priest's Rob Halford and could cook up an impressively ear-bending shriek. Inevitably, Flytrap was born.

Over at his house, I'd play my songs through Nigel's amp while he worked on lyrics. Early Flytrap standards included 'Diamond Lights',

*a critique of the seedier side of London about which we knew nothing,
'The Prodigal', based on Iain Banks' recently published debut* The Wasp
Factory, *'Flytrap' an exploration into the motivations of a serial killer
('Who's the next victim to be? You, you, you, or the newly born?') and
'Pool Shark', which was about a pool shark.*

*As productive as these sessions were, I knew if we were going to
elevate ourselves from a mere bedroom operation, Chris would need
to step up and get a microphone. That summer holiday, he phoned up
excitedly to tell me he'd just bought something important for the band
and was on his way over to show me.*

*After ceremoniously unzipping his bag, he reached in and threw down
a pair of fingerless driving gloves. Sensing my disappointment, he put
them on, held one hand up to his face, as if grasping a microphone,
and pointed the other across an imaginary sea of banging heads before
dramatically curling it into a fist, shaking it three times and returning it
to his side. 'Think how fucking cool this will look onstage,' he reasoned.*

*Returning to school as a fourth year, I set about expanding Flytrap
into a full band. While there was no one suitable of our age, the sixth
form had an impressive array of potential, including Alex Kirke, who
was in the same class as Arash. While I didn't care much for Free and
even less for Bad Company, Alex was drummer Simon Kirke's nephew
which, to my mind, increased our chances of 'making it' by approxi-
mately tenfold.*

*Alex's mum ran an antique shop nearby and lived opposite our school
in the appropriately named Wilderness Road. It was a sprawling and
eccentrically bohemian four-storey house, replete with any amount of
vintage curiosities: globes, statues, antique toys, birdcages, dressers, oil
paintings, stuffed animals, drinks cabinets.*

*'This house is a collection of collections,' a friend observed. Alex had
free rein of the whole top floor, which he likened to Andy Warhol's
Factory. As well as his own kitchen and bathroom, it was filled with
instruments, including his drum kit, amps and keyboards. Here, he and
his friends would drink, smoke and party. His mum didn't care. She'd
buy their booze.*

Alex was also in the same year as Blair Harris, an extraordinary lead guitarist with his own amp – an HH combo – a Fender Stratocaster, and the chops to play the solo to Van Halen's 'Jump' convincingly, which he'd performed as the undoubted highlight of the school's Christmas Entertainment the previous year. While I couldn't hold a candle to him as a lead guitarist, Blair didn't write songs and after playing him a cassette of a Flytrap rehearsal one break time, he agreed to join.

The closest we had to any form of music industry hierarchy at school was our English teacher Mr Gatherer, who had taken on the role of organising the Christmas Entertainment, the yearly school revue. This effectively made him A & R man, booking agent and promoter. Mr Gatherer was my favourite teacher. He'd only recently arrived at the school and seemed more akin to Rik Mayall or Ben Elton than the sadistic reactionaries running the place. He read Viz, liked rock music and, initially, seemed more like one of us than one of them. When he became a boarding house master the following year, we accused him of 'selling out'.

After being invited down to a lunchtime rehearsal, he agreed to let us play that year, provided we learn 'A Merry Jingle' for him to sing as the show's finale. Clearly, he recognised what a badass band Flytrap was and wanted in. When we came to perform it, he was wearing a leather jacket and shades. 'A Merry Jingle' was a Christmas single by The Greedies, a short-lived Sex Pistols/Thin Lizzy supergroup, both of whom I loved – what's more, it had a great twin-guitar harmony part.

Before that we'd play a plodding version of Iron Maiden's dynamic instrumental 'Losfer Words (Big 'Orra)' and the gruesome Torabi/Bertam-penned 'Flytrap'. ('Thoughtful' clean intro/chugging riff/verse and chorus x2/solo 1: Torabi/guitar harmony break/final chorus/killer final solo: Harris/outro: 'thoughtful' clean intro but with distortion/ending: whole band going duh-duh.)

I was beside myself with excitement having just acquired a red Westone Spectrum as joint birthday and Christmas present. After weeks of planning, I settled on a stage outfit of skinny black jeans, a Judge Dredd 'Judgement Day Is Today!' T-shirt, a borrowed white suit jacket with the sleeves rolled up and Rucanor baseball boots. No one could doubt my commitment to mid-eighties metal. By the time the first night arrived, nerves had got the better of me and I spent the half-hour before we were due to perform vomiting until I was so weak I had to play the first two numbers sitting down.

Thankfully, Chris was wearing his fingerless driving gloves and, utilising his signature pointing move, drew attention away from me. His canny stagecraft was wasted on the cricket-loving, 'pop muck'-hating French teacher, Doug 'Muscles' Martin, who made a point of squeezing his eyes tightly shut with his fingers in his ears throughout our entire performance as he sat in the front row. I took this as a badge of honour.

I had long since stopped paying any attention in class, spending most lessons designing band logos, ridiculously impractical stage sets or just drawing Judge Dredd with elaborate cross-hatching in the back of my exercise books.

I'd always loved comics, which I do think are the great narrative art form (not for nothing do the French call them 'the Ninth Art') graduating from The Beano through Tintin and Asterix the Gaul to Viz. But it took Madness releasing a one-off single, 'Mutants in Mega-City One', in 1985 under the name The Fink Brothers, to turn me on to the weekly dystopian fiesta of the underground British publication, 2000 AD.

I adored the beautiful ink drawings and allegorical morality tales as I pored over each page, taking in the sumptuous line work and fevered storylines. I could name any artist from a single panel. This was imagination run wild. Impressionistic, vivid and surreal fine art printed on cheap paper and sold to the masses. One hit would last me all week.

A shop called Comic Express had just opened in town. A small unit, conspicuous on the mezzanine of the Plymouth Business Centre, it was bookended by a double-glazing window showroom and a yacht broker, the staff of which would look at us disdainfully whenever we visited. More unlikely still, Comic Express was run by the mother–daughter team of Billie, an elderly Scottish woman and her daughter, Jan, who had both recently moved to Plymouth, presumably to start this shop. This pair were extremely welcoming to our enthusiastic gang and in return we spent most of our pocket money there.

They certainly knew their comics and, knowing we were 2000 AD fanatics, recommended American titles we'd never heard of. They turned us on to the DC and Marvel imprints, where many of our beloved British creators were now lucratively working, most notably Watchmen, which was created by ex-2000 AD stalwarts Alan Moore and Dave Gibbons and was just being serialised. We all came in on issue six and quickly managed to track down the preceding issues. It was a historic day when we all rushed into town to buy the climactic twelfth and final issue.

The return to school after a typical lunch break would find us talking animatedly about new books and artists we'd discovered. And never as excitedly as the afternoon we'd been told that not only were Comic Express hosting Plymouth's first comic convention, but also that they'd like us to help out.

Helping out was a vague term. I offered to make cassettes of 'sci-fi'-themed tunes to play as background music. (Anthrax's 'I Am the Law', Iron Maiden's 'Caught Somewhere in Time' and 'To Tame A Land', Metallica's 'The Thing That Should Not Be', The Fink Brothers' 'Mutants in Mega-City One', and instrumental guitar hero Vinnie Moore, whose song titles sounded sort of futuristic.) It transpired that the star guest would be Bryan Talbot. I knew and loved Talbot's work from 2000 AD. Specifically, he'd illustrated one of my favourite stories – The Gothic Empire (book four of Pat Mills' Nemesis the Warlock saga). He was top five material as far as I was concerned. Knowing my love for his work, Billie asked if I'd like to be Bryan's steward for the day. Jesus! Here in dreary, miserable Plymouth where everything moved too slowly and nothing fun ever happened was a comic convention with an actual comic celebrity – and I would get to spend the day with him. I'd never felt more important.

I had no idea what Bryan looked like and, on being introduced to him on the morning of the convention a little before the doors opened, I was struck by how much he resembled one of his drawings. Tall, rake-thin and with a shock of long, straight ginger hair framing his deathly pale face, he looked like a rock star. What came as a surprise to us both was that, clad from head to foot in black (by now I was goth-adjacent), we were dressed exactly alike; although I couldn't carry off the black drainpipe jeans, Chelsea boots and black suit jacket ensemble with anything like the natural grace and cool he exuded.

Spending the day in his booth, somewhat unnecessarily 'stewarding', I watched this gifted and articulate man chat effortlessly to the babbling stream of geeks, freaks and weirdos who filed past to get their comics signed, all the while trying to pretend I wasn't one of them, too. I listened to him patiently answer inane questions while drawing an endless cavalcade of Judge Dredds, Purity Browns and Torquemadas in an increasingly ridiculous array of poses, knowing how uncannily fortunate I'd been to land this 'job'.

As Bryan worked his way through a bottle of red wine and then sent me off to fetch him another (so that's what a steward does), I could see a feasible way out of this mundane life, a way into something more incandescent, more exciting, a pathway to an existence filled with meaning and substance. Here was an actual artist. An illustrator, writer and bona fide bohemian. A well-read, strange and otherworldly Northern alchemist.

I'd never met an adult like him before. I mean, I knew they must exist out there somewhere - I'd read about them in books. Anxious and restless, I spent my days wandering and wondering in their worlds, watching their films, listening to their music and dreaming a way out of this desperately sexless half-life.

I wondered what they made of him in Preston.

So I asked him about his life and his influences, about the comics industry. I listened as he regaled me with tales of his formative years working in underground publications, of the counterculture and how he felt about Thatcher's Britain. I told him what his work meant to me, about the kind of art I wanted to make, the kind of life I had and hoped I might have, and he didn't tell me to shut up. Quite the opposite, he was encouraging, insightful and supportive. I critiqued other writers and artists, made him laugh, we talked enthusiastically about Watchmen *still only halfway through its run and, most remarkably, he didn't seem to think I was a twat. In spite of our age difference, we got on terrifically.*

I left the first Plymouth Comic Convention long after it had closed, taking with me a signed copy of the first book of Talbot's meticulously scripted psychedelic masterpiece, The Adventures of Luther

Arkwright, *and a page of original artwork from* Nemesis the Warlock.
*I was one step further down the righteous path - these were ten golden
hours that have never since faded. Shortly before leaving, and knowing
I was a musician, Bryan asked if I was into Frank Zappa.*

*Frank Zappa? The guy with the moustache. He was one of those
boring seventies guitar heroes, right? I told him I knew who he was
but I'd never heard any of his stuff. Bryan's eyes widened and he said,
'Really? Listen, Kavus, you've got to check him out. He'll be right up
your street . . .'*

Chapter 9

Charles Hayward

Steve

I know I should be, but I've never been a devourer of music info or history. Much to my shame, reading the back cover of an album while listening to it is something I've rarely done, so I suppose it was a given that when I first became smitten with Charles Hayward's Camberwell Now, I didn't connect it with the Quiet Sun album *Mainstream* I'd enjoyed so much as a teenager. Charles Hayward had made this album in collaboration with schoolmates Bill MacCormick and (prior to his Roxy Music fame) Phil Manzanera. I also wasn't aware that Charles had been in the running to join that band, too, in their early days but lost out by one vote.

Can you imagine, in the frightening sliding-doors world we travel our paths along, if just one vote had gone the other way? Then 'The Great Paul Thompson' would have just been known to his mates as Paul. Compared to the Brexit travesty, I think this was a ballot of which we, the music fans, were beneficiaries. As a result, Charles didn't get to mime drums on *Top of the Pops* or eventually sit in the saddle next to Bryan Ferry on a fox hunt, although apparently he *was* instrumental in getting Roxy Music their first ever gig. I was also unaware that for a short period of the summer of 1972, at the age of twenty-one, Charles had been the drummer in Gong.

Regardless of my ignorance, once I started to get back to those Magma albums I'd known and loved in the seventies, I also began to investigate other music that, unknown to me, had been written about in the pages of *Ork Alarm!* and also the other publications that I'd discovered in Paul's ephemera collection. There were too many to mention, but the fanzines *Exposé*, *Audion* and *Eurock* probably packed the biggest punches. I realised there was a plethora of artists I'd missed out on who could potentially bring me the same kind of joy that Magma had. I bit the bullet and started swotting, and Charles Hayward was one of the key figures in helping me begin to join up the dots.

History now tells us that This Heat, Charles' previous band to Camberwell Now, are a post-punk outfit. OK, fair enough, although at the time, they were happy to be floating between various 'scenes' without conforming to any of them. From Punking one-off at the Roxy in Wardour Street to the late-seventies rebellious Rock in Opposition festivals, Charles' drum kit was pushing boundaries. Even to this day, as an artist, he's never sat still. That's the paradox the experimental drummer has to overcome. I finally witnessed Charles play live at the Rock in Opposition festival in Carmaux, France in 2009, when he did an astonishing solo drum set.

It was around this time that I'd also stumbled upon Camberwell Now in Paul Mummery's collection and the compilation album *All's Well* ticked boxes that I didn't even know I had. I quickly tied together the lineage and delved further back in time to This Heat. My enthusiasm for it couldn't be contained, to the point where I approached Charles at the festival and asked him to be my first guest artist on the radio show. Talk about setting a high bar.

At that point I'd been subjecting my local community to a Zeuhl-tastic feast on Phoenix FM for a couple of years – the studio in Brentwood was just a few miles from my house and regardless of what else was happening in my life and career, I'd started to value my Monday evenings with its small but enthusiastic online listenership. We never did get to find out how many people from the Brentwood and Billericay community tuned in to listen to the pressing current affairs of the area sung in Kobaïan, but if a pothole had appeared on the A12 bypass, then Christian Vander had it covered late on a Monday evening.

My newer more 'out there' show was a good buzz every week, but while I wasn't exactly running out of material from a content perspective, I was finding that my presenting style – which was basically to back-announce the track and then continue with 'Here's another one of my favourites' – was starting to bore even me. The video chat room software kept me on my toes, but I was ready to up my game and I thought if I got some guests on, it would feel more like a proper radio show. Starting this new era with someone of Charles' pedigree was a good way of putting myself on my mettle.

I decided to go for a blend of a *Desert Island Discs* format and a musical history of the man, which gave me a great excuse to delve deep into the incredible range of work he'd done – Quiet Sun, This Heat and Camberwell Now were only the start of it. Wonderful collaborations with an abundance of artists, including Fred Frith and Bill Laswell in the band Massacre, as well as participating in a superb live supergroup called Keep the Dog plus numerous solo albums. Charles Hayward has always had an ear for innovation. So I did the best Roy Plomley/Michael Parkinson/Sue Lawley/Kirsty Young/Lauren Laverne (delete according to generation) impression I could muster and thoroughly enjoyed the experience. Charles himself brought in some esoteric choices of music to play and the whole thing worked nicely enough to establish a blueprint for how future shows would develop.

I mean, fuck! I totally missed This Heat first time around. I was at musical rock bottom in 1979 when their first album came out. I'm not sure I was listening to anything much then. I was practising twenty-five hours a day and shitting snooker balls. That's what you have to do, right? I'd left school as late as I could. Failed my A levels and then stayed on for another year in the sixth form to retake them. But in all honesty, I remained at school in order to tread water and play snooker every night – and halfway through my last school year, most days as well. I didn't even like maths! It was OK at O level, but then at A level they took away all the numbers and replaced them with letters. I was great counting in base 8 and I knew a sequence of colours that added up to twenty-seven, so what else was important? I turned pro in September 1978 and appeared on TV on *Pot Black* in January 1979 as an upcoming prospect. My career was about to take off and This Heat weren't particularly high on the checklist.

This Heat only made two albums and one 12-inch, but as a way in to their brilliance I'd still recommend listening to Camberwell Now first. I realise that might seem counter-intuitive, because it's a different band, but to me, it just feels like a continuation of This Heat, rather than a new starting place. Regardless, the energy of Camberwell Now was incredible and if you buy into them, then This Heat are a no-brainer. When I got to grips with Charles' contribution, I just thought: this guy, what a fucking maverick! I didn't have any idea of the person behind the music – where he came from, either physically or in cultural terms – I just loved what he was doing.

If ever the term 'progressive' could be aimed at an artist then Charles Hayward fits the criterion. 'Experimental' is another, but I think that's too ambiguous a description. So, was it a shock to the system when one of the most 'out there' musicians I knew agreed to reform This Heat with partner in previous crime, Charles Bullen, for a mini series of gigs? Dunno! But while the fans were nostalgically knocking one out in delight, Charles was at pains to draw a stave in the sand.

Yes, This Is Not This Heat (as they called themselves) were going to play some of their previous chartbusters, but only from the standpoint of the project being the challenge of a progressive regression, at least that's what Charles told me recently. The fact that this totally flew over my head is completely understandable, because the This Is Not This Heat drummer, formerly known as the This Heat drummer, currently known as Charles Hayward, is a musical genius and I'm a snooker player!

Looking back it was a privilege to watch Charles Bullen play with him at Cafe OTO and see how, with the input of an astonishing array of guests (including none other than Thurston Moore) they somehow managed to showcase a retrospective that at the same time felt totally fresh. To his eternal credit, the only ahead-of-his-time thing Charles Hayward hasn't done is drop down dead. Long may that continue to be the case!

One interesting aspect of both This Heat and Camberwell Now is that both bands contained a member who was to a large extent considered a 'non-musician'. The sadly departed Gareth Williams completed the line-up in This Heat, and Stephen Rickard, their former sound technician, subsequently joined Camberwell Now. In doing a bit of research for this book I asked Charles about this aspect, especially since I've now stumbled head first into this rather bizarre category of artist. Charles recounted that the experience was a breath of fresh air in the studio.

While I'm probably not doing his explanation justice, there would be a scenario where This Heat would be rehearsing a piece and Gareth Williams would be expected to bring something in after a count of eight, but he brought it in on the horrifying count of seven. It would then be explained to him that he couldn't do that, to which he'd respond 'Why?' The room then fell silent for a while and with neither of the Charleses being able to come up with a better reason than 'That's the way it's always been', the rehearsal continued in a far wonkier metre.

Watching Charles perform solo at the Rock in Opposition festival, dishing out a variety of complex time signatures, gave me an insight into the mind of a brilliant musician, even though I was unable to fully grasp it. Charles was basically playing drums and firing off a bunch of sample loops with his feet. It's mind-boggling to watch, not least because as a punter you can't comprehend how this stuff is being created, let alone conceived. I know he's only got two hands, but I suspect he has two brains and two extra feet behind his kick drum, as well. To top it all, at the same time as all those shenanigans, he was singing. To my ears he's a bloody genius.

The term 'genius' is widely bandied about as an assessment of people's talent and by the commonly accepted definition, I am one. Yippee! Like Charles, I've been lucky enough to have the exceptional ability the *Oxford English Dictionary* requires of me. But surely this isn't enough? Using this as a yardstick means there's a bloody plague of us on the planet! Maybe there should be a caveat applied, stipulating that only people with said exceptional ability can judge whether one of their so-called peers has an extra amount of the stuff that then puts them into a super-category of genius.

In my previous incarnation, on 1 May 1989, I was in the top 5.2 billionth per cent of the world's population at snooker; however, even then I never really considered myself a genius. I obviously had an extremely high level of talent that I honed to as close to perfection as I physically could, but to me the term 'genius' feels more magical than that, like a sort of Tommy the blind pinball wizard. The only two snooker players I've ever personally awarded that accolade to are Alex Higgins and Ronnie O'Sullivan. The Rocket is the only player's talent I'd love to have experienced while playing snooker – channelling my actions through his brain, utilising some form of virtual reality technology as yet unavailable to the BBC. I wonder if he sees different pictures to the rest of us mere mortals.

With music, have I got a clue who the real geniuses are? Every good musician seems to be one to a non-musician. Kavus' take on it is interesting: 'A genius doesn't have any duffers in their CV.' That certainly rules out Frank Zappa and The Beatles, so Mr Torabi certainly drives a hard bargain. Perhaps he's right. If it were budding Einsteins you were assessing, you wouldn't be over the moon if they'd only got 75 per cent of the equations correct. I'm older than Kavus and a bit softer in the centre these days. So maybe a genius just needs an exceptionally high strike rate of great tracks compared to average ones. We will all choose our own heroes and, hopefully, if you seek out the body of work that Charles Hayward has produced, you'll agree with me that he should be awarded a Genius-plus rating.

Chapter 10

Voivod

Kavus

I first heard the name Voivod in 1985. I was round at Chris' house in Peverell, Plymouth. As if the debt of honour I owed his stepdad, Nigel, for taking us to that first Iron Maiden gig wasn't enough, every month Nigel took delivery of a big box in the post from Shades, the London heavy metal record shop. The pick of these spoils would usually be condensed into a couple of C90 cassettes, which he'd give to Chris – albums by Trouble, Savatage, Lizzy Borden or Warrior. Stuff that you'd only read about in Kerrang! *but couldn't afford to take a risk on.*

Inasmuch as he had a job working for the South West Electricity Board and seemed to blow his entire pay packet on metal albums, Nigel was pretty much the coolest grown-up I knew. Often, when I was round there he'd treat us to some of the purchases he deemed to be less than satisfactory.

'Listen to this fucking shit!*' he'd bellow, handing over the LP sleeve of a band he didn't feel kicked suitable ass. And so it was that I first became familiar with that futuristic logo, bizarre artwork and alien-sounding name that has since etched itself indelibly into my unconsciousness. I scrutinised the sleeve of the Canadian thrashers' second album* Rrröööaaarrr *while being subjected to 'Fuck Off and Die' at the kind of volume that only an adult's hi-fi could muster.*

'Oh my God! It's so bad,' Nigel kept repeating through genuine giggles. I had to concede that for someone who had only recently been turned on to Metallica's Ride the Lightning, *this didn't sound anything like what I considered to be thrash metal. My ears only processed a structureless, underproduced mess.*

I, too, laughed at 'Fuck Off and Die', but I kept examining the sleeve, wishing I liked it, because it was a cool-looking record.

For the next couple of years the word 'Voivod' did the work of both adjective and verb in Nigel's lexicon. It became shorthand for anything he considered unlistenable. Had this been Voivod's only contribution to Western culture, they may have become a footnote in my conversation, the way Lizzy Borden, Warrior or Savatage are now. Destiny had other ideas, mind.

Come 1988, I was sixteen, had just left school, and my listening was expanding to include Cardiacs, Sonic Youth, Killing Joke and Hawkwind. The word 'psychedelic' kept appearing in articles related to my new discoveries. I loved the sound of the word and the way it looked. It was mysterious and esoteric, and seemed to attach itself to every cherished new musical acquisition, from Loop to Fields of the Nephilim. So when I happened upon Voivod's fourth album, Dimension Hatröss, in the racks of Rival Records in Royal Parade my interest was aroused by the sticker that proclaimed 'Canada's Nuclear Metal Warriors. More Psychedelic Than Ever. THE CULT LIVES!'

'More psychedelic than ever'? Was that unfocused mess I'd heard actually psychedelic?

Once again, the cover was amazing. A sort of futuristic 2D Voivod was imprisoned within a scalpel-decorated black mechanical frame. One eye blank, the other a screenshot of redacted data. A half-exposed brain was being both syringed and drained of atomic power. All set against an eerie twilight glow. Effectively, what I was looking at here was a dystopian AI lawnmower. A dystopian AI lawnmower that screamed 'Own me!' I had enough money to obey this injunction. Buying albums based on the artwork was an occasional strategy on my part back then, with predictably mixed results. Good – White Noise: An Electric Storm, Bad – Mortal Sin: Mayhemic Destruction.

In this case, the sleeve had drawn me to some seriously debilitating music. The album was constructed from awkward mechanical riffs and strange otherworldly dissonances. It was a fucked-up, apocalyptic sci-fi concept album with impenetrable shamanistic lyrics. It completely inhabited its own world.

I could hear no precedent for this music. Although it used a little of the colour of hardcore, prog and goth, the landscapes it was mapping out were completely other – singular. 'More Psychedelic Than Ever' was *an understatement.*

Voivod's trajectory from their primitive, Venom-inspired debut to improbable space overlord visionaries three years later delivered a four-album run virtually unequalled in all rock music. Apart from The Beatles, I can't think of another band that transcends their humble beginnings with so radiant an arc. Like The Fab Four, no one member of Voivod was a virtuoso, but each album refined the strange Voivodian essence, rowing further away from their contemporaries into an eerie nowhere.

From the outset, Voivod were a high-concept band. Drummer 'Away' was responsible for the look, the artwork and the idea. A quick stock-take: while all of Voivod had noms de plume (singer and lyricist Denis Bélanger was Snake, Bassist Jean-Yves Theriault was Blacky, and guitar-ist and principal composer Denis D'Amour was Piggy), Michel Langevin, the beautiful French-Canadian sorcerer responsible for birthing the whole uncanny thing, chose to call himself 'Away'.

I see you Prince, Fish, Seal, Sting. I hear you Bono, Buckethead, Thunderstick and Demolition Man. Now you must kneel before Away.

What was the concept? Each album follows the narrative of 'The Voivod', but that's where I get off. The lyrics read like a tripping beatnik reimagining a chemistry textbook as an apocalyptic warning, which is exactly what I'm after in a band. Like the saps translating Kobaïan or giving credence to the Magma myth, for me it misses the point. The point is the music.

The first two albums, War and Pain *and* Rrröööaaarrr, *are great if you want to complete the journey, but it's like watching* Seinfeld *from the start. Effectively you only need to go in at the third series.*

Voivod elevated themselves from their auspicious metal/punk origins into telekinetic scientists in 1986 with Killing Technology. *This was the birth of the Voivod sound.*

The Voivod sound largely hinges on the flattened fifth/augmented fourth, the tritone or – if you will – Diabolus in Musica, the devil in music. To this day, my friends and I call it 'The Voivod chord'. It underpins the main riff to the song 'Black Sabbath'. It's all over Daevid Allen's Gong and Robert Fripp utilises it liberally in King Crimson, particularly the masterpiece 'Fracture'. It was popularised, if you can call it that, by Stravinsky, Messiaen and Bartók. It's the sound of chaos, the cold, desolate universe. It's the sound of being disassociated from your ego and your very sense of self. It's because of this chord that I am still, to this day, living in rented accommodation.

It's the chord of loneliness, abject poverty and - ye gods! - it's the best fucking chord there is.

The tritone is easy to play on the guitar. Form a barre chord and move the second finger down a fret so your fingers make a diagonal. Instant Voivod. Now start writing songs with it and watch your audience dwindle. Many artists use it to create tension or as a passing chord. Voivod use it as the bricks from which they build their entire cybernetic temple.

Playing chords high up the neck on the top three strings - jarring, slashing, questioning phrases that sound like crackling circuitry - Piggy utilised shapes, clusters and techniques completely alien not only to heavy metal, but also to most other rock music.

Away's propulsive drumming employed the signature hammerhead double kick of Philthy Phil 'Animal' Taylor but his tribal, pounding floor toms owed more to Bauhaus than Iron Maiden. Blacky's gnarly, distorted Nomeansno-cum-Lemmy bass tone churned out angular lines while Snake's sneering post-nuclear sermons would constantly and deliberately land on beautiful, jarring 'out' notes.

Killing Technology *is a mind-blast from beginning to end. Away's cover art is as hermetically confusing as one would expect and looks just like how the music sounds. The band looked effortlessly cool on the reverse photo, too.*

It's unfair to the rest of metal at this point even to make comparisons between Voivod and the genre as a whole. I remember a typically high-spirited evangelical rant in the late eighties being hijacked by a white-trainer-wearing dullard in a Testament T-shirt telling me that 'Voivod are shit; they sound like they haven't tuned their guitars.' Voivod was a way of finding out who the heads were.

Even today, 'Forgotten in Space', which opens side two - or, if you will, the 'Ravenous Side' - stands alone. It's pure Voivod. Descending, dissonant chords and spastic riffs over shifting metres of 4/4, 3/4, 6/8, 5/4, half-pace, double time, twisting and wriggling, riding the seismic rumble of Away's thunderous kick drums. Snake barks out the desperate plight of those, er, forgotten in space. He peppers the chaos with cries of 'Deep in the hole . . . too many echoes' and 'Cylindrical habitat modules, let me out of here, and I heard my name'. Adopting the empyrean monotone of a galactic automaton, he exclaims 'Hydrocarbonic smog, methane ice crystals, ultraviolet rays in the galaxy core, rotations and orbits of somebody, atoms and molecules through my body.'

You'll need to hear this at least five times before the underlying apocalyptic vision starts to reveal its true form. Basically, until you can sing along with this entire astronomical shopping list without the aid of a lyric sheet, there's still work to be done.

Dimension Hatröss, *where I came on board, continued the process of distillation that had been ongoing since their debut,* War and Pain. *There were four songs on each side, and the construction of the pieces was tighter, more focused with a fuller, better-produced sound. Along with Cardiacs'* A Little Man and a House and the Whole World Window, *this record was the sound of my 1988.*

While the timbre is still recognisably metal, there's spooky alchemy at work. From the opener, 'Experiment', the tension rarely lets up. A forty-minute visit into a primordial netherworld where all life begins and ends, there are no questionable moments, no point at which the music sags. It's propulsive, exciting, futuristic and bubbling with strangeness.

I couldn't have been more excited about the arrival of Nothingface. *There had been tantalising scraps of pre-release information in the metal press. Voivod had signed to MCA, a major, the album was going to feature a version of Syd Barrett's 'Astronomy Domine' and it was to continue the high-concept narrative of the Voivod. I'd already imagined the cover and what the music was going to sound like.*

When it finally arrived, I was initially disappointed. The cover was horrible. Away's instantly recognisable hand-drawn visions and iconic logo were instead replaced with a computer-graphic sleeve that looked cheap and dated even by 1989, as if Away had been given access to a ZX Spectrum, complete with dodgy power supply, and a six-hour deadline.

The graphics managed to stay awful for about the length of time it took to get the bus from Plymouth town centre back home to Crownhill. From first listen to this day, all I can see in those shitty, blurred block graphics is the glorious representation of Voivod's greatest triumph. A realisation and purification of everything the band had been working towards in those previous three years. Voivod had made this record for me, that much was clear.

The opening fifteen-second riff of 'The Unknown Knows' is about the only nod to the thrash Voivod on the entire album. It might even have been an in-joke. Like a leather jacket with studs, patches and a Tippexed Alien Sex Fiend logo shrugged off almost immediately to reveal an unrecognisable cyborg, the questionable artwork was just the outer skin that the music itself couldn't wait to shed.

Even now, listening to this album that's been so constant in my life since its release, Nothingface *is so humbling, so confident in its mad bug-eyed vision, so unshakeably out there. It effortlessly bridges the two worlds of twentieth-century modern composition with everything truly brilliant about rock 'n' roll.*

Nothingface *was as if Voivod had taken William Burroughs' cut-ups and automatic writing, added an unsettling pinch of Philip K. Dick's anxious paranoia and run with it.* Nothingface *is an abstract and mechanical realm, where all lines converge, where we leave our familiar planet and colonise an empty, bleak new world of cold landscapes governed by eccentric and cruel physical laws, where time concertinas and all logic is Mercury. That this album is barely even a cult record is ludicrous.*

Dispensing with their previous fruitful collaboration with Harris Johns, Glenn Robinson's production is clinical and squared off. The distortion has been pared back for something cleaner, more surgically precise.

The songs are tighter, with all tracks under six minutes, and, having dispensed with any residual thrash metal tropes, they exist as an intergalactic brand of psychedelic pop, studiously assembled in the cosmic Petri dish from asymmetrical structures, constantly shifting metres and dreamlike words. That Voivod came from primitive, self-taught punk/

metal to this advanced high-art composition in less than five years is a big enough deal, but it's the punky, aggressive edge that gives this music such authority.

I'd always been fairly puritanical about the inclusion of cover versions on an album rather than as stand-alone tracks – singles and especially B-sides are the place for them – nonetheless, Voivod's take on Pink Floyd's 'Astronomy Domine' is sensational. It's faithful to the Syd Barrett original yet sounds so intrinsically part of the sequence that the album would be lopsided without it. It doesn't even matter that they get a few of the words wrong.

'Pre-Ignition', though, is the money shot, the point when Wendy Torrance discovers that 'all work and no play makes Jack a dull boy'. It is that diabolical moment of revelation when we finally see the wicker man and Sergeant Howie realises the true nature of Lord Summerisle's plan. Using a riff from Igor Stravinsky's The Rite of Spring and twisting it further through an improbable path of musical trigonometry, Snake declares 'Some are set free, emotions flood their gaze, synthetic breed . . . the pre-ignition phase' and at this dazzling exhortation, for a brief, vertiginous moment, all of Nothingface makes sense, the terrifying logic is revealed and the madness is given full clarity.

Where does one go after an album like this? I hoped they'd venture further into uncharted realms. But maybe the album didn't enjoy the kind of success Voivod had hoped for, because the follow-up, Angel Rat, saw them work with Terry Brown, who was the producer for fellow Canadian band Rush. Angel Rat is apparently where Voivod 'went commercial'. They abandoned the Voivod concept and made shorter, more melodic songs, but it's a beautiful album. The 'pop' Voivod attempt is a pop only they could have made. Angel Rat is the fourth instalment in an unbroken line of brilliance that begun with Killing Technology – where Nothingface is cold, bizarre and alien, Angel Rat is warm, generous and human; the perfect complement.

Following a fallow period throughout the nineties that was marked by an unremarkable run of much more primitive albums, I'd often joke that no one 'got' Voivod like I do . . . including the band themselves, but the last couple of records have been sensational.

After the tragic passing of key songwriter Denis D'Amour, aka Piggy, in 2005, Voivod found an exceptional composer and guitarist in Daniel 'Chewy' Mongrain, someone who clearly 'gets' their music even more than I do. Down the front at the Camden Underworld in 2017, noting my gesticulating enthusiasm, Snake handed me the microphone during 'Astronomy Domine'. I sang for the beauty and sadness of Syd Barrett, of Voivod, of this crazy melancholy world and all who inhabit it, and all was as it should be in this mad old universe.

Chapter 11

yet more Magma

Steve and Kavus

Steve

I've got massive gaps in my musical knowledge, especially when it comes to the more obvious end of the spectrum. I have a sort of musical snobbery that to be honest I am comfortable with, but which has also held me back from exploring more popular artists. After all there are only so many listening hours in a lifetime (unless you're Kavus) and apart from my soul music era I've - rightly or wrongly - tended to focus on the more esoteric artists.

I was in a TV studio at the Masters snooker event in London a few years ago, sitting with fellow pundit Ken Doherty. Jason Mohammed was presenting. They were drooling over U2 and were angling to get a couple of mentions into the on-air conversation, like Chris Packham did once with Smiths song titles. No objection my end. I did a whole programme full of biscuit references on an ITV snooker event once. With twenty seconds to go until the end of the transmission (and me trailing by one biscuit against the radio presenter Russ Williams), I levelled the score when I mentioned the Wagon Wheel falling off for John Higgins' opponent. Relieved, I eased back into my leather chair, but Russ struck the winning blow with 'Yes, he truly is a Royal Scot, goodnight!'

The only problem in this case was that I didn't know the names of any songs by U2.

Ken and Jason were suggesting all these clever nods to the band, but they flew right over my head. I know every Magma track on the planet . . . Kobaïa, but I couldn't name you one by U2. They were genuinely puzzled. OK, I know the name of one album by them, but I don't want to ruin the credibility of this book by committing it to print. I don't even know if that's also a track name and I'm fucked if I'm going to waste time by looking it up. I've not been able to avoid hearing them on the radio occasionally but for me the music is so average that nothing about any U2 song I've ever heard has ever given me the inclination to hear it again, let alone find out what the thing was called.

You may have read between the lines here and surmised that I totally dislike the band. It's nothing personal. It's just not my style of music. However, *South Park*'s portrayal of the U2 frontman as the world's biggest shit came frustratingly true for me and thousands of music lovers when the dog Bono and his band uploaded doo-dah onto 500 million treasured iTunes collections. For a split second, like many people at the time, I was furious and contemplated seeking out his address and crapping on *his* doorstep to see how he liked it. Then I came to my senses and realised that this act would be giving him physical product as opposed to the virtual 1s and 0s he'd dumped into my folder. If his roses were to improve the following year as a result, then Bono would be the victor.

If I ever let someone hear the music I like, it's 99.9 per cent nailed on that they'll consider it sewage. From the opening bars you can sense they're uncomfortable and this is usually followed by a comment like 'You can't possibly like that.' You learn to expect this reaction and it's always a welcome surprise when you stumble upon a like-minded soul, especially if they were previously unaware of the style of music being presented to them. I think that's one of the big motivational forces behind doing the radio show.

Ronnie O'Sullivan came into the studio in Brentwood once. He was considering presenting a sports show on Phoenix FM, so he popped in to have a chat with me on a Monday night, while I was on air, to get a feel for the place. Not that he needs the work, though I reckon he's a decent presenter in the making, TV or radio, but he threw me a curveball when, during the Albert Marcoeur track 'Bouge Pas' from the album *Ma Vie Avec Elles*, he told me that he quite liked it. I was thinking, really, Ron? You actually like this? Well, 'every credit' as the late great Willie Thorne would have said in commentary, but the tables had been well and truly turned and it was me left by far the more unnerved by the incident.

Back in 1988, after I'd announced I was promoting Magma/Not Magma in London, my manager Barry Hearn was well impressed. 'I'm coming.' he said. 'Don't,' I pleaded. He came, along with his then friend and also rival boxing promoter Frank Warren (plus their two wives), and the four of them attended the opening night at the Bloomsbury Theatre. They had front-row seats, naturally, because boxing promoters only do ringside. As luck would have it, Barry's all-time favourite artist is the legendary Zeuhl demigod Tom Paxton. What could possibly go wrong!?

Christian Vander walked out with a big head mask on and the mesmeric strains of 'Zëss' reached the audience. The sound waves hit Barry nanoseconds before most others. I suppose that's the musical equivalent of getting the benefit of being spattered with blood in the front row on fight night. I didn't see them leave, but as far as I could ascertain a few days later, it hadn't gone well. Judging by the disturbed tone in Barry's voice as he recounted the events of the evening and me remembering the set list, they all left pretty soon after 'Zë' and just before the 'ss' bit.

There was a good line in the music press (either *Sounds* or *Melody Maker* - not all the good lines were in the *NME*) of a review of a concert Magma did in London back in the mid-seventies. At the end it said, 'Don't take your girlfriend to a Magma concert.' Generally, I'd tend to agree that this process is fraught with danger. Though that doesn't apply to Kavus - his wife, Dawn, loves Magma, which is not only fortunate for him (and for her), but also for us, as she was the person who brought us all together.

In early 2009, I went over to France to see Magma for their fortieth anniversary gigs, which consisted of a three-night residency at the Casino de Paris. I took my girlfriend at the time and she assured me that things would be fine as long as there was a champagne mouthwash area at the venue. But long-time friend and Magma and Zeuhl fan Steve Ashworth didn't fare so well.

We all met up for a beer prior to the gig, then rushed excitedly to the venue and found our respective seats. The support act was a bonus. A Magma-related band led by bass player Jannick Top were showcasing their new album *Infernal Machina*. At the interval we reconvened with Steve and his girlfriend. I took one look at her and she appeared genuinely traumatised. I tried to defuse the situation: 'Magma's going to be heavier.' I said. And that was it! She was out of there like the Bee Gees on a Clive Anderson show, leaving Steve trailing in her wake and mumbling something about seeing me the next night. Steve made the following two nights but nursing a spare ticket for sale.

Kavus

The first time Dawn saw Magma, I told her 'I'm not even going to play you any of their records. I'm just going to take you to see them . . .' In 2002, it was at the Queen Elizabeth Hall on the South Bank – they opened with 'Zëss' that time, as well.

Steve

Was that the one Paul McCartney was at? I think Heather Mills was with him that evening. You see? Fucking schoolboy - temporary secretary - error in my opinion! Never bring your girlfriend.

Kavus

No, the McCartney one was at the Royal Festival Hall a couple of years earlier, but it was before I knew you, so even though I saw you, I imagined you had enough energy drainers interrogating you about Zeuhl, so I let you be. That gig was when Dawn drank the Kool-Aid – she just became obsessed with Magma.

Steve

That's probably why you got married.

Kavus

Maybe. People have certainly got married for flimsier reasons. Dawn and I had been friends since she was going out with Tim Smith from

Cardiacs in the mid-nineties. After they split up, she was off the scene for a while, qualifying as a lawyer and becoming a grown-up, so I hadn't seen her for ages.

But then I went to The Spitz to see Tatsuya Yoshida's legendary band Ruins and Dawn was there with a couple of pals. Over the course of the gig, people were leaving, presumably because they couldn't handle the Japanese duo's gloriously full-on maximalist assault. When they walked on there were maybe about 110 people there, but by the time they got to the end of their set, there were about twenty to twenty-five people left at most. The house lights went on, I looked over and there was Dawn on her own. She caught my eye and with a wide-eyed face full of amazement at what we'd just witnessed she gave me the thumbs up. Although we didn't get together until the following year, I suppose our courtship and marriage was a done deal. Although she's not a musician, Dawn hears music like one and I'd say it still makes up 60 per cent of our conversation.

During this period Magma, or more specifically the music of Christian Vander, became all-consuming for both of us. It was all we'd listen to and all we could talk about. Neither of us had ever expected to experience again that kind of obsession with another band, like we had when we were younger, but there it was. Before we became parents, every time they were playing in France she'd take a few days off work and we'd drive down there, taking our tent with us, so we could just pitch it somewhere near wherever they were playing and have somewhere to stay after the gig. That was how Steve and I came to meet, because Magma were doing a month-long residency at a brilliant little venue in Paris called Le Triton in 2006, playing music from a different era every week. So Dawn and I bought tickets for one each of the four different shows, and because obviously Steve was there every time, that's how we became pals.

Steve

This is probably a shit story, but I'm going to tell it anyway, because it's the kind of silly thing that happens that you refer to endlessly as a friendship develops. As I might have mentioned earlier, there's an album by Magma called *Köhntarkösz*. Le Triton's capacity is 180 people max, so obviously alongside Kavus, Dawn and me, it was predominantly just French people in the audience. But we bumped into a Scottish guy and he told us, in what felt to me like a relatively strong Glaswegian accent, 'Great, isn't it? I hope they do "Kontakorus"' like it was some sort of pre-historic monster and Magma might be about to cover a Was (Not Was) song. Of course with Magma's invented language, you wouldn't have much cause to read the titles or lyrics out loud, so it was easy to see how his copy of the album had morphed from *Köhntarkösz* into something that might well have sent Raquel Welsh scarpering for cover. And from that moment on, the piece became *Kontakorus* for us, too. Would it be too much of a coincidence if one day, many years later, a band put out a track with something like *'Konta Chorus'* as the title?

Kavus

Always 'Kontakorus' . . . it's a better name. That was a funny night. We ended up going out together for the first time afterwards.

Steve

I remember the headache. Pelforth Brune was the culprit . . .

Kavus

It was Dawn who went to talk to you first. We saw you and thought, of course Davis is here, as we'd seen you at other gigs by then. She said, 'I'm going to go over and talk to him.' And once she'd broken the ice, I came over and started chatting to you, too. Within a few seconds of the conversation beginning, you stopped being that famous snooker player we'd grown up watching. Once we'd left you I remember Dawn saying, 'One of us, isn't he?' You just seemed so much like our usual mates.

Steve

I did write a review of one of those Triton shows, which was published in *Prog* magazine . . . so I thought I should include it here. First, for the sake of historical accuracy and second, to bring a moment of hope to those who seek the odd chicken nugget of more conventional musical appreciation from me, as opposed to my somewhat bog-standard, random Happy Meal approach.

Le Triton: think The Marquee or Ronnie Scott's but perhaps even more intimate. It's week three of Magma's twelve-day residency. A fan walks past with a large brass Magma logo welded to his skull – OK, perhaps it's on his hat. The queue for front-row bragging rights spills out onto the road – black attire is de rigueur. We watch the fervour build from the El Triton bistro, happy to eventually make camp at the rear bar with no sound-quality deterioration.

Our nine heroes ease themselves into 'K.A', but in no time we're hooked into this now classic opus. Philippe Bussonnet's monstrous bass demands attention, only to be upstaged by Christian Vander's mesmeric drumming before even that is trumped by Hervé Aknin and Stella Vander's vocal pyrotechnics. 'K.A' is now far better than its studio version – tonight there's more sophistication applied but with no loss of energy. The riveting 'Om Zanka' kicks in before a cliffhanger 'Hallelujah' chorus has us joyously applauding. We recover with a five-minute respite before the real onslaught starts. The mighty 'Köhntarkösz' fills the room. This seventies master-piece remains perhaps Christian Vander's greatest achievement. There are those who dare to attach the tag 'copyist' to his work, but what we are witnessing has no peers nor mimics, no elders. If 'K.A' was brilliant, then 'Köhntarkösz' is truly from another planet. Vander is in his element while Bussonett puts foot to the floor sending us into oblivion. By the time we reach the jamming section, James MacGaw is ready to take centre stage and delivers a blistering guitar solo.

Trade is brisk at the Seventh Records stall. I can smell the latest T-shirts and I'm positive the vinyl edition of 'K.A' is beckoning me, demanding I drop by at the end.

After the interval, we're treated to the mighty 'Ëmëhntëhtt-Ré'. Vander stands to deliver his legendary defiant 'Hhaï' soapbox address as his demonstrative fists crash into the cymbals. He sits to rousing applause and the piece moves through the gears until Bussonnet goes berserk on 'Zombies'. A guy behind me makes noises of appreciation usually reserved for the boudoir. I don't turn round. When Philippe's astonishing 'Grand Zombies' acrobatics kick in, the crowd are nigh on delirious.

Christian Vander's Magma are the best live band in the world. Once seen, you'll never judge another concert by the same drumstick again.

I hope I haven't let myself down by straying too far beyond my traditional mode of critique. But while I'm pushing the boundaries, I'd like to offer readers this potted guide to Zeuhl music - the whole swathe of previously undiscovered brilliance that was opened up for me by Magma's *Mëkanïk Dëstruktïẁ Kömmandöh*. Had it not been for this astonishing 47-year-old opus, I'd never have been exposed to this unique genre - a blend of rock, jazz, classical and opera whizzed up in a Magimix to create aural Marmite. Of course, it's all down to the chef. Stir up jazz, rock and classical with the wrong spoon and you'll end up in *Brain Salad Surgery*.

Christian Vander and his seventies Magma cohorts spawned an abundance of astonishing music, treading a path the like of which could never have been conceived of, let alone followed here in the UK. Magma's output under their own name was more than enough to get them on my podium, but as the band morphed and members migrated during the seventies, even more brilliance erupted from their molten core.

Bass clarinettist and saxophonist Yochk'o Seffer left with pianist Francois Cahen to form the astounding offshoot band Zao. They hit the ground running with *Z=7L*. All-round windy-blowing exponent Teddy Lasry extended his repertoire to keyboards and excelled with $E=MC^2$. Later in the decade, bassist Bernard Paganotti formed the band Weidorje and later Paga, which resulted in four more top-notch offerings, while keyboardist Patrick Gauthier produced the superb, jazzier, *Bébé Godzilla* album.

In more recent years, another cohort of Zeuhl warriors has sallied forth from the Magma barracks. Pianist Emmanuel Borghi, guitarist James MacGaw and bassist Philippe Bussonnet have been involved in the brilliant offshoot instrumental band One Shot and, as previously mentioned, even Magma's *MDK* bassist Jannick Top was tempted out of Zeuhl retirement and stunned us with the growling *Infernal Machina*.

And that's only the beginning of the riches to be unearthed. I'm talking about the Zeuhl cousins or, more accurately, bands seemingly influenced by the genre, or that have definite similarities. While Magma lay largely dormant during the eighties, the lava continued to flow. Eskaton created a buzz with, among others, *4 Visions*, and Eider Stellaire's vinyl rarities impressed those in the know. Two of my personal favourites from recent years are Neom and their superb *Arkana Temporis* album, closely followed by Setna – *Cycle 1*. Further afield, you'll be astounded by Japanese band Kōenji Hyakkei and any of their five (to date) studio albums. And if you're looking for UK Zeuhl (and why on earth wouldn't you be?), then Guapo should be your first port of call. Check out *Five Suns* and the more recent *History of the Visitation*, which sees none other than Kavus extending his compositional repertoire.

Other bands and artists that feel related to the ethos of Magma (although I'm sure the bands themselves don't feel that), are Art Zoyd, Univers Zero, Present, Shub-Niggurath, Potemkine, Bondage Fruit and Simon Steensland. The music they've produced is nothing short of astonishing. If your interest is at all piqued by reading this and you subsequently seek out Magma and start to like what you hear, then fucking hell, have you got some serious shit to enjoy with those artists listed! I'm already envying the possible journey of enlightenment you have ahead of you. On the other hand, of course . . . you might not buy into it, especially if you only give these artists one listen.

So anyway, Kavus and I met up for the first time at that Magma gig in France and a good time was had by all. At some stage, one drunken evening, Kavus mentioned that he played in a band and invited me along to see them. I said, 'Oh, lovely,' in a sort of encouraging 'Ah, bless your cotton socks' way, thinking it would probably just be something in the back of a pub. Next thing I knew I was at a Cardiacs gig at the Astoria in London with 1800 people jumping and gesturing to every turn in the music and chanting the words to songs alien to me.

I'd never heard of The Cardiacs. Obviously not, as I was still calling them 'The Cardiacs', but these crazy fans had de-definite articled the band many moons before, and amazingly, they were far more fervent and excitable than any Magma fan I'd ever stumbled upon. They were being preached to by a guy in an overcoat telling them about 'eyes and hands' and they were in awe, hanging on his every word, as if he wasn't a very naughty boy at all! It was incredible.

Then all of a sudden, my new mate who I'd hung out with in France appeared onstage with a big white guitar and Tim Smith beckoned him over and planted a big kiss on Kavus' mush. 'That's my mate! On that stage! Fucking hell!' Who the fuck were Cardiacs!? And with music as crazy as this, why hadn't I heard of them before?

After the gig, I got invited into the band room, where I chilled out with Kavus, said hello to the band members and briefly met Tim Smith. Tragically, the next time I was to see him he'd be confined to a wheelchair.

By the time I came back down into the main room, the transition into the G-A-Y nightclub – which used to come into operation after the bands at the Astoria – was pretty much complete. So the black T-shirts and beer bellies (sorry, kidz) had gone, to be replaced by what seemed to be a sea of light blue jeans and far snugger-fitting white T-shirts. Generally, the clientele appeared a lot fitter! I joined the queue to get my coat and looked along the line of guys who were also waiting to check their jackets in, thinking, I really hope the bigoted woman from the Abbey Wood fish and chip shop is working the cloakroom tonight.

Chapter 12

Cardiacs

Kavus

'Torabi!'

I recognised the mocking tone immediately and looked to see the bony finger of the deputy headmaster, Mr Veale, beckoning me over.

What could he possibly want? He'd never taught me and, while I'd never openly displayed an academic bent, I wasn't a naughty boy, either. I got through five years in that miserable school without ever having been in detention.

Standing there, pompous, stern and wiry, he impatiently scrutinised me over his glasses as I approached.

'If you're going to come back next term, make sure you get that confounded mop cut.'

Happily, I did neither.

As far as I could tell, there were five changes I needed to make to put my life in order: leave school, grow hair, leave home, get girlfriend, form proper band. I'd been biding my time, waiting for this feeling of stasis to pass until these alterations could be effected. The periodic table and Boyle's law were unlikely to be of any assistance in the life I had planned. My abiding memory of chemistry is pondering what magnesium cymbals on a drum kit might look like if ignited at the climax of a concert. There was never any question of a fallback career in case I didn't 'make it'.

I'd taken an art O level at fifteen the previous year and in 1988, took a music AS level on the grounds that the teacher, Mr Jenkins, didn't approve of the new GSCEs that were being foisted on us for the first time, having widened the definition to include the dreaded 'pop music'.

Unsurprisingly, these turned out to be the only qualifications I actually left that school with, being the only subjects I especially cared about.

I was sixteen and no law in the land could make me go back to school, but while still living under my parents' roof, leaving education completely wasn't an option. Thankfully, the thought of my returning to school and retaking my GCSEs in 'General Sixth' (sixth form for thickos) was almost as unappealing to them as it was to me. That September, exchanging tie and blazer for a leather jacket and black jeans, I stepped into the refectory of the Plymouth CFE (College for Further Education) King's Road annexe.

A jukebox blared into a cavernous, smoke-filled hall where rows of long tables were arrayed around a canteen that served eggs, chips and beans. Every day, for pennies! Teenagers of all stripes talked, preened, smoked, shouted, argued and coupled. With a jolt of excitement, my eye fell upon the furthest table on the left, by the windows, which was inhabited by goths, punks, metallers, hippies, the full gamut of the eighties alternative music subcultures. Where had all these beautiful people come from?

It would emerge that sat at this table were the outsiders from all the other schools in Plymouth. The kids who didn't get on with their folks, or for whom the education system just hadn't worked out. Here, misfits could proclaim their anarcho-left-wing politics, homosexuality, vegetarianism, impossible hopes and antisocial ideas. They could be as introverted or extroverted as they wanted – let their freak flags fly, with no fear of retribution. For the first time in my life, I'd found my people and was finally in the company of girls. I loved the CFE. That philosophy was even on the syllabus was a big enough deal, but the lecturer had long hair and wore a New Model Army T-shirt, for fuck's sake.

Sitting at that table was like being part of a club, a secret society. We may have been the object of derision for both the more diligent and vocational students at the college, but we also had strength in numbers. Our table attracted all the groovy teens and was even visited by heads not studying at the college, such was its appeal. It was a 25-minute walk from the town centre but at prices like that, who could resist the canteen? Awkward, thin, tall and bespectacled, with long hair over my eyes, here I briefly earned the nickname 'Joey Ramone', which was an improvement on both 'Paki Crap' and 'Fucking Hippy'.

It was here, also, that I met the charismatic Marcus Kielly. Marcus was confident, intense, funny and opinionated. He had an incandescent, questioning intellect and was 'not for everyone'. He was a painter and seemed to live like one, too. The very idea that this guy could have parents or anything like a normal life was unimaginable. I liked him immediately.

We initially bonded over a shared love of Living Colour, Fields of the Nephilim and illustration but soon progressed into the world of ideas and metaphysics. Following our conversations, I'd feel invigorated by a sense of infinite potential on the walk home.

I can't remember who introduced us and, given the intensity of our connection, it seems odd that our friendship was so brief. Nor can I remember what happened to him. He was in my life and then he wasn't. Perhaps he went away to art college. I've only got one photograph of him and we probably met less than twenty times. That our involvement with one another was so ephemeral only adds to his mystique. In my own myth, Marcus was the messenger who stepped through a portal into my world, giving me something that would spark the most extraordinary chain of events, alter me irreversibly and shape my entire life from that point forwards.

Marcus introduced me to Cardiacs.

One afternoon, as we walked into town together, he said, 'You have to borrow this - it's going to be your thing,' and handed me an LP.

It didn't look like my thing at all.

The monochrome sleeve was filled by an enormous white daisy. Whoever was responsible for this artwork clearly had no interest in the work of Derek Riggs.

'What's it like?'

Anyone familiar with this album or indeed the band will know how hard it is to describe music that's about everything. *Marcus gave it a decent shot, mind, enthusiastically stamping his feet and singing the offbeat horn stabs of what I later recognised as 'Dive'. I was intrigued but none the wiser.*

A Little Man and a House and the Whole World Window *by* Cardiacs had only recently been released. I was pretty clued up about *indie and alternative music, but I'd never heard of them. Nevertheless, I was flattered that Marcus had trusted me with it. Records were a precious commodity - you didn't just lend them to anyone.*

Beyond the cover, the back of the sleeve yielded few clues. A dark, murky photograph of a collection of paper flowers, song titles that gave little away, and the copy Marcus gave me had no lyrics, either.

Back home in my bedroom, I dropped the needle of my shitty jumble sale record player and sat back on my bed.

A cyclical riff started up, accompanied by what sounded like the mechanical drudgery of a factory, and then . . .

Leaving early, just before the hour.
A few moments won't make any difference.
Not to me, anyway.

Why those three lines hit me so hard I couldn't say, but immediately the spell was cast. Over the course of side one - and I must stress this isn't hyperbole for the sake of a good yarn - I experienced another profound epiphany.

This music was made for me. This music, along with the words, was aimed directly at me but somewhere deeper than the mere ego. This music resonated with something deep and subliminal. It was like being shown a film of every forgotten dream in glorious technicolour. The singer, Tim Smith, who it turned out was also responsible for the guitar playing, composition and production, had made this music for me and me alone.

In terms of the instrumentation, arrangements and Smith's cockney delivery, the closest point of reference I could make out, from my limited knowledge, was The Rise & Fall *and* Keep Moving-*era Madness, but the writing was . . . well, it was all things. It was life itself.*

Getting up to flip the album over, I already knew, beyond any question, that this was not only the most important music I'd ever heard, but it was also the most important music that had ever been made. My heart was racing, I felt woozy. Somehow, the world was different. Something that had seemed crucial a mere twenty minutes earlier had been untethered

117

and was now floating away, getting smaller and more inconsequential as it went. Whatever it was, I didn't miss it.

The unfolding revelation continued across side two and then, on the penultimate track, 'R.E.S.', following a kaleidoscopic barrage of musical shifts, a guitar solo appeared. In theory, at least, guitar solos were familiar territory for me. But this was like no other guitar solo I'd ever heard. To call it the best Christing guitar solo that had ever been played was to damn it with faint praise. It was better than that. It meant something significant, but what was it telling me? It was telling me the story of my life, the life yet to come. It was describing the following twenty years.

After gatecrashing my subconscious, reimagining my terrifying dreams as music, articulating a vision of the world that wasn't alien, phoney or corny, Tim Smith pulled me into a borderland that was frighteningly familiar, and then played that on the guitar. That!

Who was he? What did he look like? How old was he? Where had he come from? How did he arrive at this music and why had I not experienced anything so impossibly affecting before?

Something joyful and terrifying had happened. This music was deeply mysterious and yet familiar, and my subconscious responded with an affirmation: Yes, there you are, I know you. I was wondering when you'd show up.

I'd spent the last seven years trying to find that other realm revealed to me so briefly in that snatch of Stray Cats music. When I heard A Little Man and a House and the Whole World Window, *I knew I'd found it. In my suburban Plymouth teenage bedroom that evening a transformation occurred - here began my life proper.*

What exactly is music? It serves no evolutionary purpose and yet, as far as I can tell, it's the most important thing there is. Music is drenched in an essence that can't be explained with words. It suggests that there may just be more to this whole trip than the mere corporeal world. It maps out the geography of another dimension and serves as a reminder, while currently operating these atrophying temporary flesh avatars, of where we came from and to where we'll return.

With these dish-like ears containing hammers and drums affected by a limited bandwidth of noise - who knows what sonic maelstrom is occurring below and above what we can hear? Through the organisation of sound waves into order, our brain assembles this data as beautiful, profound liquid architecture, dense with meaning and significance. Music is a language of pure information. It can't be seen, it's hard to define, yet it's the best of us, the highest of all art, the idealised version of ourselves, a way of imposing order and perfection on a chaotic world.

Music is magic, musicians are magicians and Tim Smith was the high magus.

I'd been gifted a vision of something so terribly and fundamentally important that it could never be unknown.

There was no going back now.

Chapter 13

Gong

Kavus and Steve

Kavus

My first Knifeworld record was released in 2009. I'd vowed not to shave until I completed it and for the only time in my life 'wore' a beard. I also sang and played guitar, keys, bass, glockenspiel, santoor and percussion. The first time I came on Steve's radio show - ostensibly just to promote the album - was the next year. We'd stayed vaguely in touch since that first meeting in Paris - swapping the occasional music recommendation and meeting up at gigs, like that Cardiacs one we mentioned earlier, and a few Guapo shows.

Steve

By that time I'd had a few guests on and I'd begun to realise that letting them pick all the music was a great way of hearing stuff I'd never come across before. The first time Kavus came on the show, he brought eighty CDs with him for a two-hour show. Doing the maths, that worked out at $A+\sqrt{B}/C=D$, so not much per CD, but it was a good omen. It's what I'd have done.

Kavus

I just couldn't decide! I remember I opened with Alice Coltrane . . .

Steve

The whole show was superb - a real ear-opener for me - so at the end of it I instinctively asked Kavus if he fancied coming on again. Then after the second time he came on, we had such a great time I just said, 'Whenever you want to do this, I'm up for it.'

Kavus

Pretty much from that point on, I was there every week. It was only a forty-minute drive over from Hackney and what could be more fun on a Monday night than to have that lovely feeling of sitting around playing music to each other saying, 'You've got to check this out.' In the nineties, this would probably have been at three in the morning after we'd all been partying, but I was a dad by this time and I was starting to slow down a bit, so it was great timing to meet Steve moving in the other direction.

Steve

From my perspective and, wonderfully, for the third time in my life, I'd discovered a person who was turning me on to so much amazing music that I hadn't been aware of. Not only many of the Cardiacs-related acts that I'd obviously missed, but also so much more of a broad spectrum of music that I'd been a million miles away from embracing. It was fun having a co-presenter when we had guests on, too, for the extra perspective. And with Kavus being 'in the trade', we were starting to build up a good head of steam with the guests. Fucking hell! We even had Steve Hillage on! Steve-fucking-Hillage, for fuck's sake! Fish-rising-angels-egging-tastic!

He was great. He had all these different sections he'd prepared, then at one point he picked three of the most banging pieces in a row, including 'Hallo Gallo' by NEU! - which I hadn't heard since my Subbuteo years with Neil Rogers - and I was back to being a kid again for the evening. Things would have got even more surreal with Mr Hillage in 2020 had the Covid-19 pandemic not scuppered The Utopia Strong's world domination plans, but I guess that tour can wait for another day. Steve Hillage was an integral part of Gong in the seventies, so he's an ideal portal to lead into our most amazing radio show guest story, which involves Daevid Allen. I'd better let Kavus set this one up, for reasons that'll soon become apparent.

Kavus

Our Daevid Allen story is completely improbable, and not just because him coming on our radio show started a chain of events that ended up with me joining the band.

The first time I became aware of them was when Arash asked me, 'Have you heard Gong?' When I shook my head, he said, 'Oh, God, I can't stand them – they're like Cardiacs but jazzier. You'd probably like them, though,' which got me interested. I didn't actually hear them until a year or two later, when my best friend Dan – who was the guitar player in my band at the time – made me a tape with Flying Teapot *on one side and* Angel's Egg *on the other. While it wasn't exactly a jazzier Cardiacs, I understood the comparison.*

I just thought they were amazing, and it wasn't long until I'd also heard Camembert Electrique *– with the beloved tritone, the flattened fifth, in full effect – which to my ears sounded like where Syd Barrett might have gone had he continued making records. Moving on to* You *brought me into contact with 'Master Builder' or if you will, 'The Glorious Om Riff' – the greatest riff ever written, placing guitarist Steve Hillage at the apex of the Riff Writer Triangle. The two other sides are represented by Tony Iommi and Jeff Hanneman. Or Jimmy Page. Or Buzz Osborne, but Hillage on top, always. Until someone writes a better riff. Good luck with that.*

As a consequence, I'd often write riffs over the years where the extent of their influence was a little too obvious. I'd come up with a riff and think, oh yes, great – but it sounds too much like Gong.

Steve

There's a lot of what's considered to be 'psychedelic music', or hails from the psych genre, which when I hear it, I'm thinking, this is just normal. But to me, Gong are a truly psychedelic band. Not because of their nods to consuming hallucinogens, but if you'd never taken any kind of narcotic substance – and it wasn't on the school curriculum in the early seventies – then Gong's music sounds just like how you'd imagine being on drugs might feel.

GONG

A lot of the people turning up to see Gong back in the day were obviously mind-melding with marijuana, but then it was the bloody seventies, after all! Gong members were clearly indulging in psychedelic drugs, but that wasn't what the music was about – it was far stronger than that. The riffs themselves were mesmeric and the repetition was trance-inducing – Gong didn't need chemical assistance to send you into another state.

Francis Linon (aka Venus Deluxe) – Gong and subsequently Magma's sound engineer – told me that during Gong's seventies commune days in a French forest, they tried just about every drug available, while steering clear of the poppy seed variety. His most vivid memories were of taking an extremely powerful hallucinogen that saw him huddled up in a corner of the boiler room fighting off demons for two days while above ground, Steve Hillage attempted to fly out of a bedroom window.

Kavus

Although I dug Gong before I got high, once I did I thought, oh right, OK, this is what that was leading up to. And pretty much all the music I made from that point definitely had a Gong influence – my first proper band, The Monsoon Bassoon, certainly did. Once I became part of the Cardiacs family, it transpired Tim was a huge Gong fan, too. His brother, Jim, told me he'd painted flying teapots all over his bedroom walls when they were growing up. On the last tour, in 2008, we even did a Cardiacs-esque version of the Om riff. Which is why if we fast-forward to 2012, with me in my studio shed in Clapton, I was so excited to get a call from Steve saying, 'You'll never guess who's been in touch! Gong. They want Daevid Allen to do the next radio show . . .'

We'd been doing the show together for a while by that point and Steve knew how much I loved Gong. I couldn't believe it. I'd met Daevid a couple of times, but only after gigs, just to shake his hand and say, 'Hey, man, great gig.' The last time had been in 2008, when Gong had played at The Forum. So I was very excited at the prospect of spending some proper time with the shaman. We met up with Daevid at The Premises, the rehearsal studios in Hackney Road, and Steve drove us out

125

to Brentwood. First, we took him to an Italian restaurant there called Tarantino, which was where we usually ate with guests before the show.

Steve

It was also used as a venue for some of the filming of *The Only Way Is Essex* - I think someone in the cast is related to the owner - but in terms of the mood of the place and the way customers are normally dressed, it tends to be quite a conservative environment. So even when Kavus walked in, maybe wearing his red velvet jacket and with rock star hair, there'd be a few eyebrows raised . . .

Kavus

'Who's this dandy?'

Steve

Exactly, but when we strolled in with Daevid Allen, the reaction was akin to a scene in a western movie when the gunslinger first walks into the town bar. Mouths were opened but food was still firmly attached to forks. Spaghetti strands froze in mid-air like pasta stalactites. As Daevid pushed open the swing doors, the gunslinger the patrons were presented with wasn't so much Billy the Kid as Catweazle. And tonight, Matthew, he was wearing a long greatcoat and a red top hat with a black cut-out paper hand stapled to the back of it . . .

Kavus

He looked amazing - exactly like you'd expect Daevid Allen to look. What you've got to understand about Daevid Allen was, right up until the day he died - and he died at seventy-six - this was a guy who carried himself like a man in his mid-thirties.

Steve

The expressions on people's faces were fucking hilarious. By that point, the staff of the restaurant had got used to me turning up there with a variety of 'artistic types' they didn't normally see, but the punters, not so much. We asked Daevid why he was keeping the top hat on and what the black paper hand stapled to the back signified. He said, 'It's all right, it's to ward off evil spirits.' That was good enough for us.

So we sat down at the table and started chatting and he was just such a great character - he was so easy to talk to. Not only that, but he also definitely took a shine to Kavus.

Kavus

Half an hour into the meal, he stood up and told me, 'Hey, man, you're a poet,' which of course I was very happy to hear, given how much of a poet Daevid was. I'd been friends with Tim Smith a long time by this point so, while not completely immune, I knew when I was being flattered or charmed.

Although it was one of my favourites, the radio show itself wasn't as good as it could have been. Because we'd already spent a couple of hours together and the conversation was really up and running, by the time we'd had the meal and turned up at the station to do the show, it almost ended up feeling like the broadcast was an interruption.

We were talking about far more interesting stuff over the music Daevid was playing than anything we managed on the mics between tunes. To be honest, I don't even remember much about the music. Daevid had picked the songs he wanted to play but what he really wanted to do was talk - he was asking Steve about snooker and the three of us were firing off each other. I wish we'd recorded that conversation.

I do remember Daevid played a track from Robert Wyatt's Rock Bottom *and he told us - quite rightly - that* Rock Bottom *is one of the greatest albums of all time. But because Robert made that record when he was in the very early stages of recovery from his accident, Daevid said all he could hear when he listened to it was the pain of his friend trying to get better.*

Afterwards, Steve stayed behind in the studio to lock up and turn everything off, and Daevid said, 'Hey, man, you want to get high?' So we had a smoke together while Steve did the responsible thing, and - as you'd expect - Daevid's weed was ridiculously potent. Steve gave us a lift back in his car and Daevid sat in the front talking excitedly to him the whole journey while I sat silently in the back seat texting some of my friends – including Mike York, who I was playing with in Guapo, saying, 'I'm sat in the back of Steve Davis' car. Daevid Allen has just got me high. My life is ridiculous.' Before we got to his hotel, Daevid and I swapped numbers . . .

Steve

And the next minute, out of the blue, Kavus phones me up and says, 'You'll never fucking guess . . .'

Kavus

Well, actually, there's a build-up.

Steve

Not from my perspective! It was such a bromance. They were texting each other and I never knew – before you could say 'have a cuppa tea', I'd become the third wheel!

Kavus

Daevid would come to London and say, 'Gong's playing, do you want to come along?' So I went to see them at Shepherd's Bush Empire and had a chat with him afterwards. Not long after that, he was going to be improvising with Marshall Allen from the Sun Ra Arkestra at Cafe OTO. I already had a ticket for that and I was excited by the idea of the two Allens playing together. The two righteous elders had never even met before. Then Daevid asked me to come down and hang out before the show and . . .

Steve

Without even hearing him play the guitar! He'd never heard him play a fucking note!

Kavus

Jesus, man. Don't pull the rug out from under my anecdote! So I came down early and Daevid seemed slightly agitated. Then after about twenty minutes, he said, 'Oh, man, I've been thinking, I really want you to play guitar in Gong.' I didn't have to think this over for long. This guy was older than my dad, but he had such an amazing amount of crackling electricity coming out of him. Daevid wasn't some old rocker whose heyday was in the past. He lived in the present, was fully aware. He was all about now. I thought, I want to know what this guy's got. This is how I want to be when I'm his age, you know?

So I said, 'But, Daevid, you've never heard me play.'

And he said, 'Oh, I don't need to hear you play.' Then added, 'I'd never heard Mike Howlett play, I'd never heard Pierre Moerlen play, I don't need to hear you play. I just need someone to bring fire. You're going to bring fire.'

I said, 'You know I can't play like Steve Hillage?'

And he said, 'Oh, I'm not interested in what you can't do; I'm interested in what you can do.'

So, there it was. I walked home from that gig and texted a few friends: 'I think I might be in Gong.'

I'd already been in Cardiacs by that time, so I suppose it wasn't completely unprecedented. In a strange way, I had sort of expected it. I was already pretty busy with my own group, Knifeworld, which was doing OK, so I wasn't especially looking to join another band, but this was Gong and Daevid was a wise elemental whom I knew I could learn from. These things happen for a reason and I couldn't pass it up.

A couple of weeks later, Daevid came to a gig I was playing with my other band, Guapo, at Corsica Studios in Elephant and Castle. He was dancing down the front throughout, totally into it. Afterwards, he told me, 'Oh, man, it's exactly what I thought it would be!' And not long after, we had a get-together at a rehearsal place in New Cross. I was early, as usual, and came up with a riff while I waited for the others. Daevid walked in and almost immediately started singing along, and that ended up becoming a song we did together called 'When God Shakes Hands with Devil'. The title came from a quote by Neil Young, who described rock 'n' roll as being just that. I told Daevid and he loved it. The funny thing was that – going back to what I said at the beginning about how I had loads of riffs that sounded too much like Gong to use - after we did that song, Daevid said, 'Hey, man, that's a great riff. Got any more of them?'

'Fucking hundreds!'

So that was that. It was perfect.

I went to Brazil with Gong and did some gigs over there, the first of which was headlining a psychedelic festival to 5000 people, which was something of a trial by fire. We returned to the UK while Daevid went back to Australia and we continued working on the new album, I See You, remotely. During which process - somewhat unfortunately, given that we had a 48-date European tour booked - Daevid slipped over and broke his arm.

'Oh, guys, a bit of a bummer - I've broken my arm, so I'm not going to be able to play guitar on this tour. But that's no problem, because we already have two guitarists.'

Then when he went into hospital to have his arm checked, they found cancer. He already had skin cancer, but this was much more virulent and quick-spreading, around the throat.

After our first ever rehearsal together, Daevid had taken me outside for a smoke and was saying things like, 'Well, man, you know, I can't go on forever. I never wanted Gong to die with me. Gong was always an idea - it wasn't a band - and I've always thought you could do it, because you're not very English, you're not reserved, you're all up front. You've got to carry the band on.' At the time I kind of brushed him off: 'Yeah, yeah, Daevid, yeah, yeah.' I'd just joined - it was like discussing marriage and kids on the first date. It wasn't until a year or so later when this situation arose that it came back to me and I saw that his enlisting me was part of a larger plan.

While we expected Daevid to recover, he couldn't do the tour. Once the promoters knew that, most of the dates were cancelled, but we still had about eleven shows to honour.

I didn't want to do those gigs. In fact, no one in the band was particularly enamoured with the idea of a Gong without Daevid Allen. It seemed totally bogus - with no original members, no one's going to buy into it at all. It wasn't where I was at in any way. There were a lot of emails and Skype sessions. But we had a new album out and, as much as I hoped they would be, the remaining gigs weren't being cancelled, so I said, 'OK, I can front the band. I know how to do this. I've got previous. I'll honour the shows but then I'm out.' Everybody agreed. Everybody except Daevid, that is, who was insistent that we should carry on.

The rehearsals went really well. At the very least, I knew we sounded good, but leaving the house on the morning of the first show, I felt like a condemned man. I thought, how on earth did I get here? This wasn't what I signed up for.

Up until now, I'd been in control of my so-called musical career, only ever doing things I felt 100 per cent about. But this was being foisted on me and, short of just quitting – which I would never do – I felt powerless to stop it. I wasn't looking forward to playing at all. The atmosphere in the van on the way to the first gig in Châteauroux, France was pretty subdued. That feeling lasted right up until the moment we walked out onto the stage and then it was if someone else took me over. I became the frontman of Gong.

Over the course of the small tour, we sent desk recordings to Daevid in hospital in Australia, who would respond positively the following day. After the tour, we thought, God, that was really good. And Daevid said, 'Guys, you have to carry this on, but you've got to do your own thing now.'

As his health deteriorated, I started to think maybe there was something in this idea. So I told Daevid shortly before he died: 'Yeah, we'll do this.' But if we were going to make this work, we'd have to write our own tunes and if people weren't into them, then I didn't want to do it, because I wasn't going to be in a tribute or a covers band: I wanted us to be out there doing our own thing. We'd play some old stuff as well, but it had to be something ongoing, so that we'd taken on the baton. And that is basically what happened.

The bizarre thing is that it's not a band I'd ever have conceived of myself. It's an impractical arrangement – we live all over the UK and the guitarist, Fabio Golfetti, lives in São Paulo in Brazil. This was something Daevid had conceived. He'd put this band together and it worked so well, like it was his final artwork.

Obviously, we've lost the 'No Daevid, No Gong' contingent, but I feel like those who have stayed or got on board anew understand that our love for Daevid's ethos, for the kind of band he created, is the motivation at the heart of the music. And that's why, to me, at least, it still feels authentically 'Gong'.

There's some extraordinary footage of Daevid from about two weeks before he died – it's on YouTube. We were still in email contact at this point, his hair was short and he was performing in a beachside cafe in Byron Bay, where he lived. He read a poem by Kahlil Gibran called 'On Death'. 'For what is it to die but to stand naked in the wind and to melt into the sun?' Even though he only had days to live and he was as skinny as a little willow tree, his eyes were twinkling the way they always did. The last email he sent me said, 'I'm going to go now. They've told me I need more treatment, but I'm a believer in what will be, will be.' He went into his death open-armed.

Daevid was the real deal, not some bullshit merchant. He'd talk about cosmic stuff and you'd believe him – it wasn't a put-on. When you think about all that he did throughout his life, Daevid Allen is an incredibly important figure in the counterculture. The history books celebrate people like Ram Das and Abbie Hoffman. But to my mind, Daevid Allen was every bit as significant a figure in that generation – this was the guy who was collaborating with William Burroughs in 1964, the guy who turned all those Canterbury guys on to LSD, the guy who started the Soft Machine. It would be wrong for him to be written out of this whole great story just because some people find the 'Pothead Pixie' element of Gong a little unpalatable.

When we met up for the meal, it wasn't like talking to somebody who was old; it was like talking to a teenager. He still had the enthusiasm of youth, but with all the knowledge of a much older man.

It was like he was thirty more times more evolved through the cycle of rebirth than the rest of us.

Steve

It was like he was outside time, in a way. And for me it was amazing to have another guest on our radio show who had chaperoned me through my adolescence and who had affected my musical path in the way that Daevid had. To me, at fourteen, Gong was otherworldly and Daevid Allen was this mystical entity (like Steve Hillage and Christian Vander) that I was never likely to meet but was feeding a need in me. The fact that I was now having dinner with him felt like it was me who was having the out-of-body experience that Daevid had so often sung about. That in itself was more than enough – it didn't have to go any further. But then the beauty of the consequence of him asking Kavus first to be in the band and then to carry on holding the torch . . . if someone asked me if I believed in fate, I'd say there was no such thing, but what an amazing piece of sliding-doors history.

Kavus

And it must be said that this saga takes a very profound turn towards the end – when Steve comes back into it again. It's a real crescent-shaped moon of a story. So when Daevid eventually died, we were doing the radio show together every week on Phoenix FM. I can't remember the exact day of the week he died, but it was two or three days before the Monday night, because we got in touch with each other and said, 'Well, we know who the show's going to be about this week.'

We went on the Facebook page and told everyone that we'd be doing a special tribute show for Daevid and that people could suggest anything from any of the many projects he did throughout his career that they wanted us to play, which they did. We went to Tarantino before the show and ordered the same meals we'd had when he came with us. We were talking about how sad it was, when I got a text saying that Daevid's ashes were going to be scattered in Byron Bay at 11.11 a.m. Australian time.

With the time difference, we worked out that that would be eleven minutes after our show normally finished – at midnight – so since we were the last show of the night, Steve suggested we extend the show so we would still be playing his music at the point Daevid's earthly remains went back into the cosmos. We sat there in the same positions we'd been with Daevid, remembering our time with him and listening to his music, and wondering what track to finish with. Then it hit me: 'I know the very one!' Because there wasn't really any possible choice other than: 'Thank You'.

It was the last track on, I See You, the album we made together, and it's basically his goodbye song, where he just lists everything he was thankful for in his life: 'Thank you for the music [. . .], thank you for the children . . .' I'd come up with this kind of glam rock riff over Daevid's chords. It was the ideal finish, because the tune wouldn't have existed in that form had we not had the initial meeting in this very studio that led to my joining the band. It was our own farewell ritual. Orlando, his son, who was the drummer in the band at the time, had mixed in all these old tape loops and cut-ups over the end of the outro that Daevid had made back in the sixties like the 'Gong, Gong, Gong' loop that appears at the start of Camembert Electrique and a load of other stuff he'd done from four or five years before that.

At the time, we thought it was a nice touch but hadn't really placed any great importance on it. We put the song on just after midnight. It's ten and a half minutes long and as the clock clicked to eleven minutes past midnight, all these samples of Daevid when he was younger started coming in, so at precisely the point where his ashes were being scattered you could hear him at his most powerful. The beginning, end and continuation of Gong in a mad Möbius strip. The eternal wheel. Just as it should have been.

I looked at Steve and I don't want to embarrass him, but he was crying. We could feel Daevid's presence so strongly. It was one of those rare occasions when you think, I don't believe in ghosts, but this is a pretty crazy moment of serendipity.

Steve
And in Brentwood, a place that couldn't be less Daevid Allen if it tried!

Chapter 14

Pink Floyd

Kavus

Once I'd heard Tim Smith's music, I spent the next couple of years attempting to convert everyone I knew, like a turned-on Timothy Leary. Here did I learn the hard truth of subjectivity. This music wasn't for everyone. Insanely, some people didn't even think it was music. Others absolutely fucking hated it.

Cardiacs were barely covered in the music press and on the rare occasions when they were, it was (with the occasional honourable exception) with derision, mockery or scorn. This music was so important that I believed it would only be a matter of time before the NME abandoned their obsession with The Stone Roses and woke up to the glory of Cardiacs. How wrong I was.

This was a relatively prolific time for the band. Cardiacs Live *was released in 1989, followed by the lead single 'Baby Heart Dirt' from the forthcoming album,* On Land and in the Sea.

Rival Records was my favourite record shop. It was part of the Chain With No Name distribution network and sold pretty much everything I was interested in. All of the staff were in their late teens and early twenties, and represented the provincial city subcultures of the late eighties: goth, indie, metal and rave.

Neil (who represented 'indie') was on the counter that day.

'Is On Land and in the Sea *in?' I asked.*

'Don't think it was in the boxes,' he replied. 'Let me just check.'

Nothing. I walked despondently back to college.

This routine went on for at least a month and a half until one Monday, as I entered around 11.25 a.m., Neil caught my eye and gestured towards the display shelf. There, on the top right, were ten copies of what I'd soon come to know as the greatest album of the twentieth century.

There was no way I was going back to college now. I headed straight for the bus home.

It was lunchtime, I was at home alone, both of my parents were at work. Sat in my room, I turned it up loud. The opener, 'Two Bites of Cherry', is one of those rare songs where the music and vocals start together immediately:

Any real egg has a shell has a shell an egg
So break it killer fisty
killer fisty beat his head.

On Land . . . *wasn't as immediate as* A Little Man *and the first listen was a different experience, but then I came to it with an expectation.*

On Land . . . *delved much deeper into the darker recesses of the sub-conscious, seemed more singular again than the previous year's* A Little Man. On Land and in the Sea *was truly a psychedelic album, and for me and my coterie of tripping friends, it would be* the *psychedelic album.*

On Land and in the Sea *is an odyssey into the human psyche. Tim Smith dredged up everything – the scary, the grimy, the blissful, the ecstatic – whether you wanted him to or not, crystallising the way the world looked in childhood but with the knowing dread and fear of an adult perspective.*

Cardiacs would mete out a scorched-earth policy on everything I previously liked and for a while, few artists I'd previously listened to made it through. Instead, I wanted something that scratched the same sort of itch and entered a musical labyrinth that led to artists like Steve Reich, King Crimson, Shudder to Think, John Zorn, Bunty Chunks, Etron Fou Leloublan and Magma.

I eventually got to follow up on Bryan Talbot's recommendation a year after he gave it to me – hearing Zappa for the first time on what turned out to be a very pivotal compilation tape made for me by my friend, the musical heavyweight Richard Larcombe. It was a 'Well, if you like Cardiacs, you should get on board with this . . .' sort of compilation called Pink Floyd: The Wall, *complete with a hand-drawn approximation of Gerald Scarfe's iconic sleeve.*

There was no Pink Floyd music on the tape and especially not The Wall, *which Richard disliked anyway. Punctuated by Brian Cant's dreamlike announcements created out of cut-ups from a* Play Away LP, *both sides were filled with tunes from Captain Beefheart's* Trout Mask Replica, The Dog Faced Hermans, *both Bastro and Bastard Kestrel, 'Berkshire Poppies' by Traffic, '11 Moustachioed Daughters' by the Bonzo Dog Doo-Dah Band and a selection of Zappa instrumentals from* Uncle Meat, Hot Rats *and* Burnt Weeny Sandwich. *I'd never knowingly heard a single note by any of the artists before and* Pink Floyd: The Wall *became my soundtrack until I could locate the albums the music was culled from.*

Zappa was the biggest surprise. Boring seventies guitar hero, my eye! Here were sped-up drums, 'found' sounds, tape manipulations and bassoons all intricately arranged and sewn together – a musical box stuffed with brightly coloured jewels and exotic-tasting fruit. 'Project X', 'Holiday in Berlin (Full-Blown)', 'The Dog Breath Variations' and 'Peaches en Regalia' blew away the rain clouds and heralded bright, sunny and hope-filled planes. An optimistic and generous galaxy of magnificent Lydian melodies.

Pink Floyd: The Wall *catapulted me further into the spiralling cosmos of visionary music I'd been exploring since Tim Smith had rerouted my neural pathways. With its help, I leapfrogged years of potential blind alleys and musical cul-de-sacs into a treasure trove of deliriously wonderful music way, way behind the looking glass.*

Yet, the biggest influence at this time didn't come from music at all. With rave ushering in the second summer of love, by the late eighties, LSD was everywhere in Plymouth. Friends were trying it and, while I'd been vehemently anti-drugs, the further I got into head music, the more the collision course with acid was unavoidable.

Like many others before me, I'd become enamoured with the music of Syd Barrett. The singular way he used melody and chords had no precedent, that I could hear. Like John the Baptist to Tim Smith's Jesus. Over his scant discography, The Pink Floyd's The Piper at the Gates of Dawn, *solo albums,* The Madcap Laughs *and* Barrett, *plus a handful of songs like 'Jugband Blues', 'Dolly Rocker' and especially*

The guitar remained in Iran, but I never went back.

Hard to believe I went on to win 'Hair of the year' in the mid-eighties.

My other car was a Lada.

Get in the back of the van. Note the guitar carelessly leant against the back.
Die Laughing in 1991 from left: Dan Chudley, Carlos Parsliffe, Kavus, Jim 'Sicky'
Parker, Tim Floyd.

Cardiacs big band, 2005 tour line up. Back row: Cathy Harabaras, Melanie Woods, Sharron Fortnam, Claire Lemmon, Dawn Staple. Middle: Kavus, Bob Leith, Jim Smith. Front: Tim Smith.

The only gong I was interested in came with a Gliss guitar.

'They are like nothing you have ever heard before' SOUNDS
'bloody great' MELODY MAKER

The day I joined Magma.

*The Monsoon Bassoon,
brief and implausible
darlings of the* NME, *1999.*

What I would give for just one more kiss? Onstage with Tim Smith.

LEFT: *The expensive guitar. Onstage with Knifeworld, 2012.*
RIGHT: 'The red wire . . . no, the blue wire.'

Outside Cafe OTO with Daevid Allen after being asked to join Gong, March 2013.

The Utopia Strong marking their territory.

Be seeing you. At Festival No. 6 in Portmeirion, 2017.

Going upwards at 45 degrees. Onstage with Steve Hillage in Aylesbury, 2019.

The Utopia Strong, Cafe OTO, December 2019.

The Utopia Strong heading towards The Crow's Nest, Glastonbury Festival, June 2019.

'Opel', Barrett had mapped out a unique musical world.

The songs on his solo albums had a spectral, unfinished quality, but what beautiful, haunting music this was. His use of modulation, alluringly unusual top lines and darkly poetic lyrics were the work of a rare master.

Crazy Diamond, the first biography of Syd Barrett, had been recently published and I was captivated by the story. There was only one thing for it.

My girlfriend, Andrea, obtained two purple Om blotters. We dropped them that evening and decided to head into town. It was midweek and the only club open was The Ritzy, formerly the Top Rank venue that had once hosted both Iron Maiden and The Sex Pistols (as S.P.O.T.S.: Sex Pistols On Tour Secretly). In between it had been Fiesta, the indoor ice-skating centre where I'd been to a few kids' parties. Now, it was a club for what we referred to as 'townies' – not somewhere we'd usually visit. We paid our two pounds and entered.

The Ritzy on a Thursday night wasn't the ideal location for a psychedelic experience. From the relative safety of a darkened table in a corner, we spent the next few giggling hours watching strange courting rituals play out against a background of horrible-sounding music. As we left, our overall assessment was that it had been fun and it was something we'd do again. There it was – I'd crossed the Rubicon and taken LSD. Nonetheless, I was left with an unshakeable feeling that this wasn't what had 'sent Syd Barrett mad'.

The following week, we repeated the experiment with two green microdots and wildly different results. Within the hour, I was rendered near speechless, gazing into the yawning maw of an unfolding abyss. As my ego fragmented, the previously amusing surroundings were transformed into a grotesque carnival. Andrea withstood the psychic onslaught a little better. Back at her flat, a long night of revelation followed.

LSD was the making of me. It exploded my mind and let me examine the shards of the wreckage as a detached observer. The bad ideas, faulty thinking and pretensions I'd been holding on to, the hang-ups and opinions I'd once thought important, that I believed defined me, now seemed gaudy and cartoon-like. Jesus, I'd been taking life so seriously. And while what I was unearthing sometimes made me uncomfortable, over each eighteen-hour workout I was able to reassemble the pieces of my smashed-up psyche, effectively leaving out anything that I saw as unhelpful. Following a trip, I'd feel buoyant and weightless for days afterwards, reborn and charged with an enthusiastic zeal.

LSD came along at just the right time, undermining my fundamental beliefs, razing the chaff of nagging, circular anxieties and reframing unpleasant memories. All that before I even discovered the effect it would have on music.

Chapter 15

Surgeon

Steve

'As one door closes, another opens' is a well-known saying, but I could never have envisaged the wonderful way it would come to apply to me. I was still wet behind the ears when I fell in love with snooker – before I knew it, I'd turned professional, and by the age of twenty-three, I was Champion of The Wooorld! The whole wide world! Well, the UK and a few other countries that we'd raped, pillaged and enslaved our way through in times gone past. By the age of thirty-two, I'd been awarded an OBE for 'services to my hobby' and had rampaged my own way across the globe numerous times on snooker crusades of one kind or another. During this phase of selfless service to our shameful empire, I'd also learned to become an adrenaline junkie – not something my *Spitting Image* puppet was widely assumed to have been, but the thrill of competitive snooker was exhilarating and highly addictive.

Not only was that happening, but between competitions I'd also be playing snooker exhibitions and later in my career, after-dinner speaking. Plenty of sports 'personalities' are also hired for corporate motivational speaking, though I always preferred to consider the impact of my speaking as fundamentally demotivational. After all, what is remotely inspiring about sitting listening to someone spouting off about how they made it to the top, while highlighting how obviously unsuccessful you, and all the other chair-sitting nonentities, have been?

All of these supplementary activities at least aspire to the condition of entertainment and as dull as they might have been for the audience, for me, performing has always been a massive buzz. When I finally ran out of competitive puff in 2016, I converted my cue to a tomato cane and left behind the spoils of green baize

endeavour for the millennials to fight over. I knew I'd never experience that competitive thrill again, but there was no denying
I'd had a good innings. Little did I know what was in store for my
adrenals!

The Interesting Alternative Show had been gathering momentum,
kudos and interest ever since Kavus and I had first teamed up,
but we hadn't considered the possibility of doing any more with
our favourite music other than listen to it, while giving the artists
featured some much-needed (and well-deserved) airplay. Then, a
slow-burning hand grenade was thrown into our lives when we
were asked if we'd play some records at the taproom of a newly
opened craft brewery in Bethnal Green called Redchurch Brewery.

It was more of a listening and social space than a dance floor
area, but it turned into a bi-monthly set that started to gain some
attention. Out of the blue, we were contacted by Alex Benson and
George Hull from Bloc Weekend, an iconic electronic music festival
that was sadly hosting its last ever weekender at Butlin's, Minehead.
Apparently, Alex and George had popped in to the Redchurch for
a beer one evening and liked what they'd heard. What we knew
of techno could be written on the back of Autechre's *Chiastic Slide*
CD case, but we were assured that it wasn't necessary for us to fit
the mould and that the festival itself was more than just four-to-
the-floor doofing, anyway.

When you say no to things, nothing happens, but when you
say yes, there's no knowing what the consequences will be. So
in a mad moment of 'Fuck it! What have we got to lose?', we
decided to give it a go. And then once Bloc Weekend announced
our appearance at their 2016 finale, things got stupid. BBC Sport
wanted to cover the moment and make a short documentary
about the snooker world champion, whose nickname was
'Interesting', and his musician buddy who played experimental
psychedelic rock, turning into techno-rave DJs. Radio, magazines
and newspapers also thought it was a great story. Our homespun
endeavour was getting far more exposure than we could possibly
have envisaged.

We were assured there'd be no pressure to fill the dance floor at Bloc, but hey, who wants to be a strokey-beard DJ!? So we set about sourcing alternative floor-fillers – first from our recent Redchurch Brewery sets and then from the deepest recesses of our record collections.

The brief for Redchurch Brewery was a pretty broad spectrum. There was no demand for any type of music (can't get much broader than that) for the simple reason that it wasn't really a bona fide music venue. We quickly came to accept what we'd later come to recognise as the DJ's nightmare scenario – people would have the cheek to come to the taproom to drink beer and chat to each other, with no intention of even listening to what we were playing. It was as if some of them didn't even know we were going to be there. The upside was that this completely took any pressure off our formative mutual DJ'ing endeavours.

We understood the rules and kept the volume relatively low early on before attempting to crank it up slowly, while every now and again a member of staff would suggest we turned it down a bit. Familiar scenario? Meanwhile, we got fed the best Redchurch Brewery could offer, fresh from the barrels below. The Old Ford Export Stout at 7.4 per cent is a dangerous fucker indeed and lends its delicious self more to spinning CDs than rare, expensive vinyl. The DJ area was pretty tight, so for logistical and social reasons, we took it in turns to DJ, starting off with relatively chilled-out ambient material early doors and progressing to the meatier cuts later on. I tended to gravitate towards electronic stuff and liked the idea of going on first in order to play the more laid-back variety, with music from Prefuse 73, Biosphere and Vakula springing to memory. Kavus would then come on and change the style a bit with a general rock flavour . . . although I use the word 'rock' in its loosest sense. Then we'd alternate and build to a frenzy as the beer kicked in.

This was how our radio shows had dovetailed so nicely; while we obviously had common ground, there were other areas of music one of us had delved into that the other hadn't. No mean feat when it comes to Kavus, because boy that guy has listened to a shitload of music in his years on the planet.

I'm convinced you can be a musician (even a great one) and be obsessed with playing music, without being a 'music fan'. Maybe not when you first start, but certainly as the years drag on. Weird, eh? And possibly a bigger proportion of musicians would fall into this category than you'd think . . . which is why there's a good few of them you'd want to keep as far away from the turntables as possible. Rumour has it that Christian Vander listens almost exclusively to John Coltrane, which obviously works brilliantly for him but might not go down such a storm at the 100 Club on a Saturday evening. Not Kavus, though. I can honestly say I've never met anyone who has more passion for music – whether it be his own or produced by others – than Kavus. It's often said that DJs are frustrated musicians – otherwise they'd be playing instruments instead of DJ'ing, right? I think it's pretty much nailed on that DJs love music and want to *inflict* their preferences on others. So when a DJ starts to get into producing music, at the very least you know you'll have an enthusiastic participant. And when you get one with a real sense of musical empathy, you can get some amazing results. Look no further than the colossal (and sadly missed) Andrew Weatherall . . .

Operating at a slightly lower technical level, I think our time at Redchurch was invaluable as a testing ground for DJ sets where we needed to get people dancing. Crazy tracks from the hurdy-gurdy of Valentin Clastrier to the frantic Kōenji Hyakkei have great memories for me, but there was one selection where Kavus excitedly informed me that he'd found a banger to unleash. Towards the end of the evening, the people who had wanted to chat to each other had fucked off to do even more chatting, or whatever else we didn't care about. So we could then hold court, more or less exclusively, to the hardcore heads and our musical buddies. It was at this moment, as I was standing watching Kavus play the last leg of the evening, with the amplifier nudging twelve, that the familiar magical sound from Patrick Gauthier's fingertips hit my ears.

I was in a relaxed state, being on maybe my eighth bottle of Old Ford Stout. That's like having a 60 per cent beer! Admittedly, they're only halves, but it wasn't long before I was bopping along to the sound of a track I'd heard plenty of times in the past but had never considered as a potential floor-filler. The track and the artist in question was 'Vilna' by the seventies French band Weidorje. The amazing thing about this track is that once you hear it in a dance-floor context, it just makes total sense. I don't think there's ever been a DJ set where we've played this track to an audience who were anything other than astonished by it. The Redchurch faithful loved it.

Back to Bloc. Even though no specific dance gauntlet had been thrown in our direction, we chose to pick up the sequinned velvet glove, albeit with a slight tingle in our veins. There's nothing quite like a journey into the unknown. We decided to remain in Red-church mode and take twenty-minute turns at the decks during our four-hour set – something that in hindsight, now we're relatively experienced campaigners, was a stupid decision.

So, with a full BBC film crew in tow, we arrived at Sir Billy Butlin's gates . . . (To be continued after a brief digression into the enchanted realm of Berlin record shops.)

OK, I lied about my techno knowledge earlier. I'd started to get into more electronic music. Obviously, back in the day I was aware of – and liked a bit of – Tangerine Dream (not so bothered by Kraftwerk, though), but when I returned to my prog first love, twenty years after cruelly ditching her for the glossy sheen of soul music, I found my past desires largely taking me down a more angular 'Rock in Opposition' route and hadn't considered what the electronic genre might have been up to in the interim. Kavus was more au fait with some of the more recent stuff in that area, but it wasn't anywhere near the top of his list of musical priorities.

One of our early guests on *The Interesting Alternative Show* was The Joff Winks band (soon to become Sanguine Hum). Both Joff Winks and Matt Baber were electronic music fans and the playlist they chose for the two-hour show reflected that, with a Boards of

Canada track among the many choices that particularly caught my ear. My interest was piqued enough that I asked Matt Baber for his recommended ten artist and album entry-level electronic potpourri.

His list included records by Autechre, Oneohtrix Point Never and Tim Hecker. Here was 'music that I never knew existed'! All of a sudden, I started to delve into the electronic genre. Fast-forward a few months and finding myself with a day off in Berlin during a snooker event, I planned a tour of local record shops, including the legendary (although unknown to me at the time) Hard Wax store in Kreuzberg. Walking up the four flights of stairs (there were no lifts - which seemed an astonishing logistical and physical nightmare for the staff lugging boxes and boxes of vinyl up higher than the Brandenburg Gate), I sensed there was something special about the place.

I walked into the shop and started flicking through racks and racks of names and labels I had absolutely no history with. The process was futile. I had no idea what I was looking for beyond the names of the artists whose work I'd already sampled. Fortunately, a member of staff sensed my plight and after I asked for recommendations in the vicinity of Oneohtrix, Tim Hecker et al., the first record he pulled out was *Breaking the Frame* by Surgeon, stating that while it wasn't in exactly the same vein, it was undeniably a great album. He wasn't wrong and the techno-tinged joy of having that record on my deck for the first time is still with me today. I'm not exactly sure what the British Murder Boys fans thought of it when it came out, but it was the techno legend spreading his wings of desire further afield than just the confines of Berghain's difficult-to-access dance floor.

So by the time we played at that Bloc Weekend, I was in a position where I could have a slightly more informed chat with Anthony Child (aka Surgeon) on the event's Boiler Room radio residency without feeling completely out of my depth. I also got to do an interview with the amazing Holly Herndon - who was also performing and showcasing her rightly acclaimed LP *Platform* - without totally embarrassing myself. That part came later, when the BBC crew filmed me in the main room headbanging to Surgeon and Blawan's amazing double act.

Kavus and I have become good friends with Tony since and I do think we missed an April Fool's opportunity by not starting a folklore rumour that Tony and I used to DJ in some dark Berlin nightclub snooker dungeon and that now that I'd broken cover as a techno fan, it was time to spread the word that *Breaking the Frame* was our collaboration. This wouldn't have been my first offence. I was once on Piccadilly Radio in Manchester back in the eighties and with the help of the DJ who was interviewing me, I managed to convince a number of listeners that prior to turning professional, I'd founded The Spencer Davis Group along with fellow snooker pro John Spencer.

It was Tony I have to thank (I think) for bestowing me with my unofficial DJ name. He and his wife, Doris (aka DJ Bus Replacement Service . . . only the best DJ and DJ name in the world!), had been big fans of the TV comedy series *The Increasingly Poor Decisions of Todd Margaret*, in which I'd appeared in a cameo role. The plot revolved around a health drink called Thunder Muscle, imported into the UK from North Korea, where they were using it to dispose of their nuclear waste. Not too much different from chlorinated chicken, I suppose. Shortly after the Bloc gig, a few people on Twitter started asking if I had a DJ name. Tony chipped in with 'DJ Thundermuscle'. Had we actually been spinning techno, it would have been a killer handle, but the upshot would have seen Kavus gagging to up his DJ name game, too. Kavus nearly got an upgrade around the same time anyway, when a mate of mine asked me, 'Who's this Tarkus Varkoni bloke, then?'

Maybe we should have gone with the Varkoni-Thundermuscle pairing. We could have been headliners at Bloc weekend!

Sometimes the lines between star and fan get a bit blurred. I've always embraced the fact that one minute you might be a master of proceedings but the next moment another person takes over the mantle. Or - to aid sales for the 2022 *Oxford English Dictionary* - one minute you're a punter and the next you're the puntee.

Let's take, for example, Nicko McBrain. The legendary drummer of the band Iron Maiden is a big snooker fan. He proper loves the game. Not only does he play it regularly, but when he's not bare-footing his way all over the globe, he also turns up to the World Snooker Championship in Sheffield. He's even been known to get behind the drum kit at the after-final party, although I'm not sure that Mark Selby is a worthy replacement for Bruce Dickinson.

At a recent world final at the Crucible Theatre, Nicko was sitting with Stephen Fry in the VIP/press seats and a tactical exchange between the two players ensued. From his vantage point, Nicko spotted a two-ball plant into the middle pocket and he realised that neither player had noticed. In his excitement, he whispered to the *QI* host to alert him, too. The only trouble was that Nicko's whispers aren't as quiet as they used to be. Smashing the fuck out a drum kit with Iron Maiden for thirty-eight years had obviously taken its toll on his three speeds, because the audience, and players, got the full force of '*Stephen there's a plant on!*', Whether or not this town crier announcement changed the course of snooker history, we'll never know, but the incoming player had a look and agreed with Nicko's assessment. The only part of this story Nicko didn't tell me was whether the player made the plant or not.

A while back, Iron Maiden were touring and playing a few shows at the giant O2 Arena in Greenwich. Prior to this, I was in the illustrious company (at a much smaller gig in London) of Kavus, Mike York and Mike Vennart (Oceansize and hired axeman for Biffy Clyro). I was taking a back seat and enjoying them holding court, when they started drooling over the remote possibility of being able to get tickets for Iron Maiden. I casually dropped Nicko's love of snooker into the conversation, spiced up with the revelation that on a number of occasions, he'd told me that if I'd ever wanted to go to a show, it would be no sweat to arrange tickets.

In a heartbeat, without being able to play a chord on a guitar or get any coherent noise out of any wind instrument, I'd made myself the centre of attention, progressing in an instant from punter to puntee. The diamond geezer who is Nicko duly sorted out tickets and also VIP backstage (platinum backstage, no less) passes, and we were all set. Once we'd negotiated the merchandise queues and top-notch security screening, we were into the arena and revelled in the spectacle that was (and hopefully one day will be again) an Iron Maiden show. As the crowd happily left, singing along to the strains of Eric Idle's 'Always Look on the Bright Side of Life', my friends were like schoolkids on a day trip, bracing themselves at the prospect of meeting these legends.

We rolled up to the VIP area and all the Maiden lads to a man duly showed their faces at the incredible aftershow party. Nicko bumped into us and I introduced my now overawed, incredibly talented musical stars to one of their heroes. They contained themselves to a degree but eventually cracked and went all fanboy on Nicko. The only problem was that Nicko had been having a bit of trouble with his technique that week. He felt he was getting a bit of unwanted sidespin on the cue ball and needed advice, so we chatted about snooker while Kavus and the two Mikes bit their knuckles in frustration.

My favourite punter-puntee switchback to observe is a truly wonderful thing that combines snooker with British contemporary art. One of Ronnie O'Sullivan's biggest fans and friends is the artist Damien Hirst, who I assume likes snooker in general but who *really* loves snooker when The Rocket is playing. Ronnie (who, coincidentally, shares the same date of birth as Kavus) doesn't let many people into his inner circle once he's in competition mode, but Damien has AAA clearance, including - the ultimate compliment to their friendship - access to Ron's dressing room during a match.

The word 'gofer' is widely considered a derogatory one, but in times of need or under great strain or just being in a position to have a 'gofer' because someone wants to be one, they do exist. So in this wonderful scene at the Crucible that I've witnessed too many times for it to be just coincidence, Damien trots off and gets Ronnie a coffee and while that's happening, someone is sent off to get Damien a coffee. It's performance art at its very best. And if for some unknown reason, the long-distance Olympic gold medallist

Haile Gebrselassie had been in the dressing room, then Ronnie would have been fetching him a 'capachoochoo' in turn. Obviously, my coffee run would be for Christian Vander and Christian's would be for Bob Nudd or an equivalent French fishing legend.

Back to Butlin's . . . Little did I know that my state of punter-ship was about to flip within a matter of minutes. I'd just finished hosting a fun pool tournament for some of the performing artists and DJs. While they were masters of their CDJ-2000s, this was my office and with a cue in my hand instead of a microphone, I became the surgeon on duty.

While we were stood chatting to a couple of people in the bar afterwards, one of them spilled the beans that her friend, who she was standing next to, was Rob Brown from Autechre. He was hanging out at the festival incognito (until she blew his cover) and there we were next to him. I turned to Kavus, nodded towards Rob Brown and whispered far quieter than Nicko: 'Kavus, royalty!' After we'd bowed, we hung out with him for the evening – rubbing shoulders with the IDM deity.

As the hours ticked down to our debut festival DJ set, I could feel the all-too-familiar queasy sensation rising in the pit of my stomach that had been part of my life since I first competed on the green baize. It was eased by sharing the load with Kavus and helped further by downing a few beers for a bit of Dutch courage, but then, far too quickly, the moment was upon us. God knows why we didn't DJ together, but I went first regardless. We were playing in a large pub-style room that was jam-packed, especially in front of our ground-level DJ area. Crowds were nothing new to me – obviously, I'd played snooker in front of thousands of people countless times – but this was a totally different experience.

The Bloc team had had a brainstorm prior to the event. Upon check-in and registration, people were presented with their wrist-bands, chalet key and information pack (the donkey derby and putting competition were cancelled for the weekend), and as an addition, everyone was given a cardboard mask with cut-out eyes and mouth of . . . my face!

Back to the decks. I walked forwards to a rousing cheer – which was encouraging before I'd actually done anything – and slotted in my first CD (we've never used USBs . . . it feels like cheating). Vinyl is great, but you never know how stable the staging is, especially when Kavus starts jumping on the table to incite more crowd participation. I pressed Play and Frank Zappa's 'Night School' from *Jazz from Hell* was unleashed onto the masses. There was no clever mixing planned and by the time I'd eased into the second track, the show was off and running.

It felt strange. In front of me were people starting to get into the music and I could sense they were dancing but I didn't dare look up because I felt too self-conscious. Eventually, I cast my eyes out to the throng in front of me and I was confronted with a sea of me. They'd all put their masks on, guaranteeing me a frisson of the kind with which watchers of Aphex Twin videos and the film *Being John Malkovich* will already be familiar. I've had a bundle of surreal moments in my life, but that one was top ten material.

One of my two most lasting memories of our stint was watching the whole bar losing its shit when Kavus' inspired choice of Black Sabbath's 'Supernaut' kicked in. Playing this track and the reaction it got was not only an insight into the Bloc weekend ethos (that it was all about great music regardless of genre), but also evidence that we had something to offer as DJs by presenting a unique cross-section of obscure music right up to Birmingham's best.

The other satisfying moment was playing a track from Kavus' own project, a superb CD called *The Exquisite Corpse Game* – where he got a succession of artists on standby. The first artist recorded a relatively short track and then only the last twenty seconds were sent on to the next artist to interpret the progression. The outcome is a musical journey that I'd recommend to any forward-thinking music fan who wanted not only to experience something original in a musical context, but also be introduced to many new artists in the process.

The track in question was made by long-time friend and band member of Kavus' nineties outfit The Monsoon Bassoon, Laurie

Osborne. Laurie had moved in a slightly different direction to Kavus at the turn of the century. The Y2K virus had affected them in different ways. Kavus went all Cardiacsy and Laurie took a fruitier path into dubstep and techno, rebranding himself as Appleblim.

Later that weekend, Laurie was going to be Appleblimming brilliantly with his partner in electronic crime, Second Storey, but it was lovely to see Kavus and him reunite when he'd turned up to support his ex-bandmate. Laurie was close to the decks and it was worth all the butterflies in my stomach as I started to fade up his 'fold' from *The Exquisite Corpse Game* and then watched his face and ears prick up from first thinking, I know this track, to then realising, it's my track! Obviously, this was absolutely nothing special in itself, but it made the world seem like an even lovelier place . . . although the general bonhomie at Bloc was close to unsurpassable anyway. But when you're least expecting a treat, they always taste sweeter.

After the set, we went back to our apartment to film a full debrief. We were as high as kites. It was a great buzz and even though Kavus had had plenty of previous experience of being in various bands, I sensed he'd felt a new type of adrenaline surge. As the night drew to a close, we mused on the possibility of future engagements.

'Now what do we do?' offered Kavus.

'Er,' I replied commandingly, 'I suppose we wait for the phone to ring.'

It turned out that our friends from the BBC were doing their best to help that happen. The film crew who had come with us were very accommodating. The next morning at the crack of dawn, they went out doing aftermath interviews with the punters.

BBC: What did you think of the masks?
Bloc Punter: Great! We'd run out of clean plates, so we used them to eat our food off.

BBC: What did you think of Steve and Kavus' set?
Bloc Punter: Yeah! I've found a new buzz. You get a pitta bread, fill it with cocaine and poppers, and stick it up your arse. It's fucking brilliant!

While the experience of being followed around by a camera crew was nothing new to me, the response to the documentary would see my public image deviating from reality in a totally different way. Though far from being one of the wild men of the snooker circuit, I'd certainly not been as much of a choirboy as my *Spitting Image* caricature had led people to imagine – in some ways, it was quite a useful cover. In contrast, the publicity generated by that short film majored on the non-fact that I, a total ingenue in the electronic realm, had somehow become a 'Techno DJ'. OK, so I'd started to get into a few Autechre records, but let's put it this way, I don't think Carl Cox was losing too much sleep over me.

Chapter 16
Die Laughing

Kavus

I first met Carlos Parsliffe in Wants when I was fifteen. Wants was a small but crammed buy, sell or loan shop in the centre of Plymouth that dealt in musical and electronic equipment. My second guitar, a red Explorer-shaped Hohner, was bought there when I was thirteen and I'd been visiting regularly ever since, gawping at the chaotic array of guitars hung up on the walls or piled against amps. Unlike many music shop proprietors, the owner, Roger, was happy to let me try instruments out, knowing I'd be unlikely to purchase them. He was an encouraging and friendly guy, happy to have a busy shop, I think, and as a consequence, Wants was a hang-out of sorts for local musicians.

Following the release of Metallica's seminal Master of Puppets *in March 1986, I spent the summer holiday attempting to master James Hetfield's extraordinary palm-muting, right-hand technique. While the main verse riff to 'Disposable Heroes' required superhuman strength to play convincingly, I could certainly make a decent fist of most of the album – enough at least that I found myself scrutinised by a swarthy long-haired rocker while trying out a guitar during a school lunch break. He looked like an outlaw, wiry and tattooed, unlike anyone I'd ever met. In a broad Plymothian accent, he grilled me with a pushiness that put me on my guard. Was I in a band? Er, yes, I have one at school. Did I fancy a jam? Um, no, actually, I'd better not. Anyway, I have to go back to school now. Nice to meet you. Bye.*

I attended my first rock festival in the summer of 1988, just after leaving school. Donington 1988 is now notorious for the tragedy that led to the death of two fans in the crush. Amid the cavalcade of piss-filled plastic bottles, the whole experience had been both terrifying and exhilarating. Another attendee, unbeknown to me at the time, was Carlos, who I ran into a second time, again in Wants.

Now, dressed in black, free of school uniform and with longer hair, I was more confident and felt less intimidated by him. He enjoyed recalling our previous meeting, telling me his ears had pricked up at the metallic riffing coming from the back of the shop; exactly the kind of playing he and his drummer friend, Tim Floyd, had been looking for. He'd seen a typical-looking Plymouth grebo holding a guitar and went up to speak to him, only to realise the guitar wasn't plugged in. Peering beyond into the darkened recess of the shop, he'd seen me, surprised to discover that that unholy racket was coming from a geeky-looking schoolkid. He asked me what I was up to. I told him I was looking to put a band together and he invited me over the following day for a jam. He was like a pirate, quite unlike anyone I'd been to school with – the thought of being in a band with someone like that was thrilling.

He picked me up in his Toyota Tercel and we talked music while he smoked foul-smelling Berkeley cigarettes, the cheapest brand available. He was six years my senior and had been turned on to punk as a boy in 1977, before moving on to metal. While he liked a lot of thrash stuff, he was by and large into more traditional rock. In his flat in Lipson, where he lived with his girlfriend, a huge poster of The Cult hung over his bed, while the walls were adorned with posters of semi-naked women, motorbikes and semi-naked women on motorbikes.

I was fine with satanism, murder and the apocalypse, but this kind of rock sexism had always made me uncomfortable. Nevertheless, there in front of my eyes, resting against a genuine Marshall stack, was a Fender Precision bass with a holographic skull between the pickups. This was exciting. No one I knew had this kind of equipment. Or a car.

Once we started playing together, it was clear we had something. He gave me a tape of his previous band (Dirty Virgin . . . dear Lord!) rehearsing and there were a couple of tunes, 'Chasing the Dragon' (drugs = bad) and 'Yesterday's Hero' (war = bad) that I thought could work. I learned them quickly and suggested some modifications, which he liked.

I showed him a few of my songs in return: 'When Hell Freezes Over' (the media/governments/the system = bad), 'The Wheels of Time' (ageing/death = bad) and 'Only the Toughest Survive' (everything = bad). Although he was clearly influenced by Steve Harris, Carlos played the bass with a pick and, unusually, favoured a trebly tone. Melodically, while his chops were limited to blues runs, he played fast and accurately. He was only the second bass player I'd played with and we sounded excellent together. His girlfriend told us.

Carlos was serious about wanting to get a band going and insisted this project should progress as a matter of the highest urgency. This was the kind of guy I'd been waiting to meet – 'Man, Sid Vicious was younger than me when he died,' he reasoned. 'I can't wait forever.' He had excellent equipment, long hair, his own pad and a car. What's more, he worked as a draughtsman ('Like Steve Harris,' he noted) and had access to a photocopier, which would later prove invaluable in our attempt to conquer if not the world then at least Plymouth.

Carlos was very much 'from the streets' and a bit of a fighter. His Spanish heritage meant he'd been picked on while growing up and like me, this had made him headstrong. If I was a little intimidated by our age difference and his volatile temper – I'd generally relent on potential conflicts – when it came to the music, I'd never back down on a disagreement if I knew I was right. While prudence and moderation are fine in small talk, music is far too important to be held accountable to the same rules as polite society.

I was still awkward and unsure of myself, but in the context of a band, I was bullheaded and confident. I knew how I wanted us to sound and had a good idea how to get there. It turned out, through playing gigs with Flytrap and later, Marshall Law – effectively a covers band but a gateway to playing parties and underage drinking – that I already had at least as much live experience as him. I soon established myself as the principal songwriter.

Carlos brought Tim Floyd along to our next rehearsal and we took to one another immediately. He was a tall, skinny and long-haired eighteen-year-old, articulate and funny, who thought deeply about music. He had an enormous blue Pearl drum kit with five toms, two roto-toms and two kick drums, which would take him seemingly forever to assemble.

His influences as a drummer were Sabbath's Bill Ward and Budgie from Siouxsie and the Banshees, and he had a canny knack with a *rhyming couplet which, along with his bleak outlook, made him an excellent source of nihilistic lyrics.*

He lived with his brother and stepdad halfway between my place in the suburbs and the town centre. It would take me forty-five minutes to walk to his house and a further half an hour to get to town. I'd call on him every Friday and Saturday and, over a few cans in his bedroom, get schooled in Celtic Frost – today's lesson is To Mega Therion – before we headed into town to go clubbing.

At my suggestion, we'd settled on the name Psycho Dirt Perps (I know, I know). 'Perps' I got from 'perpetrator' in Judge Dredd. I've no idea where the Psycho Dirt part came from. Now imagine it said in a Devonian accent. It became the first in a long line of band names I'd grow to regret.

We needed a singer and Tim suggested a guy he'd met from Horrabridge, twice voted the ugliest village in the UK, called Ian Johnson. He was twenty years old, rode a motorbike and looked pretty cool with long, curly Robert Plant-like locks. He had a suitably rough-sounding voice that could hold a tune. Ian was infatuated with the Bristol thrashers, Onslaught, particularly the singer Sy Keeler. He'd often point out that the two of them held the microphone in the same way, something he took to be of great significance. Although we shared a love of 2000 AD and Hawkwind, Ian resented being in a band with a cocky and opinionated kid, and would sneeringly refer to me as 'Mowgli' whenever I got above my station.

We spent the next year playing what few gigs we could get, opening for rare visiting metal bands (Foxx, anyone?), playing at charity events and organising our own shows, including one at my old Scout hut. We weren't especially good but stood apart from most local rock bands on the strength of both original material and having a singer who performed shirtless. Within a couple of years, Plymouth would have its own burgeoning underground metal scene – Cadaverous, Teratogenic, Psychastorm – but in 1989, we were the only thrash band in town.

Tim would present beautifully handwritten sheets of gloomy verse for me to write music to, which in turn was becoming darker and heavier. After Ian had turned us on to Coroner, we wrote 'Crying Is The Sea,

Dying Is The Land' (the planet = fucked) and marvelled at how it didn't really sound like anyone else. Not that it was all smooth sailing. Over the next year, I'd experience our particular version of the much-celebrated 'singer versus lead guitarist' tension every time we were together, as Ian would mutter snide asides about me to the others. 'What was that?' I'd ask. 'Nothing, Mowgli, settle down.'

This bad feeling came to a head upon arriving at St George's Hall in Exeter. We'd driven up that afternoon in Carlos' trusty Toyota Tercel while Ian followed behind us on his motorbike. Somewhat excitable at the prospect of playing in a big hall outside Plymouth, even if it was supporting Tawny, a muso rock covers band, I spent a great deal of the journey leaning out of the window pulling 'Joey' faces at Ian.

Joey Deacon had been born with severe cerebral palsy – a heroic figure who, despite his condition, wrote an autobiography providing an insight into the lives of those with physical disabilities. During the last year of his life in 1981, he was featured on Blue Peter, *presented as a man who had achieved a great deal, in spite of his disabilities. Despite the sensitive way* Blue Peter *covered his life, they couldn't account for the cruelty of schoolchildren and the following day, 'Joey' became a commonplace insult in playgrounds across the country.*

It came as something of a surprise, then, once we reached the car park, when Ian removed his helmet and come flailing at me, roaring, 'You little shit!' He was incandescent with rage and, had Carlos not intervened, would certainly have kicked the crap out of me. I was never more grateful to have an actual fighter in the band.

Ian's dad was in the advanced stages of Huntington's disease and, unbeknown to us, Ian had been diagnosed with it, too. Typically thoughtless, I hadn't made the connection. I felt like such a cunt.

My friend Jane had coined the term 'the tact of a Torabi' and it still holds true for everyone I know with this surname.

'Well, this is our last gig,' he announced as we walked onto the stage, much to the surprise of Carlos, Tim and me. 'You'll probably never hear of us again . . .' It was our final gig – as Psycho Dirt Perps, at least.

From Iron Maiden onwards, I loved the sound of two guitars and, although we had a few shows under our studded belts as a four-piece, we'd been looking for a second guitarist since we started. We'd tried out a couple of people but, whether overly combative in their lead playing or simply turning up in blue jeans and white trainers, they weren't right. I was still living at home when Carlos called round accompanied by a gaunt sixteen-year-old with a Marlin Sidewinder guitar in one hand and a fifteen-watt Ross practice amp in the other. His face was obscured by a curtain of lank, greasy hair and he wore a leather jacket, tatty black jeans, an oversized black sweater covered in food stains and Doc Martens boots.

'This is Dan,' announced Carlos. 'He's here to try out for the band.'

Dan, barely looking up, followed us upstairs to my room. We plugged in and, under Carlos' watchful eye, went through a few standards: 'Paranoid', 'Seek & Destroy', 'Whole Lotta Rosie'. He played well enough, mimicking the solos of Tony Iommi, Kirk Hammett and Angus Young, but he wasn't particularly better than me and after an awkward half-hour, in which he barely spoke, we went downstairs for a smoke and coffee. I just couldn't visualise this bloke playing in our band and resented Carlos for bringing him round without asking me first. I didn't want to be the one to turn him down. Inscrutable behind his hair, Dan puffed away on a cigarette as I attempted to get the measure of him by engaging him in conversation.

'So, Dan, do you like Carcass?'

'Yeah, they're mental.'

'How about Sabbat?'

'Yeah, they're all right.'

Eventually, Carlos suggested we go back upstairs and show him some of our tunes.

Reluctantly, I showed Dan the opening riff to 'Only the Toughest Survive', which he immediately played back confidently. It wasn't a hard riff but, previously, C&A snow-wash and Nike high-tops matey had required me to explain the picking pattern before he could play it properly. Next, I showed Dan what I envisaged to be the harmony lead and he added his part instantly. Now it sounded like the music I'd always heard in my head. Having explained the structure, 'All right, it does eight of the first riff, into the verse, then a half-chorus, followed by the double-paced riff,' and so on, we ran the eight-minute song from the start. Without prompting, Dan played it back as if he'd been performing it for months. Next, we moved on to the more complex 'Shadows on the Grain'. The same.

Within the hour, Dan had learned seven of our songs in almost the time it took to play them. I'd say, 'Do a solo here,' and he'd rip out something melodic and unusual. It wasn't just his ability to learn, Dan was also inherently musical with his own unique voice. He may not have verbalised much, but playing together was a fluent musical conversation devoid of small talk. I'd played with other guitarists before, but it had never felt like this – it opened up a world of possibility. Dan was the guitarist I'd been waiting to meet since we'd started the band two years earlier. It required no further thought – Dan Chudley was in.

I'd seen Jim 'Sicky' Parker around at the metal and alternative clubs (Connections on Friday night: rock; The Warehouse on Saturday night: indie). He was cool as fuck – tall and striking, with dyed black hair and intense, piercing blue eyes. Dressed with much more style than your average metaller, he looked like a raven. We'd spoken a few times and I really liked him. I had no idea if he could sing, but he looked like he should be fronting a band. Whenever he was out, I couldn't stop looking at him. He had a kind of magnetism that I supposed was star quality. It transpired he was an artist who had moved away from Leamington Spa, where he'd been part of Bolt Thrower's scene, responsible for their initial logo and early artwork. While I was taken with his charisma, I knew a portent when I saw one and, noticing a Voivod tattoo on his upper arm, asked him if he wanted to try out as a singer in Die Laughing (the new, Killing Joke-inspired name we'd settled on).

A year older than Carlos, Sicky had also come to metal through punk but was now more entrenched in grind and hardcore. While he wasn't one for melody, his urgent and intense bark radically altered our sound, immediately making us more vital and edgy. His attitude and delivery inspired us to play more aggressively. It was unanimous – we'd found our singer.

We collectively bought a small vocal PA, which we set up in a corrugated iron shack above a pig barn in Chilsworthy, Cornwall, that belonged to 'Gren', a farmer whose wife was in a relationship with Tim's dad. We never got to the bottom of how this worked domestically, but freed from paying rehearsal rates at the Plymouth Musicians Cooperative, we never questioned the fortuitous arrangement. 'The Cornish are weird,' Dan explained. 'They punch walls.'

Now driving to Cornwall at weekends, we took a few months off gigs to work on a new set. The volume was so intense that Gren cheerily informed us that he'd received complaints from Devon. He didn't seem to mind, though; he was always happy to see us.

It transpired that Dan was a terrific writer and together, we began to develop the sound that would eventually alienate the rest of the band and despatch us to London. But for the next couple of years, we were largely in agreement about where we were headed.

We recorded and mixed our first cassette EP, 'Omnigod', in two days at the Daylight Studios, a sixteen-track recording studio in Honiton, East Devon, built in a beautifully renovated old mill and bakery. 'Cassette EP' is a more romantic term for demo. Carlos and I spent days overseeing the duplication of copies with our tape-to-tape cassette players set on 'high-speed dubbing' mode. Carlos used his draughtsmanship skills to tidy up my artwork, while Sicky had created a fashionably unreadable logo that looked more like 'Diet Crugring'. Once all the covers had been photocopied, I airbrushed a spectrum of impressionistic swirls over all the sheets before cutting them up, making each one unique.

With 'Omnigod' as our currency, we began tape trading with underground metal bands across the globe and soon found ourselves being reviewed in fanzines and metal magazines. At Carlos' suggestion and taking advantage, once again, of his access to a photocopier, we launched our own fanzine, Extreme Diabolism, which covered the local metal, punk, crusty and noise bands that had started to emerge. Many underground LPs would include the home address of members and over the course of six issues, we ran the first ever interview with Pitchshifter, as well as Hellbastard, Decadence Within, Prophecy of Doom and Bolt Thrower, including album and demo reviews, rants and artwork by ourselves and our friends. Metal was undergoing a transformation in the late eighties and early nineties. Still derided by the music media at large, *it was taking in influences from avant-garde industrial music, hip-hop, prog and hardcore. Labels such as Earache in the UK, Germany's Noise and Roadrunner in the US were regularly putting out incredible albums and between us, we bought almost every release. Traditional metal was sounding increasingly boring and staid, so it was exciting to feel that we were, in some small, provincial way, part of a new dawn.*

In the year 1991, the country turned crusty and the fractal was king. I'd finally finished college and, with my long hair now dutifully matted into dreadlocks, left home to begin my life proper. I moved into a bedsit in Greenbank (PL4 - postcode of the gods!) and got my nose pierced in the same week Cardiacs released their magnificent 'Day Is Gone' EP.

PL4 was a hive of squalid bedsits, flats and shared houses inhabited by musicians, artists, dropouts and dealers. Plymouth wasn't part of any real circuit and while there were a handful of good venues, there were very few good promoters, which meant touring bands rarely played. Nonetheless, over the few years Die Laughing were operational, I saw gigs by Fields of the Nephilim, Hawkwind, Prophecy of Doom, Silverfish, Zygote, RDF, De La Soul - if you can believe it - Poisoned Electrick Head, U.K. Subs, Culture Shock, Acid Reign, Creaming Jesus, Decadence Within. Even Celtic Frost came to town; although touring the not especially visionary Vanity/Nemesis *album.*

By the early nineties, Plymouth had its own vibrant, internalised scene, with a hierarchy of about twenty bands, all of whom lived together, drank in the same two pubs and went to the same clubs. Die Laughing found ourselves in the centre of a network of creative and fucked-up freaks. Our local venue, The Cooperage was home to this collision of styles - death metal, punk, rave, dub, folk, hardcore and psychedelia - and all the bands played regularly. Every Tuesday night, Roots, a tiny club off Union Street, would spin tunes by Fugazi, Spacemen 3, Psychic TV, N.W.A., Big Black, Front 242, Into a Circle and The Young Gods. Unbeknown to anyone outside Plymouth, and most of the people who lived there, we had a hell of a thing going on.

Die Laughing's audience was increasing - we were attracting up to 200 people at our shows - and through selling the tapes, T-shirts and fanzines, we saved enough money to buy a cheap second-hand transit van, retiring Carlos' Toyota Tercel. Having taken to promoting gigs ourselves, getting bands down that we'd connected with through our fanzine and tape trading, we were now playing gigs outside Plymouth and before long, engaging in something that started to resemble touring. I wasn't yet twenty.

On top of these various entrepreneurial activities, Tim Floyd and I were making an additional £20 each Friday by DJ'ing, playing out the same ear-bending records we were buying, at a night we called 'Beelzeklub' in The Academy - an enormous old theatre, split into two clubs. What's more, as DJs, Rival Records gave a 20 per cent discount.

If I was going to commit to the musician's life properly, though, I'd need a proper income. Visiting the DHSS office for an interview, a woman not much older than me asked what sort of work I was looking for. 'Well, you see, I've got a band . . .' Her laughter cut me off before I could get any further and she handed me a form to fill out. It was that simple.

Being on the dole was living, all right. Although only £25 every fortnight, with the addition of the weekly DJ'ing money, it was more than adequate. By this point, the whole band was signing on. We'd heard that in Norway, musicians were given an actual grant, so we viewed our giro as basically the same thing. Now, Dan Chudley and I could see each other every day, so we immersed ourselves in writing and playing. Our listening was becoming increasingly diverse and we attempted to shoehorn our new ideas into the metallic framework of Die Laughing.

Although I was technically unemployed, the DHSS put me on an art scheme, which meant that because I was 'in training', I wasn't officially on the dole, which kept the Tory government's unemployment figures down. Although attendance every weekday from 9 a.m. to midday was mandatory, I had access to the biggest array of art equipment since leaving school and while some attendees were clearly there under duress, I loved it.

Most importantly, the art-scheme studio - which my friend Justin Lish referred to as 'the mental home' - had screen-printing equipment. I'd use Die Laughing money to buy bags of cheap T-shirts from the local wholesaler, Barbican Discounts, and screen-print designs rendered by myself and Sicky, which we'd sell at gigs. We soon had quite the collection on our merch stall.

Of course, as in any small-city scene, all was not entirely harmonious. There was a particularly dire Bon Jovi-inspired band called Karrallon, beloved of Plymouth's right-wing rag, The Evening Herald. Their exploits were fawningly documented, week in, week out in the local paper, as if they were on some kind of fast track to international success. They were a joke – the drummer wore a wig and a couple of them were in their early thirties, for fuck's sake.

When Karrallon opened the Radio 1 Roadshow on the Hoe, Plymouth's historic seafront, The Herald proudly printed a photograph of the guitarist (short strap, guitar on chest) wearing a baseball cap backwards next to the bass player, who was using a Phil Collins-style 'hands-free' mic. Enough was enough. I cut out the image and along with the caption 'Don't Come to Plymouth', printed them as A4 posters. That night, after a few drinks, I fly-posted them all over the city centre using wallpaper paste.

As soon as I woke up the following morning, I regretted having done it and avoided going into town for the remainder of the week, scared I'd run afoul of the ghastly soft rockers on the warpath. I never found out if they saw the posters or even connected them with our band, but we hadn't exactly been retiring in our assessment of them.

Either way, Karrallon sadly endured.

Chapter 17

Mixmaster Morris

Steve

I'd already planned to announce my retirement from competitive snooker shortly after Kavus and I rocked the house at Bloc, and when the BBC unleashed the iPlayer feature during the World Snooker Championship a month later, it got a bundle of hits online. From this point on, my management started to be inundated with people wanting Kavus and me to DJ. My agent at the Matchroom Sport offices was fielding queries from a variety of sources, none of which were the usual fodder of snooker clubs or corporate dinners needing my services. Instead, plenty of weddings and birthday parties were requested.

Initially, we were all pissing in the wind trying to determine a hit gig from a potential foul and a miss. Beyond that, what on earth should we be charging? Kavus and I quickly worked out that we weren't wedding DJs – quite the opposite, given the style of music we were intending to play. We also sensibly decided to pitch our price slightly below the rate that Calvin Harris was going out for.

The most important phone call came in from a little festival in the West Country situated in a few fields on a site called Worthy Farm. *Fucking hell!* We were reeling with excitement. Our second ever DJ booking was about to be at Glastonbury. Not fair, is it? What about all the hard-working DJs who've grafted for years, dreaming of a slot at Glasto? The moral dilemma we faced was quite frankly overwhelming. Should we, as rookies, take up a slot that a far more deserving DJ should have? Kavus and I sat down for a serious discussion. Yeah, like fuck we did. 'Let's party!' was our immediate battle cry without even knowing what the fee was.

We were booked to do a ninety-minute set at the Stonebridge Bar – a 500-capacity tent in the Park area of the festival. Our Bloc

Weekend stint had been a sequence of twenty-minute individual slots and neither of us had had a playlist planned after the first few tracks, but ninety minutes at the UK's biggest music festival needed a lot more preparation. We called upon the talents of Ben Jacobs (aka Max Tundra) to run our planned order of attack past his experienced ears. As a testament to the value of his guidance, I still have our set list written on a piece of card with authentic Glastonbury mud on it.

We'd also realised we needed to up our performance level by not only DJ'ing together, but also by making sure it looked like we knew how to operate heavy machinery. This came easier for Kavus (as a natural performer), but I had to try to step up to the plate, as well. Our set was early evening on the Thursday, which is a great day to DJ (although we didn't know it at the time), because the punters have usually all arrived and set up and are ready to get stuck in. Even though they're planning to have a quiet one and ease themselves in gently, once they get there, that all goes out the window and it's foot to the floor from the moment the tent ropes are secure.

It certainly was for us - and the fact that we were crapping ourselves did nothing to slow our alcohol consumption. We were DJ'ing at 5 p.m. We started on the gin at eleven in the morning. By two in the afternoon, we'd drunk two bottles between four of us, but with all the adrenaline pumping around our veins, the alcohol hadn't even taken the edge off our nerves. Hendrick's needed to up their game if they thought just half a bottle of gin was going to shore up a Glastonbury debutant's sphincter.

We arrived at the Stonebridge Bar in plenty of time at 4 p.m. The place was empty. A feeling of dread came over us. What if nobody turned up? At 4.30 p.m. - still nobody. Shit, what a let-down. We walked into the empty tent and through to the artist area backstage feeling a tad deflated. We met the crew, drank as many beers as we could find to pacify the still-bubbling nerves and had ten pisses in the higher-spec Portaloos. Melanie Woods, a member of Kavus' band, Knifeworld, had come down for moral support, but she was

169

even more pissed than us and slipped arse over tit after stepping out of the loo into a huge puddle of what she hoped was only mud. It didn't bode well for our upcoming performance.

We walked out to a rammed tent. And I mean truly rammed. It was one out, one in on the gate. Curiosity had got the better of the Glastonbury crowd and with no main bands performing, it seemed like we were one of the hottest tickets for that early evening slot. We'd even been mentioned in the festival guide as a show not to miss. Not only was it packed inside, but by all accounts there were also three times as many people standing outside waiting to get in (I'm not making this up – there are photos on the internet, so it must be true). Of course, we were oblivious to all this at the time, not least because we were totally smashed.

I do vaguely remember it being ninety minutes of pure enjoyment. At one stage, out of the blue, Suggs from Madness appeared onstage to great applause and even though I was drunk, both of him looked just like Suggs should. We chatted, although I haven't got a clue what he said, as all of my brain cells were occupied trying to stand up straight and read what the next planned track was.

Finding a happy medium between Barry Hearn's well-oiled Matchroom merch machine and Kavus' DIY beginnings in Plymouth, we'd had a selection of tote bags printed up and threw a bunch out to the crowd, rock star style. There were four different designs: 'The Interesting Alternative Show', 'Tonight Steve Davis Is a DJ', 'Last Night Kavus Torabi Saved My Life' and 'Last Night Steve Davis Bored Me Shitless'. They're destined to be collector's items once we've cracked Vegas.

We're still relative greenhorns DJ'ing-wise, but within the brief of not compromising and only playing music that we like and believe in, it's interesting to recall what we started out playing and see how much the set lists have changed in a relatively short time frame. One thing we have learned is that a key early indicator of likely success is when the women in attendance start dancing. The girls definitely know before the boys if the unknown music they're listening to is cool or not.

The most difficult thing is playing a set to non-heads. Heads get it. They're keen to listen to new music and once they trust the DJ, then they'll happily be guided on the journey. The tougher gigs are festivals that people go to as an 'event' rather than a music experience. We've certainly got a small advantage inasmuch as we may get a slightly longer pass before a punter wanders off in search of other fodder owing to our novelty aspect. It's not the usual career progression for ex-snooker players and former members of Cardiacs, but that advantage only buys us a few tracks extra.

We can't (and don't have any desire to) keep them in the room at all costs. 'Come On Eileen' is never going to get a look-in and it's a fascinating challenge trying to juggle obscure tracks into a compelling set that can keep a dance floor occupied. It's also fun delving into our record collections and listening with a different ear. A track you might have disregarded as a home favourite takes on a completely different aspect when played live in the wee small hours of a Saturday night. Charles Hayward's 'Speculative Fiction' from the Camberwell Now album *The Ghost Trade* is a case in point. Sitting listening on a sofa, other tracks take centre stage on this album, but bring 'Speculative Fiction' to the party house and you've got a techno-tinged Hydra that gets every head in the room nodding in appreciation. The crowd are usually none the wiser about its roots, but to be honest, who cares! It's all just about the music in the moment.

It could be you want something a little more simplistic or visceral the later the evening goes on, as the booze and disco biscuits kick in for the crowd, but that doesn't mean you need to pander to the techno mentality of a mechanical beat only.

Here's a controversial statement – something Kavus observed. You can't dance sexy to techno. Yeah, you can put your hand above your head, bend your wrist in homage to Rod Hull and Emu and then give it a shake . . . but you can't swing your hips to the genre. Considering I've never 'danced sexy' in my life, I don't see the issue here, but in essence, we've never wanted to kowtow too much to the basic four-to-the-floor beat. Conversely, we hope that when we DJ we don't *just* appeal to the trainspotting guys, either, and as a general rule, it's everything in moderation - and so far so good on that front.

One venue where nobody was dancing sexy was a gig we did on a boat from Newcastle to Amsterdam. It was a scheduled ferry crossing, but the promoter had reserved a certain number of berths on board (although the gig was open to anyone travelling), hired a couple of local bands and decided that we might like to DJ. Considering our then operational 'if you say yes then things happen' strategy, we were only going to give him one answer. Let me first say that we've never yet regretted agreeing to do a gig, even one recently in Leicester when, genuinely, only my two friends turned up, but obviously some are more successful than others.

So we checked in on board at 3 p.m., set sail at 5 p.m. and hung around with the promoter, bands and the other DJ. Meanwhile the passengers, who included a healthy - or unhealthy, depending on your viewpoint - mix of stag and hen parties on course for oblivion in Amsterdam, set about getting some practice in by downing the alcohol they'd smuggled on board. A couple of hours later, the stag-ees had morphed into staggers and by the time the opening band launched into their first number mid-evening, they had to fight off five women determined to sing 'I Will Survive' a cappella onstage. By the time the headliners Frankie & The Heartstrings came on at ten thirty, things had calmed down in one respect. The stag parties had caned it so hard they were comatose back in their cabins.

Meanwhile, above sea level, one type of carnage had been replaced by another. The more hardcore among the passengers were still ready to dance, but the North Sea had other ideas. Frankie & The Heartstrings were serving up some nice chops, but the choppiest moves were made by the increasingly turbulent sea. As they launched into their hit single 'Hunger' and their fans took to the dance floor, the rolling of the boat, and the unfortunate heaving of one person's stomach, caused a certain amount of mayhem as the throng lurched from side to side in front of the stage and a couple of unlucky dancers lost their footing in a puddle of vomit. Other than the one fight that broke out between two guys over a girl, the rest of the night went pretty well, but come midnight, most people were shipwrecked from nine hours' solid drinking.

We tried our best but to no avail. One woman did approach us and ask if we had any Nickelback, but sadly, I'd forgotten to put that CD in my case, so other than one couple who jumped up in excitement when we put on Julian Cope's 'Upwards at 45 Degrees', we were resigned to performing to some diced carrots that were heading eastwards at 21 knots. Peter Brewis of the excellent band Field Music was DJ'ing after us at 1 a.m. and we watched as he dropped the needle on King Crimson's 'Elephant Talk' with a sinking feeling on a *Titanic* level looming for the rest of his hour slot.

It was also around this time that I did a solo DJ spot at the Islington Assembly Hall, the headline act being Tom Jenkinson's (aka Squarepusher) jazz fusion band Shobaleader One. I had the luxury of playing an eclectic set in between acts with zero dance-floor expectation.

The next day, I got a call from the band's booking agent, Rick Morton, telling me he'd enjoyed the unusual music and was interested in solely representing us. Kavus and I were initially sceptical but told Rick we were still happy for him to find us gigs. At that time, my snooker agents were fielding phone calls on a subject they had little experience of and after a couple more questionable bookings combined with a few excellent ones from Rick, we bit the bullet and haven't regretted it since. I'd never experienced a rider before. It's brilliant - all the IPA we can drink and whole bowlful of brown M&M's.

He's an absolute star. Totally professional in his field - but when it comes to a Worthy Farm field, it's a different story entirely. Kavus was raving about Rick to some of the crew at the Spike Bar just before our second DJ'ing spot there, when at that exact moment, Rick rolled up in a wizard's outfit. He was only missing a Nimbus 2000 for the complete kit. The timing was perfect and he went up in our estimation no end.

As a snooker player, I always remembered my missed shots and losses more clearly than my successes and it seems to be the same with DJ'ing. The most frustrated I've ever seen Kavus on the decks was at a festival that came with a great reputation but was frequented mainly by 'straights' who thought the most important thing about going to a festival was putting glitter on. We can now see a correlation between the success of our sets and glitter. The closer the festival is to a Ryman's, the worse things will probably turn out. The equation is $G \times 1/P = X$, where G = the number of punters who apply glitter, P = number of punters attending the festival and X = the percentage chance that we'll go down about as well as flatulence at the baulk end of a snooker table during a bout of safety play.

We rocked up at this festival just as the heavens opened. With no obvious place to hang out and thinking that we might as well get as close to our ultimate destination as possible, we arrived at an open-air space in a wooded area of the site and looked for cover backstage. The only protection seemed to be a piece of leaking tarpaulin, draped over a few branches, with two soggy old sofas half underneath. We were soaking wet and cold. An older couple (older than me, even!) were already marinating on the sofas. The guy seemed OK but his wife was a total fucking pain. She was pissed and kept offering us red wine, insisting on blowing 'good luck' into our faces as if she were some kind of wistful soothsayer.

We escaped to the DJ booth to meet up with the guy who was on before us and also curating the stage. He proceeded to initiate us into the mystical brotherhood of forestry DJ'ing.

'Have you ever DJ'ed in the woods before? It's not the same as a club. You have to take into account the trees. It might help if you took some psychedelics before you go on in order to be in tune and at one with your surroundings.'

I sensed that Kavus wanted to knee him in the bollocks, but to be honest, it was the driest place around and he was nearing the end of his set anyway - a set that was about as psychedelic as stepping on a dog turd just before your driving test. The writing was on the wall for us, because the bland music he was churning out had attracted a good kilogramme of glitter that was two-stepping around in the space circled by the trees. We gave it a go and played some properly psychedelic music, but it turns out that the glitterati don't like it that much and they're only treading water until they're old enough to listen to Heart FM.

We must have done something right on our second-ever gig, because the following year we got our first rebooking . . . at Glasto! We were booked to play the Spike Bar in the Glade area. It turned out to be a brilliant couple of hours. We'd also agreed to play a ninety-minute afternoon charity set in the Greenpeace field in a wooden tree house. Actually, it wasn't so much a tree house as a fabricated tree, built out of wood, that housed some DJ decks. No doubt the wood had been ethically sourced, even though there was a certain irony in building a tree out of the stuff.

To get in or out of the DJ booth required a ridiculous level of contortionist prowess. Once in it, trying to get out was akin to an underground trial in *I'm a Celebrity . . . Get Me Out of Here!* That, combined with the considerable distance to the nearest toilet, and the fact that the organisers had kindly loaded us up with five pints of real ale each, meant that we both had logistical bladder concerns. Not a problem when you consider that we had ten reusable plastic glasses that weren't going to be full forever. I was three pints in when just as I prepared for my first moment of relief, a spanner was thrown into the mix. Or rather, a master mixer was thrown into the tree in the shape of Mixmaster Morris, a living legend of underground DJ cool, who had limboed in to say hello.

It was a Sunday afternoon and the area surrounding the tree house was more of a chill-out space than a proper venue. There were a few families with kids hanging around, which was great. Kids are far less judgemental when it comes to music. We had a fair few toddlers bopping away to Alec K. Redfearn and the Eyesores' 'Fire Shuffle', even though it had started to rain a little, but my main concern was inevitably somewhat closer to home. That didn't stop me drinking, though. Morris said hello and was chatting about all things 'music', but I couldn't concentrate and, between digging out tracks and trying to focus on my pelvic floor muscles, I more or less ignored him.

I suppose I could have just said, 'Morris, I need to refill this glass I've just drained,' but I was too embarrassed. This confession is a sort of apology for basically having tried to use my Jedi mind powers to (ever so politely) get him to fuck off. Morris wasn't going anywhere as we'd just started a great conversation about the Basic Channel record label. Perhaps I should have offered him an empty glass and invited him for a communal piss. If you'd picked this card up in a game of Scruples, what would you have done?

Finally, he did make his exit - and to my eternal credit, I pissed more than a pint. This is no mean feat and, usually, if you lay the bet as a bookmaker throughout the festival season, you'll end up well in front. By the end of the set, considering they weren't the first pints I'd drunk that day, I'd ended up with three full glasses. OK, they weren't a real ale hue - they had more of a lager look to them. We finished our set and handed over the DJ reins to another contortionist.

There was nowhere in the booth to pour these babies away and regardless of the fact that it might have looked strange taking them with me, escorting them to the nearest urinal would have moved the scenario on from *I'm a Celebrity . . .* to *It's a Knockout*. So I left them there, shutting my mind to the thought that the incoming DJ might have turned up a tad thirsty.

Chapter 18

more Die
Laughing

Kavus

The free festival scene was still burgeoning at the start of the nineties and having our own van meant it was now accessible to us. We'd hear about these underground events through fanzines, flyers or word of mouth, assemble a crew to help chip in with the fuel, pack our tents and backline, and head off. Our first was The White Goddess on Bodmin Moor, where we shared a bill on the Wango Riley's Travelling Stage with Citizen Fish and folk/punk collective Good Grief, who I briefly played guitar for.

Free festivals were an extraordinary scene – wild and totally lawless affairs. Ad hoc stages and performances sprouted up between buses offering Trips: £1.50, Brew: £1, Hot Knives: £1, Haircuts: 50p, Egg Sarnie: £1. Following The White Goddess, I was smitten for a while with the romance of this lifestyle, or at least what I imagined it to be. I dreamed an idealised future touring from one free festival to the next, living on the proceeds of T-shirt and tape sales and donations, inhabiting a beautiful old bus, getting high, playing guitar and writing poetry, liberated from the constraints of straight society.

As it turned out, the barely disguised animosity I experienced over the two days I spent on an actual traveller site in Cornwall would be even more of a downer than the prevailing conditions in the straight world I hoped to leave, as I ran up against a hierarchy of who was the hardest, or had the hardest dog, and an undercurrent of aggression, criminality and anti-intellectualism. A couple of the site's numerous canine denizens were actually called 'Resin' and 'Mushroom'.

In early May 1992, we came into the possession of a flyer detailing the location of a free festival at Chipping Sodbury in Avon. Still a couple of weeks off, there was excited talk about it among our mates. It promised to be a big one and we all agreed Die Laughing should be on the bill. The relevant Friday arrived and we headed off around midday, hoping to arrive later the same afternoon. As we neared, we stopped off at a payphone, dialling the number on the flyer to clarify directions, only to discover the festival had moved. An hour of winding country roads later and we joined a large slow-moving convoy of colourful and probably untaxed buses, next to which our battered white transit van looked positively aristocratic.

It was dark before we got onto the site at Castlemorton in Malvern. The entrance was swarming with police but thankfully, given the sheer scale of the event (there seemed to be hundreds of similar vehicles arriving), the forces of law and order were contenting themselves with just ushering everyone into the field – containment, presumably, being the safest policy.

We parked up in the nearest and most obvious space and erected our tents before venturing further in. Night one was relatively sedate and we wandered around for a couple of hours. I was a little taken aback by a dreadlocked child, no older than ten, trying to hard-sell us some LSD. 'Good clean trips,' he insisted, but it was late, I was tired from our day's travelling in a slow queue of traffic (squashed in the back of our hot van, sitting on one of Tim's kick drums), so I headed back to where our tents were.

I returned to find that in our absence, Spiral Tribe, the notorious crusty rave crew, had now set up their stage adjacent to where we were camped and the volume was punishing. There was nothing for it – I couldn't face taking down my tent and finding a new pitch at 2 a.m., opting instead to spend the night horizontal and awake while an MC instructed 'Rush your fucking bollocks off.'

In the spring daylight of the following day, I discovered that in the dark, I'd set up my tent on a substantial dog shit – at least, I hoped it was from a dog – so we moved our van and camp to a quieter spot. Once successfully relocated, over the continuous and ululating thrum of dub, digeridoos and djembes, we set about finding some breakfast. Thankfully, pretty much the entire site was vegetarian or vegan and after we'd eaten, we went looking for the stage to secure a slot for our band.

The festival was enormous, far larger than any we'd been to before. We located Wango Riley's, which was the main stage in the travellers' area, where we were camped. Their operation had deep roots in the peripatetic rock underground, going back to Hawkwind and the first Glastonbury.

Built into the back of a flatbed truck, the PA was powered by a generator and between acts, someone would come out with a hat, asking for 'diesel for the genny' donations. Looking at the chalkboard at the side of the stage, I saw that Tin Tin Tin, Stormed, Poisoned Electrick Head and Back to the Planet were due to play that day. While I didn't care for Back to the Planet, we loved Poisoned Electrick Head and thought this would be the ideal bill to play on. The friendly, hobbit-like stage manager remembered us and said, 'The bill's full today, but we can get you on tomorrow afternoon.' So he chalked up 'Die Laughing 2 p.m.' on the board under Sunday.

On the way back to the tent to tell Carlos and Tim, we scored some powerful acid, from an adult, and later bumped into one of Sicky's old mates, the singer from the punk band Bad Beach. I had a song of theirs on a Manic Ears compilation album. Tasting metal in the back of my mouth and gritting my teeth as I felt the first wave hit me, I couldn't stop staring at his angular, chiselled face as the sun reflected from his sunglasses. He looked like a deity. My stomach clenched. This would be a good day.

During Tin Tin Tin's late afternoon set, one of the Wango's crew found me and began to say words at me. He was looking at me for a response, but I hadn't been listening. I was staring at his face, and particularly the self-transforming geometry of his interesting beard.

'Hey, nice to see you, man.' I smiled in complete incomprehension.

He tried again and this time, I really tried to concentrate on what he was saying. If I understood him correctly, there was an opening on the bill for us to play in an hour if we wanted it.

The thought of merely tuning my guitar, let alone finding the others, loading onto the stage, setting up wires and pedals and then performing was completely ludicrous. As best I could, I managed, 'Yes, we're fine with tomorrow. Thanks, man.'

Poisoned Electrick Head were from St Helens. Their sound and per-formances were a fabulous mix of Devo and Gong. They'd played at The Cooperage in Plymouth a couple of times and were always brilliant but here, tripping, among a friendly throng of fellow psychonauts, they were monumental. This was the last time I saw them play before they took to wearing HR Giger-inspired masks and, in retrospect, my favourite period. Their Castlemorton set remains one of the most mind-bending performances I've ever witnessed. Knowing nothing could beat that and certainly not Back to the Planet, Dan, Sicky and I headed off to explore the rest of the festival still very much in a state of heightened awareness. It would transpire there were 40,000 people in attendance and making eye contact with the procession of faces darting, stumbling or streaming past us, around us and behind us, one thing was clear - everyone here was tripping. It felt joyful and deranged.

'Hey, look! Let's check that out.' We followed Sicky's finger to where distant strobes were flashing and pulsing with a warm, deep bass throb. As we walked away from the travellers' field, we became aware of a massive rave in full flow. This was so much bigger than anything we'd left behind us. Instead of the monolithic parked vehicles, there was a sea of dancing revellers. It was like walking into the future, or rather, walking out of the past and into the present.

Then the realisation hit me that this was actually the main event - a dazzling light show illuminated an enormous PA, the music coming out of which was sensational. How could we not have noticed this? Did anyone we'd left behind actually know this was happening? It was unreal. We made our way further into the heart of the throng to dance with abandon among a giggling crowd of wide-eyed and gorgeous-look-ing people.

I'd been to a couple of raves in Plymouth before but tonight, outdoors, the experience disclosed itself on a much deeper level. This was it - that propulsive, insistent rhythm and everyone around me smiling. And then noticing how much my face hurt from smiling, myself and those squelchy, lyrical synths - snaking through my body and through everyone's bodies - were communicating nothing but love. A whole beautiful separate event on the same site. Free festivals were the greatest and I was so lucky to be alive. Right then – in the only moment there was and the only moment there had ever been.

I threw my head back and shook my stupid dreadlocks for all I was worth.

We eventually tired of frugging and headed back out to the periphery of the crowd, but now the atmosphere felt different. Perhaps we just hadn't noticed, but something wasn't right. A thick smell of cooking meat hung in the air. There were vans offering burgers, stalls selling hot dogs and a whole pig's carcass roasting in half an oil barrel. What a bummer. We found ourselves among parked BMWs and Mercedes, circled by mean-looking coke dealers in puffa jackets. Coke dealers at a free festival? This was ugly.

By 1992, the rave scene had changed from free parties into a money-making machine. The travellers were resentful that their festival had been co-opted by these capitalistic opportunists and I didn't blame them. It all felt so at odds with the psychedelic Arcadia the previous few hours had presented. Bad vibes pervaded, which the acid now only amplified. I was confused, and there was only one thing for it. Back in the familiarity of the travellers' area, I found our friends Darren and Emma in their live-in ambulance and spent the next couple of hours downing medicinal Special Brews in an attempt to feel normal.

After too little sleep, I was woken by the competing collision of sound systems and vacated my tent into the sunlight to find Carlos already up, fag in mouth, scrutinising me from the back of the van. 'Good night, was it?' he smirked, triggering memories of that rural Gehenna as I looked upon the familiar idyllic vista of an English free festival.

Dan and Sicky arose next and finally, after much prompting from Carlos – 'Get up, Floydy, you lazy cunt,' Tim's scowling face emerged from his tent. It was one o'clock before we were all vertical. We moved the van to the side of Wango Riley's to begin the slow process of loading on our backline. Not for the first time, I was struck by how needlessly large our live set-up was, especially on a relatively small stage such as this.

Wango Riley's skeleton crew rolled their eyes as they watched us produce drum after drum from the back of our van. On the stage, Tim was assembling the enormous Pearl kit at his usual torpid pace.

Then we brought the amps on. Naturally, Carlos had insisted on using his entire stack. As we set up our gear, a small crowd began to congregate at the front. I peered out but couldn't see anyone I knew.

I'd once seen a photo of Johnny Ramone carrying his Mosrite guitar in a carrier bag, which I thought looked so cool that I used it to justify the preposterous corner-cutting of not actually owning a case.

I never cared for that white Kramer Focus anyway, with its awful sloping headstock and a stupid locking trem that necessitated carrying Allen keys in case a string broke. Carlos had pressurised me into buying it because the idea of being in a band with a guy who played a Westone horrified him. After a gig or rehearsal, I'd load it into the back of the van like it was an amp head and just hope for the best. Dan used to do the same for no other reason than we were anarchists and anyway, who can afford a hard case?

Line checks at festivals were especially stressful. Beyond just the guitar, there were so many variables that could go wrong: broken amp valves, loose jack sockets, dead batteries or dodgy leads – and given that I used to travel with everything in a plastic Tesco bag, broken pedals, too. Having to set up in front of an audience added considerable pressure. I had the usual rush of anxiety as I flipped my amp from 'standby' to 'on', rolled up the guitar's volume knob and strummed an open E major chord. To my relief, the sound emerging from my speaker cabinet confirmed that not only was my amp working, but the guitar was also in tune. I stepped on my distortion pedal, offered a few perfunctory chugs, checked my delay settings and, hitting the phaser pedal, was greeted with a satisfying whoosh. I was good to go.

With too few mics to accommodate both of Tim's kick drums, we had to find a compromise. Using only one wasn't an option. Aside from the pummelling barrage, essential to our sound, Tim had painted 'EXTREME' on one of the skins and 'DIABOLISM' on the other in spiky letters. We foolishly opted for a single mic between the two drums, knowing they'd probably be inaudible, before proceeding with the ridiculous set-up. Tim would just have to play them louder. Unsurprisingly, once we were ready, we'd overrun our allotted line-check time by twenty minutes and the crew – and now much larger and increasingly rowdy crowd – were keen for us to get on with the gig.

I turned round to look at the unattended drum kit. Where the fuck was Tim?

No one had seen him. The stage manager looked at us impatiently from the sidelines. Now we were taking the piss. Carlos returned to the van to see if Tim was in there. Nothing. Dan and I ran to the back of the stage, shouting, 'Tim? Tim?'

This was awkward – he'd disappeared.

I ran back onto the stage and was presented with the entirely reasonable ultimatum: 'You guys are going to have to either play or get off.'

How could this have happened? What the fuck was Tim thinking?

I picked up my guitar, hit the phaser and delay, and started some 'dotting' in an Eastern mode while Dan faded in some sympathetically atmospheric drones. Dotting is an essential space-rock guitar technique. Playing against the delay transforms the guitar into a kind of human sequencer, while adding some phasing or a flanger, preferably before the delay, gave it the authentically Steve Hillage flavour I was going for.

Yes, this would buy us a couple of minutes, but it wasn't going to work indefinitely. I turned round again to find the throne still empty, so I walked up to the mic and joked, 'Can anyone play the drums?' A strategy I soon came to regret. As if he'd just been waiting to be asked, a toothless meths-drinker sprang up, to cheers and whoops from his mates, and, waving his arms at me, began lurching towards the stage.

In desperation, I ran to the back again and opened the tarpaulin flap. Squinting back thirty metres or so, I saw a familiar lanky figure dressed entirely in black, oblivious to any drama, puffing on a joint and walking back towards us at a leisurely pace.

'I was busting for a piss,' he explained before powering into the drum intro of 'Siamese Child' as Carlos ran back onto the stage straight into a hanging incense burner at head height.

We played well, though, and following the performance, we set up our stall at the side of the stage and managed to sell a few cassettes and T-shirts. A skinny, bare-chested traveller with blond dreads said he only had a quid but pushily asked if he could have a tape anyway. Feeling good about our performance, I said, 'Sure.'

'Yeah, proper fucking punk rock, that's what you guys are. You know the score. None of this bleep-bleep rave shit!'. He leaned in aggressively. 'Fuck that rave bollocks. That's what this festival needs – a proper fucking punk band.'

While I was happy to be called a proper punk band, I wasn't about to take sides in a bogus war. I gave him a weak smile and awkwardly managed, 'Well, you know, man, music is music. Who cares how it's made!'

The rest of the band had categorically run out of weed and, despite scouring the site, had found no one with any for sale. It would be another two years before I fully understood the urgency of this problem. Tim was particularly miserable. 'Can we please just go home?' he pleaded.

The mood of the site had truly darkened, too. We packed up our tents and started on the long drive home. As we were leaving, we heard that flare guns were being fired at the swarming police helicopters.

Following the Castlemorton festival, the police charged thirteen members of Spiral Tribe with public order offences and the following year, the Criminal Justice Act made events such as this illegal. It felt like a kick in the guts.

That was, as far as I can tell, the end of the free festival scene. Our band didn't last much longer, either.

Chapter 19

Henry Cow

Steve and Kavus

Steve

If you ask the rock cognoscenti for their favourite supergroups, I'm sure the consensus would point towards Cream or ELP, but let's face it, everyone really knows that the daddy is National Health. How can you argue with a melding of great minds from Egg, Gilgamesh, Gong, Hatfield and the North and Yes? The fact that National Health also contained the amazing keyboard player Alan Gowen is proof enough on its own.

While good supergroups are few and far between, I assume creating a supergroup is relatively easy. A few phone calls and behind-the-scenes nods at festivals and hey presto, Transatlantic! What more could you not ask for?

However, there's another type of supergroup. A band that hits the ground running – and it, and its members, seemingly never put a foot wrong. I think we've reached the right point to bring Henry Cow into the medical-grade equation now. Championing the significance of this band is massively important to both of us.

Kavus

I'll put my hat into the ring right away – Fred Frith is my Elvis.

After Henry Cow, he, Dagmar Krause and Chris Cutler did three albums as the Art Bears, each mind-blowing. He moved to New York during that incredibly fertile late seventies No-Wave period and became part of the downtown music scene, working with Bill Laswell, Brian Eno, The Golden Palominos, Eugene Chadbourne, The Residents, Zeena Parkins, Ikue Mori, John Zorn – basically everyone – forming all these different projects. Skeleton Crew, Massacre, Keep the Dog. He composes classical music, he improvises, he does noise stuff, he plays in other people's groups, and he also played on Robert Wyatt's Rock Bottom.

He has the most enviable career – as an improviser, a composer, a performer – spanning multiple genres, and everything he does sounds like Fred Frith. He ended up as Professor of Composition at Mills College in California before retiring in 2018.

But, yes, Henry Cow is where he first comes onto the map. I think they're unlike any other band I can think of, both the sound and the way they operated.

Steve

I wonder if it's just coincidence, but so many of the bands I drool over have drummers at the helm. Christian Vander, Daniel Denis, Charles Hayward, Tatsuya Yoshida, Robert Wyatt, Dave Kerman, Greg Saunier, and of course Chris Cutler. Regardless of writing credits, I doubt Henry Cow would have been the same beast without his input.

Kavus

Despite the fact that Frith is writing a lot of stuff in Henry Cow, it's clearly a group thing. It's in the Art Bears where the signature Frith sound really appears. That kind of Bartok-y, Hungarian folk flavour that seems to run through much of what he does afterwards, I think you hear it much more in the Art Bears. Henry Cow is a lot more like an avant-garde, serious composition version of the Canterbury stuff – there's definitely a crossover with Hatfield and the North . . .

Steve

Off the back of the incredible success of Mike Oldfield's *Tubular Bells*, Virgin Records' A & R man Simon Draper went into over-drive and for a few years the label was my go-to for cutting-edge progressive rock. Eventually, Virgin realised Henry Cow weren't commercial enough and the band became ever more frustrated at the lack of support they were getting and left the label. Even so, the release of their first album was a moment of inspiration on both of their parts.

Where did I first hear *Legend*? I assume Mr Peel had something to do with it. Was it an automatic buy? I'm delighted to say yes. From the moment I heard 'Nirvana for Mice', it's been part of my life. As a way in to their catalogue, *Legend* is probably Henry Cow's most accessible album, even though you could also make a case for *Desperate Straights*. For me, *Legend* is a *Desert Island Discs* shoo-in.

Kavus

I'm so glad you've said that Legend *is your favourite, because it was my way in, too.*

My introduction to them came from reading a fanzine in the eighties called The Organ, *which when I look back on it was my equivalent of Steve's education via* Ork Alarm! *Henry Cow would pop up in that a lot – nothing conclusive, just a mention here and there – and they really intrigued me. Then Earache Records put out* Torture Garden *by Naked City. I used to buy pretty much everything on Earache at this point. Naked City was a project John Zorn did with a load of brilliant jazz players: Wayne Horvitz, Joey Baron and Bill Frisell, and also Yamatsuka Eye from The Boredoms. Fred Frith of Henry Cow was on bass. That album was my gateway to jazz.*

So their name kept coming up and I'd always be looking for them in second-hand record shops in Plymouth, but I could never find anything. I'd ask people who were older than me who liked funny music, 'Have you ever heard any Henry Cow?'

I'd already built up an idea of them, imagining that they were going to be my new favourite band, because they just sounded so intriguing, and there was such a funny atmosphere around them, but no one else seemed to know much about them. At that point in Plymouth, it was actually easier to read about them than to hear their music.

Anyway, about a year before I moved to London, a friend of mine at a party said, 'You've been asking about Henry Cow, talk to that man over there.' And they introduced me to someone who said, 'Oh, yeah, I've got a cassette. I don't listen to it any more.' They gave me a tape of the first two albums: Legend *on one side and* Unrest *on the other. I listened to it every day, again and again.*

The music was everything that I'd hoped for. I knew them and the Art Bears were an influence on Cardiacs, and that came through clearly. But there were also a Zappa-esque element to their sound and a hint of Beefheart, but with a Canterbury-ish undertow. The whole thing was quite austere, and incredibly through-composed. And no matter how many times I've listened to Legend, *and how much I've read about it, I can't unravel the mystery of that record.*

The first time I heard Trout Mask Replica, *I knew we were going to be friends: we hit it off from the first listen. But I thought: we're going to have to spend a lot of time together before it reveals itself to me. It was so full-on and dense, it would be a while before I could sing along with 'Dali's Car'. Not so with Henry Cow: from the moment I first heard* Legend, *I was in. All the pleasure receptors were open and it just lit me up. It rarely repeats itself – it's just this beautiful, detailed unfolding narrative.*

I'd known this album for about six months before I listened to it on LSD for the first time. I was in the room with two other friends and before we got to the end of side one, I said, 'Man, this album needs three of us just to hear it properly.'

Steve

Back in the seventies, when I was listening to *Legend*, the only tripping I was doing was in the penalty area while playing Subbuteo. I'm pretty sure I wasn't even aware of LSD's existence back then, but it's interesting to consider how surroundings and states of mind might influence musical judgement. I read an article once reviewing the truly psychedelic White Noise's *An Electric Storm* album. It was, from a collector's point of view, bemoaning the fact that it was nigh on impossible to find mint-condition first issues with Island Records' original 'Eyeball' logo owing to the folklore fact that everyone was off their tits listening to it and butchered the process of flipping the record over.

Kavus

The funny thing was, in terms of the way the different realms of music in this book overlay each other, that sometime after I'd moved to London – when I was fully into my Henry Cow phase – I went back to Plymouth and popped round to my friend Chris' house. Nigel was there and he asked me, 'What are you listening to now?' I said, 'Oh, I'm all about Henry Cow.' And he cracked up, having remembered them from the time, and said, 'Oh! you were the one guy who bought their album, were you?'

Of course, after Legend, *Lindsay Cooper and her bassoon are in and the whole thing takes a different turn. Although Lindsay Cooper doesn't start writing until the last album, she brings in a more formal sensibility. Where on* Legend *there are familiar elements used in an unconventional way, on the second album,* Unrest, *what you're hearing is Henry Cow really cutting their ties with the recognisable stuff. They move into even more unusual territory, less Canterbury-ish, I suppose, which I don't think has been explored by any other band.*

In fact, I don't even like to use the word 'band' for Henry Cow. They're just a thing that happens – an entity, a way of thinking about music, about how much can be done with a smallish ensemble. Each part keeps snaking off on its own little path, only to meet up with each other for a while every now and again. Maybe ten or fifteen bars later, something else will appear, which might be a melody that was first hinted at a minute and a half before. It's truly psychedelic, this stuff.

Steve

'Deluge' is my personal go-to on *Unrest*. It's one of the bleakest pieces of music I've ever heard. I love it. It's a soundtrack in waiting for an apocalyptic blockbuster. When Chris Cutler came on our radio show as a guest, he told us they had 2-inch tape loops running all around the studio when recording it. The album has a different feel to its predecessor. 'Solemn Music' is the track we've played the most on the radio shows, though. It offers a fraction more hope for the human race, despite its title.

Kavus

It has everything – absolutely exquisite. Just that minute alone knocks half of my record collection into a cocked hat.

Henry Cow merged with Slapp Happy, another band on the experimental fringes at Virgin, featuring cartoonist and lyricist extraordinaire, Peter Blegvad, keyboardist Anthony Moore and vocalist Dagmar Krause. They joined forces to make two albums, the first of which is Slapp Happy but with Henry Cow as the band, and that's Desperate Straights. *The other one,* In Praise of Learning, *is more Henry Cow but with Slapp Happy sort of bolted on. Both of these records are the goods, but I think Steve and I agree that* Desperate Straights *has a special magic.*

Steve

I know Dagmar Krause is something of an acquired taste, but the songs are so strong they entice you back for another listen and before you know it, you're in love with Dagmar. 'In the Sickbay' is just an astonishing track and they're a band that Tim Smith obviously loved, as he doffed his cap to them with the track 'Nurses Whispering Verses' on the Cardiacs album *Sing to God*.

Kavus

After Western Culture, *the last Henry Cow album, which Hodgkinson and Cooper wrote, they were going to do another all written by Frith and Cutler, but then that ended up not being Henry Cow, so that's what started the Art Bears, who were a trio of Chris Cutler, Dagmar Krause and Fred Frith. Their first album,* Hopes and Fears, *is like what Henry Cow would have done and still has the others on it as guest musicians, so is really Henry Cow in all but name. And the second one,* Winter Songs, *is great in a way that's all its own.*

Steve

I absolutely love Art Bears. 'The Summer Wheel' is a banger. And 'The Slave', and 'The Hermit'. I adore these tracks now, but the first time I heard them I thought they were awful. I'm sure I'm preaching to the converted, but don't disregard these bands after just one listen. Henry Cow are a supergroup in reverse. They were born a supergroup and proof of that is what happened once they disbanded in 1978.

Kavus

Is there a single other band in rock - or whatever you want to call it - that's had such a good hit rate as Henry Cow once the band split up? All of the members went on to make brilliant music.

When you look at the diaspora of Henry Cow, it's not just about the Art Bears, or Frith's career. Chris Cutler wrote the book File Under Popular *which, while a bit of a grind at times, was essential for the discography at the end alone. He founded Recommended Records, which was basically the motherlode as far as Rock in Opposition was concerned, and has been involved with countless projects since. Lindsay Cooper went on to become this incredible composer scoring for theatre, film soundtracks and everything. Her band, News From Babel with Chris Cutler are essential. Dagmar Krause collaborated and released solo albums throughout the eighties, and Tim Hodgkinson formed The Work. John Greaves, after he left Henry Cow, made the album* Kew. Rhone. *with Peter Blegvad, which is another one of my favourite albums.*

And it's not just about what they did, it's also about what they didn't do. None of them went on to forge a career in soft rock in the eighties as so many of their contemporaries did. Everyone in Henry Cow, almost every single record they made post-Henry Cow is, if not remarkable then always interesting, and always done in their own way. For all the ideological tussles they had, they were all equally committed to making this extremely detailed, personal music, and they've carried on doing it to this day. It's not like any of them ever said, 'Oh, there's a big offer from Europe to tour the first album, let's get the old band back together.' They walked it like they talked it.

Chapter 20

yet more Die Laughing

Kavus

By the early nineties. I'd try to see Cardiacs perform at every opportunity, either getting lifts or hitchhiking. The portal their music opened up to Dan and me became a major factor in the split of Die Laughing.

The sound of our band was changing and fissures were appearing, but so long as we were gigging regularly, we didn't pay too much attention to them. Although Carlos and Sicky were sceptical about the non-metal influences creeping in, they were OK about our 'weird' new compositions, as long as we still had 'heavy bits'.

'Do you guys listen to Yes?' Ian Dent, the friendly studio owner and in-house engineer, asked not unkindly. Inspired by our recent lysergic odysseys, Die Laughing had returned to Daylight studio to record another cassette EP, 'Artificial Playground'.

While still recognisably metal, 'Artificial Playground' was a more expansive affair than its predecessor. Having had my eyes opened to the possibilities of recording, back in this lovely residential studio, we had bigger ideas about what we could achieve this time and we arrived with Tim's flatmate, Steve Patterson, from local space rock warriors Our Fate, whom we'd recruited to pepper Hawkwind-like modular synth swooshes over a couple of tunes, such as 'Artificial Playground' (LSD = good) and our Castlemorton opener 'Siamese Child' (domestic abuse = bad).

Steve would guest with us occasionally and brought an unpredictable electronic edge to the already challenging sound. We'd decided the songs ought to include interludes and had brought along an acoustic guitar specifically for that purpose. Effectively, the interludes involved our friend Justin Lish blowing delirious digeridoo drones while accompanied by a strummed 'mysterious-sounding' C#, over which Sicky recited poetry, backwards. It was 1992, after all.

Before we even reached the mixing stage, we'd gone way over budget and Ian, knowing we were skint, kindly allowed us the extra time to finish, on the proviso we returned the following week to dig bricks up from the studio garden. If this served a wider purpose, we weren't party to it. That night, on the journey back to Plymouth, we listened to the tape repeatedly in the van, amazed we'd actually created it ourselves.

We dutifully returned the following week to settle our debt. As we dug, Ian plied us with beer before taking us out for dinner and more beer at a local pub then putting us up in his house. Given that we were all signing on, this seemed a good deal for just the cost of the fuel to Honiton and back.

I turned on fairly regularly at this time, usually with Dan. Once we'd come up, we'd pick up our guitars, invent a hypnotic riff, and cycle it round and round while evaluating the weight and density of every phrase, making small adjustments along the way until it shone like a polished jewel. Acid allowed you to see both inside and behind the notes, to understand the motivation behind musical decisions. Psychedelics brought a greater understanding to our writing and arranging and, with ego dissolved, Dan and I started to fuse as co-writers. For the next few years, many of our songs started like this. Each experience was meta-programming a new system into us and sometimes I couldn't tell which one of us was which. Here began the development of a style our friend Nick Evens called 'One mind, four hands'.

I loved the sound of our two guitars together. What had begun with Iron Maiden's Smith and Murray had moved into the gamelan-like techniques of Fripp and Belew of eighties King Crimson and the chaotic, argumentative playing of The Magic Band's Antennae Jimmy Semens, and Zoot Horn Rollo. Further inspired by the 'systems music' of Steve Reich, Dan and I forged a style where each of us would play colliding parts, usually in differing metres. Riffs in opposing orbits would then meet and chime with one another at contrasting points in the bar, throwing up unusual and unpredictable new shapes. Once we'd got these into our muscle memory, we'd write melodies, often in a different metre again, and have to learn how to sing them over the top.

Increasingly, keeping our anchor in the sonic mud of heavy metal was limiting where we wanted our music to go. It wasn't just the

197

tunes this applied to. In the psychedelic state, songs with a message sounded clunky, heavy-handed and self-important. Lyrics are not poetry, I concluded. Poetry stands up as words alone, but with music, or at least what I think of as psychedelic music, the lyrics serve a different function: to increase the mystery and strangeness, to imbue the music with a further charge.

The more expressive and far out the music, the more inconclusive and opaque I wanted the lyrics to be. Abstract and mystical words would serve the music rather than the other way round. The music itself should be the message – the words are merely there to help contextualise it.

By 1993, Die Laughing were fragmenting. Adding a keyboard was still a cardinal sin in metal, but we thought the songs we were writing required another element. Matthew Lovett had joined us the previous year. Fundamentally, he was on board with the new music Dan and I were writing, which made him an essential accomplice in the widening schism. Unlike Steve Patterson, Matthew, a trained pianist who had studied music, was able to explain to us exactly what it was we were doing.

Singing the lyrical puzzle 'It's better than what he said you said's better than what he said you said' over a jagged Gong-meets-Voivod riff obviously made more sense than ranting against the ills of corporate greed over a chugging E. Inevitably, not everyone in the band agreed.

'You know how we're supposed to be a cross between death metal and Cardiacs?' Carlos questioned Tim during a phone call to the Cornish cottage he was staying at with his girlfriend, knowing he didn't especially like Cardiacs (the description had come from a favourable review of 'Artificial Playground'). 'Well, forget the death metal.'

Tim had been summoned back to Plymouth for a crisis meeting, resentfully terminating his holiday prematurely. That morning, clearly pissed off, Carlos and Sicky visited me in 'the mental home'. I arrived at Carlos' mum's house that afternoon to find the rest of the band already there. Apart from a few dejected nods, no one spoke. Sicky glowered silently in the corner as Carlos pressed Play on a rough-sounding demo of 'Glassing the Eye That Bleeds', which we'd made in Tim's absence – the first endeavour of our new writing process. Like naughty schoolboys called to the headmaster's office, Dan, Matthew and I sat sheepishly on the bed. Tim stared at the floor inscrutably, avoiding eye contact with Carlos, who was examining his face for any hint of a reaction.

'Fear not, the bridge and my smile are not real,' the song ended, leaving an uncomfortable silence.

Carlos sneered, 'Well?'

The band was now a six-piece and, at three against two, Tim's opinion was the decider.

Eventually, he looked up. 'I think it sounds brilliant. Put it on again.'

Beyond a couple of gigs in Plymouth, the six-piece version of Die Laughing lasted long enough for a short UK tour. We included 'Glassing the Eye That Bleeds' in the set – a highlight for me, but Sicky's heart wasn't in it.

His aggressive punk delivery couldn't or wouldn't accommodate the melodies we were writing by then. Shortly after we returned to Plymouth, we parted ways. Well, Dan and I suggested we take over the vocals. I'm not sure how badly he took the decision at the time, because I was too much of a coward to tell him myself. Carlos admirably bit the bullet, possibly fearing, not for the first time, intervening in a potentially volatile situation between singer and gobby, outspoken guitarist.

I managed to avoid Sicky for a few weeks, but Plymouth is a provincial city and the freaks flock together. Inevitably, I ran into him in the King's Head, one of the two acceptable pubs, his hair now in dreads under a mauve top hat, around which he'd painted a ring of magic mushrooms in his recognisable style. He'd seen me – I couldn't leave now – and besides, the unresolved situation had been gnawing at me and I wanted to move on. I was visibly shaking as I offered an apologetic 'I'm so sorry, man, I was a real cunt back there.' And I meant it. For a brief moment, he gave me the same intensely piercing look that had made him such a magnetic frontman before he broke into a smile and told me to relax. He wasn't pissed off any more. He'd started a new band anyway, Bark, which was much more his kind of thing. I saw them play once. They had a djembe.

Not long into 1993, I had the 'Vision of the Bent Path', which would confirm me on the course I've subserviently followed ever since.

Dan and I, having dropped a powerful 'strawberry' blotter, had set to work on 'Aladdin', a new tune based around a cyclical Eastern-sounding riff in 7/8 that Dan had written. Once we'd entered what we used to conspiratorially call 'the Iceman's back garden' - the point at which we were seeing evolving arabesques behind our eyelids - we rapidly composed the melody, structure and a middle section. There was no question, this was the closest to the bullseye yet. Whenever I hear it, I'm back in my bedsit, staring at the mutating geometric lizards spiralling over the cheap grey carpet where they usually lay dormant, disguised as grubby marks, still full of wonder at what we'd birthed.

'Aladdin' encapsulated everything we'd been trying to do - two guitars played an insistent hypnotic riff against one another, over which we sang a dervish-like hex: 'Taste breathe the spice open your eyes, I'll take your eyes, I'll take your teeth, I'll take it all, contaminate your nest, surprise . . .' We played it over and over, punctuated only by occasional incredulous laughter that we'd somehow sculpted this mad new prismatic universe.

This was the evening we realised Die Laughing was no longer the optimum vehicle for what we were writing. Plymouth seemed increasingly local. It wasn't that we'd outgrown the place necessarily, more that the kind of kindred spirits who dug where Dan and I were going were thin on the ground. There was no going back to 'straight rock' now. We needed to find our people.

We listened back to our recently recorded cassette EP, 'Six New Songs by Die Laughing'. Our increasingly knotty compositions just weren't what Carlos, an avid Wolfsbane fan, wanted from rock 'n' roll.

He didn't especially like our new music and had become listless and disinterested. Once a fastidious motivator, an engine at the heart of the group, he hadn't even bothered to learn some of the basslines when he showed up to record his parts this time. He was already playing in a couple of other bands to which his deft, galloping bass style was better suited. I think he felt betrayed at being unseated from the venture the two of us had started together five years earlier - a venture he now hardly recognised. I'd even 'de-metalled' the logo.

Tim was more open-minded about where we were going, but his style was pounding and tribal. The polyrhythmic intricacies of Pierre Moerlin and Christian Vander hadn't been his original motivation for picking up the drumsticks and it was unreasonable of us to present him with an 11/8 riff and expect him to make it bounce.

I can't remember which one of us suggested moving to London. It wasn't an idea I'd given much thought to, but once said, it couldn't be unsaid.

The evidence was unavoidable, and what bands of any note had come from Plymouth, anyway? We thought Carlos would probably be relieved.

On the other hand, Tim was clearly still invested in the band.

And then it hit me. Everything I'd been gravitating towards since inventing songs for my toys and first watching Top of the Pops, since picking up a guitar and starting a band, all of it had all been for this decision. Every failed exam and shameful school report, the disappointment I was causing my now separated parents, all of it had led to this single moment of bizarre realisation. This glorious, swirling, angular and dissonant music, all heartbreaking, bursting with light and breaking up our band, this was my music. The otherworldly Lydian mode that had drawn me into its sphere was more than a mere design for life - it was the sound of me.

I was answerable to a higher power.

And there it was, in a flash of remarkable cosmic scapegoating, I'd absolved myself of any responsibility. I was merely following the will of the universe. I saw three silver sixes and three silver sixes saw me. It was clear now. Where there is clarity, there is no choice. And where there is choice, there is misery.

'What about Tim, though?' I asked Dan. 'He's our mate.'

'I know,' said Dan sadly. 'But how many "mates" do you think Frank Zappa has?'

By the time the sun came up, Dan and I had vowed to end the band and relocate to the capital, following the only pressing commitment in our calendar: a support slot at The Cooperage with the groovy UK rapcore band, Papa Brittle.

In the interim, Dan and I secretly began putting together a new band. Justin Lish was a former classmate of Tim's and his closest friend. With an extraordinary command of the English language, he was also the best drummer I knew. We sounded him out; we were going to leave Deadsville, move to London and do this properly, no fucking around.

Did he want to come? Along with Darren Mcveigh, a Cardiacs nut and my favourite Plymouth bass player, he was game and we worked on 'Aladdin' and a more complex piece, 'The War Between Banality and Interest', over a couple of clandestine rehearsals.

Then I received the fateful memo in the post from Sean Worrall, who along with Marina Anthony, was responsible for the fantastic London-based fanzine, The Organ. *The Organ had been supportive of Die Laughing, putting 'Artificial Playground' on their compilation cassette album,* Goosebumps. *They had printed a big feature about us, having conducted the interview at a Tufnell Park bus stop, following our London debut supporting Hellbastard at the Boston Arms the previous year.*

Along with the London promoters, TLF (Tortoise Liberation Front), they were staging an event called the Eight Day Itch – eight separate music events, culminating in a big all-dayer at The Venue in New Cross. Cardiacs were headlining, with Poisoned Electrick Head beneath them on the bill, and they wanted Die Laughing, too. The gig was still two months away.

This was too much. We couldn't split the band yet. We had to play this show. Utterly unscrupulously, I said yes.

With a set list almost exclusively comprising music we'd written post-Sicky, the Papa Brittle show turned out to be my favourite gig we ever played. Sharing their drum kit and borrowing a double kick pedal, Tim Floyd was on fire, which was fantastic news for the forthcoming Cardiacs show but would make the now inevitable dissolution of the band even harder. I put that out of my mind. We were going to be on a bill in London with Cardiacs.

A few days later, I answered the door to a regretful-looking Justin. 'I couldn't help it, man,' he began. 'I'm not a dishonest person and I couldn't do that to a mate.' As he went on to explain what had happened, I experienced a noxious wave of guilt at my own next-level cuntery. I'd really done it this time.

Tim nodded silently as he opened the front door to me and we walked up the three flights of stairs to his flat.

'The thing is, I don't blame you,' he reasoned sadly. As a fellow drummer, he was Justin's biggest fan. 'To play in a band with you and Dan is just what he needs.'

YET MORE DIE LAUGHING

Die Laughing was over. We duly pulled out of the Eight Day Itch, but then over the following weeks, Justin got cold feet about the move. 'I'm a country boy,' he explained.

I left my flat and along with my girlfriend, Andrea, we moved into a tiny box-room in the shared house Dan lived at rent-free. Andrea and I spent the next few weeks working in a T-shirt wholesalers for ten pounds a day to save money for the move – just around the corner from the dole office, too. Now I was living dangerously.

Sarah Measures was energetic and free-spirited. She was always down the front at Die Laughing gigs and was one of my favourite people in Plymouth, so I was delighted when she and Dan got together.

But now in a new relationship, Dan remorsefully broke the news he wouldn't be moving to London, either. The grand plan had collapsed, but having set our minds on it, Andrea and I hitch-hiked up to the capital anyway, staying with Richard Larcombe in Leyton, and returned four days later, having put a deposit on a spacious two-bedroom flat in Grove Green Road, a five-minute walk from where Richard lived.

The Saturday before we left, we decided to go out to The Studio, for old time's sake. The Studio was a small club adjoining the much larger Warehouse at the top of Union Street. It had been the first club I'd ever attended at the age of sixteen in 1988, astonished that I'd actually managed to get in. It was where I could dress up, judgement-free, in full goth regalia – eyeliner, Chelsea boots and a forearm full of bangles – where I finally kissed a girl for the first time, could get served at the bar, and where I got my first schooling in punk and alternative music.

Now, five years on, I was there to say goodbye to the city in which I'd come of age. Naturally, I dropped acid beforehand.

Tripping with our little clique, which included Dan and Sarah, I stood on the edge, an observer rather than participant, as the dance floor bounced to such indie disco anthems as 'What Do I Get?', 'Preacher Man', 'Blister in the Sun' and 'New Rose', blaring out of the tinny PA. Against the soundtrack of The Pogues' 'Sally MacLennane', I watched with a curious sense of detachment as my first girlfriend flirted with a guy, just as she had done with me four years earlier on the same dance floor.

Then I got a shock as a stranger's hand shook my shoulder aggressively. 'We should get a pressurised gas canister and throw it in there . . .' Dressed in black combat trousers, German army boots and a leather biker jacket, a rough-looking guy who I'd never seen before was shouting gruffly in my ear, flecking it with spittle. I looked up to see him gesturing towards the dancing throng.

I had no idea what his reasoning was but smiled anyway. He was clearly mad.

'. . . And get rid of all this scum once and for all.'

Drunk people are confusing enough when you're tripping, but this was a new one on me. Cautious as to how I ought to proceed, I tentatively offered a noncommittal, 'Oh yeah?'

'Yeah, you'll see!' he promised. 'The rave generation are gonna take over and kick all this lot out. Not now. Not for a few years. But it's gonna happen. Then, all of this will change.'

I was struggling to make sense of his argument. Was he pro-rave or anti? He didn't look like a raver. In my experience, tripping people are a magnet to nutters and he'd clearly marked me out as an ally. I was in no hurry to contradict him, at least until I could understand his point.

'OK,' I said.

Then he dropped the chilling bombshell – the lesson that has never left me. Grabbing me again, this time he stared directly into my eyes and, pointing at himself, ordered, 'Look at my face!'

He backed off a little and, behind his lanky hair, I saw a network of welts, scars and bruises. A roadmap of torment. I saw a broken man. A man at odds with the world, with himself.

'All I ever told was the truth!'

I was speechless. This was the way of the world, the clandestine, unspeakable code. He'd spoken his dark philosophy and I understood it implicitly.

He followed this with, 'I'm a Viking, you know.'

I had to leave. I managed an 'Oh, that's nice,' but made my excuses while he explained how they'd 'whipped the Saxons' ass'. I needed to get on with the rest of my life. Two days later, I was in London alphabetising my record collection.

Chapter 21

The Utopia Strong

Steve and Kavus

Steve

If there's one online publication on the subject of music that you financially subscribe to, then make it *The Quietus*. John Doran and Luke Turner and the rest of the contributors provide an astonishing service. It's not hidden behind a paywall and has quickly become the single most important musical resource out there. On 3 August 2015, it was the catalyst for a life-changing transformation of my musical landscape.

The Quietus Phonographic Corporation had just put out their fifth release. The Chrononautz' 'Noments' 12-inch was an interesting techno-tinged effort that the Quietus lads had played when they guested on our radio show. The record launch was held at Cafe OTO in London, with the amazing Sly & the Family Drone as headliners. Chrononautz were on before them, and starting off proceedings was a band called Hirvikolari, a side project by two members of our future label-mates Teeth of the Sea.

Sam Barton played trumpet and effects, and Mike Bourne juggled a modular synthesiser. Kavus told me their name means 'Deer that has been killed by a car' in Finnish.Who wouldn't want to go and see a band called that? The whole event was great, but I was particularly smitten with the roadkill support band. This was my first visual exposure to someone just playing a box with a load of wires coming out of it and, crucially, no keyboard. I was transfixed. There was no keyboard! You didn't need any dexterity! As Special Agent Dale Cooper would have said, 'Hellooo-ooo!'

It wasn't that I was desperate to play a musical instrument – I'd given up on that years before. I'd had a few attempts along the way. During the eighties, I made a futile effort at learning to play piano and then after that the harmonica, with equally underwhelming results. In fact, these brief flirtations with musical endeavour led to some of the most embarrassing media appearances of my life (obviously, competition is quite hot in this category), the last of this trio of painful incidents being when Jools Holland came round my house.

It was in the early eighties. I'm not sure exactly when but I do know where – in a terraced house that I'd recently bought on Plumstead Common as an upgrade to our council flat in Abbey Wood. Things had gone ballistic my end. Snooker was fast becoming flavour of the decade and I was the hottest property in the game. I had a Porsche 928 parked outside the house. They both cost roughly the same.

Looking back, it was a crazy time in my life. I was on countless TV shows and regularly doing newspaper and magazine interviews. Anything I said was magnified out of all proportion. I was asked once if I thought snooker was better than sex. My answer to the journalist was 'What is more important to you? Your job or sex?' So when the tabloid ran with the headline 'I Prefer Snooker to Sex', it was just adding fuel to the fire for the creation of my *Spitting Image* character a few years later.

I'm not sure why out of the blue I decided to try to learn to play the piano. Maybe it was the regular trips I'd been taking up to Ronnie Scott's to watch great jazz pianists from all over the globe, or perhaps it was the subliminal impact of all those new-fangled five-star hotel automated pianos I'd been subjected to in the lobby.

I had yet to be introduced to Conlon Nancarrow's amazing *Studies for Player Piano* series, wherein this twentieth-century programming visionary threatened to create pandemonium among the ladies wot lunched at the Waldorf Astoria by punching a few extra holes in his automated instrument's piano roll, and thus upping the ante from the usual fare of Mozart that was spewing out of them.

Either way, the next minute I'd bought a Yamaha CP-80 (which was obviously 'the nuts', as Shakatak had one on *Top of the Pops*) and started practising my scales. Like everything else I did at that time, my new hobby got publicity, and the next thing I knew I was on Leo Sayer's TV show attempting to accompany him on a version of the Bill Withers soul classic 'Lean on Me'. This was not one of music's definitive moments. I gave it my best shot but I withered more rapidly than planned and consigned Leo to a cappella duties.

It was no surprise I was shit – I'd only had the piano a few weeks. A couple of months later, I went on some TV show that was (much to my subsequent relief) only being aired in Australia. The comedy duo French and Saunders were also on the show, as well as Annie Lennox. I attempted to play 'Birdland' by Weather Report from the album *Heavy Weather* and got about twelve bars in before collapsing into a heap of sausage fingers. I wasn't particularly upset, but back in the green room, Annie Lennox was kindly trying to sweeten my dreams that night by reassuring me that I had good syncopation!

Scaling down my musical ambitions somewhat, I made a sideways move to the harmonica. Fuck knows why, but was it possibly to relieve the boredom (and maximise usage of my time on the planet) by multitasking on long car journeys back through the night after snooker exhibitions. In this case, my schoolboy error was to plump for a chromatic version, which was a tad trickier playing one-handed than the normal variety.

The fact that I was attempting to emulate Larry Adler wasn't something I was shouting from the rooftops but still, word got out and then things got silly. Jools Holland's people got in touch with my people and suggested we explore the possibility of recording some music together. I know this is totally ridiculous, but it did happen.

The next minute, Jools was there in my terraced house playing my electric grand (which was jammed under the hall stairs) while I was trying to come up with some sort of blowy-sucky-riffy thing. After a couple of hours, we said our goodbyes. As we shook hands and he turned to wander off (unaware of the fact that *Jools' Annual Hootenanny* would one day beckon), I'm sure the same thought crossed our minds: what the fuck was that all about!?

Although the omens weren't auspicious in terms of my previous musical endeavours, this no-hands synthesiser thing was an interesting prospect. It felt like proficiency might be achievable on an instrument that you just rammed wires into like a fifties telephone exchange. So a few weeks later, I bought one. Then soon after, I had a change in my personal life, becoming a bit more nomadic, and for about a year this thing was more or less sitting in its box, doing very little. Well that's my excuse, anyway.

Human beings are an astonishing plague on the planet. Apart from the warmongering and exploitation and slavery and racism and cruelty to animals and not looking after our elderly and vulnerable and being happy to see people homeless aspects, we've been incredibly inventive in harnessing nature for our benefit. Nowhere more so than in the field of electrickery. Now, a light bulb has been pretty useful since its invention, but let's face it, pop-pickers, it's not in the same league as a synthesiser.

But what is a modular synthesiser? There's a clue in the name, but here's a brief history. Clever people started making electronic music-making stuff. These people were called electronic pioneers. The electronic equipment that started to gain traction among non-electronic pioneers (who were called musicians) back in the mid-sixties was a product made by Bob Moog. By the start of the seventies, he'd correctly identified that for mass-market appeal, a synthesiser needed more emphasis on the keyboard as opposed to all the other gubbins. So, knobs to do the twiddly stuff were plonked on top and all the wires connecting any twiddling knobs were under the hood. Great!

Wendy Carlos produced *Switched-On Bach* and also the soundtrack to *A Clockwork Orange* on the Moog synthesiser, and then it all kicked off and the synth keyboard became cemented in the history of music. But obviously this wasn't the only way of making electronic music. Shit, no. Whether some pioneers were pants at playing the piano, I don't know, but some of them fucked the traditional keyboard right off. Nice.

More importantly, these renegades and manufacturers wanted

to make electronic instruments that were more inventive and versatile, rather than just adhering to one signal path. Cool! So, keep all the wires on the top of the unit and then the punter can choose what route the signal takes around the system. Think guitar pedals – they're modular. Guitarists can effectively route them in any order they want. So each module had a specific role and, with help from Alessandro Volta, stuff could also be automated, so things got far crazier than your standard Yamaha DX7 could ever dream of. You may find more accurate historical documentation of the facts presented here elsewhere, but who gives a shit?!

Fast-forward to my own modular acquisition. My initial experience with it reminded me of the story of the funeral for Larry LaPrise, the guy who wrote 'The Hokey Cokey' and after they'd got his left leg in the coffin, that was when all the problems had started. So there I was with a bunch of modules and a bunch of wires. I'd occasionally get the box out and do an impression of a dog staring at a card trick and then put it away again. I carried it around over much of the UK with me – I lugged it to Sheffield when I was working for the BBC at the World Snooker Championship for seventeen days – and the only modulation I did with it was lid off, lid on, lid off, lid on. I was overawed by it.

I know my traits. There's a part of me that does this. I'll buy new clothes and then not bloody wear them. I've got a great T-shirt I bought probably fifteen years ago that I still haven't fucking worn. In the case of the modular synth, I just knew it was going to be a steep learning curve. I've always admired people who take something out of the box and dive in with a hands-on approach right from the off. Eventually, I mobilised myself – 'What's the point of having it, otherwise? Get stuck in. You might enjoy yourself, Steve.' – and tentatively switched it on. Straight away, I realised it was a bit of a mindfuck, so I shut the lid again and sought out some expert help.

Online tutorials are great. Except they aren't great. Or at least the ones I was initially stumbling upon weren't. My biggest Achilles heel with them is the gradient of the learning curve they expect the viewer to follow. It's one thing understanding a subject, but it's a completely different skill understanding how to convey this knowledge to a layperson. Some of these tutorials felt like the equivalent of teaching someone to swim a width for the first time in the shallow end of the pool and then for the next part of the lesson expecting them to cross the English Channel. As a consequence, I'm now a modular expert - not so much in modular synthesis itself, but in knowing where to look for good online tuition.

Around this time, I informed Kavus that I was off and running. He told me, 'Well, I'll reserve catalogue number fourteen for your solo album on Believers Roast.' He was referring to his record label. There's no apostrophe in that, by the way - apparently, things like this are massively important in the music world! So I advised him not to hold his breath and things went quiet on this front until destiny brought us Mike York.

Kavus

Mike York used to play with Coil, but I met him through Guapo. He played pipes on our album Obscure Knowledge *and they sounded so good, he ended up joining. He's in Current 93, too, and has a terrific modular synth band called Teleplasmiste. And as a sideline, he makes English bagpipes, which he plays beautifully. So when Steve and I got asked back to DJ at Glastonbury in 2017, because neither of us fancied camping in a mudbath again, I mentioned him to Steve: 'Look, my mate lives one mile off-site and he's given us the offer that if we can blag him in, we can stay at his.'*

Three people can be a funny dynamic to get right: it doesn't always work. But this was the exception that proved the rule, because Steve, Mike and I got on famously - we basically had a five-day-long party. And because Mike's a modular synth player, he gave Steve that bit of encouragement that he needed.

Steve

Mike's a lovely, generous, dry, funny fucker. While we were wandering around Glastonbury festival trying to find places and people and venues, he took control of our diva-dithering angst and calmed us down with the now immortal words 'Don't worry, I'll tour-manage the fuck out of this!' Then he proceeded to go to the backstage area of the venue where we were due to play and asked, 'Is there any chance the guys could get a mixed mezze?' I realise you probably had to be there, but at the time we almost pissed ourselves.

A month after our second Glasto, I was fortunate enough to witness Mike York and Mark Pilkington perform as Teleplasmiste at the Delaware Road festival at the Secret Nuclear Bunker in Kelvedon Hatch, right on my doorstep in Brentwood, Essex. I love the Secret Nuclear Bunker – there are signposts to it all around the Brentwood area. The decommissioned nuclear fallout hideout was the perfect location for a twelve-act electronic get-together. Four levels underground, I witnessed Mike and Mark's undoubted prowess on their wonderful Fénix II synths. Apart from hallucinating that I was actually experiencing the apocalypse, on account of standing next to a mannequin wearing a gas mask and holding a book (placed in its hand by Mike) called *Ecstasy is the New Frequency*, the whole event was a wonderful experience and showcased a myriad of methods for making experimental electronic music. I was finally ready to learn more.

A few weeks later, the two of us met up and Mike gave me a more relaxed, handheld run-through of how a modular synth worked than anything I'd previously encountered, so I didn't feel too self-conscious about my own stupidity when it came to asking the same basic questions.

While Kavus is like a musical version of Tigger (without the stupid bit), Mike's exuberance is more restrained but no less inspiring. He was full of encouragement: 'Listen, now you can play modular synth, the three of us can have a live jam!' I couldn't 'play modular synth' but fuck it! We could at the very least continue our Glastonbury partying. So he and Kavus came over to my place in Romford and on New Year's Day 2018, Mike sat in on our radio show on Phoenix FM and picked some tunes. Then on the second of January we sat down to jam together.

Kavus

So I'd brought up my harmonium, a guitar and an amp and loads of effects pedals. Steve and Mike both had their modular synths, and we set them up in the front room of Steve's house. We thought we were just going to spend the day fucking around - there'd been no thought of recording anything - but Mike brought his laptop and recorded it. We had one channel each, three tracks. That was our first session.

Mike and Steve were at one end of the room, hunched over their modular synths, and I was at the other, with my harmonium and very gentle guitar, none of us wanting to overplay. We didn't really know what to make of it all. At the end of each improvisation, one of us would say, 'That had a couple of good bits,' or 'Oh, that was nice, let's do another one.' And over the course of that day, we improvised nine pieces of six to twenty-one minutes in length.

Steve

Knowing what I know now about my instrument, I was about as much in control of it as Frank Spencer would have been with a chainsaw in his hands. Having said this, that particular day, I had enough sense to leave well alone when my synth was making empathetic noises and turn the thing down when it was having a strop.

At one stage, we'd been doing a series of what I thought of as fast ones, so I suggested that we should try something a little slower. But we were all in agreement after we'd tried it that it was a mess and power ballads obviously weren't going to be our thing . . .

Kavus

Afterwards, we went out for dinner before going into Steve's snooker room for the playback. Mike put a generic 'expensive' reverb over everything to soften it - no mixing, just a bit of panning to separate the channels. Dear Lord! What a surprise - eight of the nine pieces had something really going on in them.

But as we listened for a second time, we became more excited, talking about overdubs: 'God, imagine how good that bit would sound if we put some acoustic guitar over it . . .' We went in with no expectations of how it was going to sound, or that we might end up having a band, but the whole experience was just very positive. If I'd hazarded a guess, knowing what we liked, I'd have predicted we'd make something dark and dissonant. Instead the music was, for the main part, joyous and uplifting.

Steve

Overnight, we were sufficiently inspired to envisage these raw tracks being good enough to be the basis of an album. We did a bit of editing to put what we had into a more useable form, then sat back and had another listen. Even the slow track turned out to be great! I was pretty chuffed. Basically, the fact that I had kind of held my own and played with these two great musicians and not fucked up had come as a wonderful surprise.

We worked out our roles without even knowing we were doing it. I was basically rhythm and Mike was melody (and more) that he took from my rhythm, then Kavus had free rein on guitar to work his magic as well as adding drones on harmonium. I can't put into words how exciting it was for me personally. A musician reading this would be correct in thinking that three people sitting down to this recording process was no biggie, but think again. One of these three wasn't a musician and furthermore, this music wasn't just average improv fodder. It was something that had the potential to be totally psychedelic and there I was in the middle of it! I'd been part of creating music that even in this basic state, I'd have been delighted to have bought in a record shop.

Kavus

It was exciting for us, too, because from mine and Mike's perspective – as people who have done a fair bit of improvising and had played together in that framework in Guapo – you don't normally get that kind of hit rate. Whatever the reason, and maybe it just came back to the nice dynamic between the three of us, and the fact that we were really listening to each other, the music just seemed to flourish into something that sounded unforced and very beautiful.

Steve

Immediately, I felt protective of our recordings. I'd never been involved in creating something this way before. I had a copy of this raw two and a half hours of music that I was listening to in my car thinking, 'I want this to go out just as it is. Don't anybody touch it, because it's brilliant.' My naive enthusiasm probably became a little overbearing, but Kavus was adamant and reassured me that we could improve it further. I was concerned about losing the spontaneity of the pieces, but I needn't have worried.

Kavus

So we ended up editing that two and a half hours of music down to about three quarters of an hour. At first, because he hadn't done it before, Steve was saying, 'No, no, no, leave it as it is.' But eventually we talked him round. 'Just trust us on this one.' The exciting thing was that we were all contributing to the overdubs - Steve would sing a part and I'd try it on the guitar, or he'd play a bit of Fender Rhodes. Mike would add some bagpipes or I'd put a big drum in there. Listening back, I can't remember who wrote what. It was the product of a hive mind.

Steve

The thrill of being involved in a creative project with other people and watching it grow in this way was another new experience for me. Obviously, the other lads were used to it, but for me, this fresh buzz was something I couldn't quite quantify.

Then we got the name. We decided that much of the music conjured up images of a utopian landscape and I vaguely recall an early working title for one of the tracks having the word 'utopia' in it. We'd also decided that we had a strong friendship . . . so voila! The Utopia Strong was born.

The process of turning long-form improvised pieces into tracks was for me another immersive stage in this journey. The decision-making process of what to keep and what to throw out was an exciting challenge. For most of 2018, at intermittent and mutually agreeable times, we met up to discuss and further refine the arrangements. Finally, when we felt like we could improve them no more, we decided we needed them mixing professionally.

Antti Uusimaki had previously worked with Kavus and Mike and they both felt he was the best pair of safe hands for the job. It was fascinating to hear how he managed to improve things from what, once again, I thought was the perfect album to an even more polished, three-dimensional work of art. Antti was a great fit and his ability to withstand the concoction of ten cans of Guinness and a bottle of Shiraz in an evening meant that the fermenting Finn was guaranteed honorary membership of The Utopia Strong. The end result was a fair amount of liver nursing the following week and on top of that, a finished album. At each stage of the process of refinement we'd become ever more excited at the realisation that we'd created something special. Now, our attention turned to trying to find a record label sympathetic to our psychedelic debut.

Once again, the (Mike) Bourne connection played its part. Kavus and I had built up a pretty good reputation as no-compromise DJs by early 2019. If your bag for a night out is music you've never heard before with a possibility you'll like it enough to boogie the night away, then I reckon we've nailed our colours to that mast and you won't be disappointed. All-round champion Anthony Chalmers (of Baba Yaga's Hut promotions) had previously booked us for his excellent Raw Power Festival in 2017 and we were delighted to be signed up as the DJs to close a gig to launch the new album by Teeth of the Sea and also a new project by Sepultura-founding drummer Iggor Cavalera called Petbrick.

Both bands were signed to Rocket Recordings, and label owners Johnny O'Carroll and Chris Reeder were there to show support as well as let their hair down. It was a bloody fantastic night. I lost half a dozen CDs, couldn't remember getting home and vowed never to drink again. But on a more important note, at some stage during the evening, somehow Kavus remembered to give a demo copy of our album to Johnny O'Carroll and more amazingly, Johnny actually kept hold of it as the night degenerated.

Every band and musician who makes music surely likes (if not loves) what they make. They all think it's worthy of either a physical product, or at least being put up for grabs on Bandcamp as a digital download. We were no exception to this rule. Our album was better than brilliant! How could any record label not want to bite our hands off? Given how amazing the music was, surely it would instantly add credibility to their imprint and they could pat themselves on the back at how good their judgement had been. But then there was 'The Thing' - a nameless horror way more insidious than the one John Carpenter came up with in 1982, in whose grisly shadow we might have no option but to start our own label if we ever wanted to release our album.

'The Thing' in question was . . . me! I'd never previously considered myself as a liability, but that's what was staring me in the face every morning while I was brushing my teeth. What credible record label, in their right mind, would put out an album by a trio, one of whose members' only previously recorded output had been singing one line in a verse of 'Snooker Loopy' by Chas and Dave & the Matchroom Mob?

Regardless, fate had played a trump card. We'd stumbled upon a record label who were brave enough to take a chance on us. Unbeknown to us, Johnny and Chris had accepted our demo CD on the condition - arrived at between themselves - that they wouldn't be touching it with a bargepole . . . unless, by some miracle of lottery-winning proportions, it was something extra special.

We met up with Chris at Cafe OTO a couple of weeks later and shook hands on the deal. All of a sudden, I was being advised by Kavus to register for PRS as a musician and composer. Pinch me! Chris was asking us if we were prepared to do a tour to promote the album and Kavus was saying, 'We've got to do live shows!' But I wasn't listening by then. All I was thinking about was I can't wait to give a CD to John Parrott and Stephen Hendry, because they already think I've lost the plot as it is.

Chapter 22

The Monsoon Bassoon

Kavus

I'd just turned twenty-three when I made the decision to move back to Plymouth. Andrea and I had been in London a little over a year and I wanted my old life back.

While Camden may have been buzzing with the birth of Britpop, a mere eight miles away in sleepy Leyton, I was inactive, miserable and bored. Richard Larcombe and I had started a new band, Monocle, attempting to pick up where Die Laughing had left off, but aside from a handful of rehearsals, it never got much beyond a good idea.

I'd known Richard since I was seventeen. A year younger than me, he had a prodigious talent that he could seemingly apply to anything. Back in Plymouth, he'd hosted two surrealistic revue shows, 'Eat Your Shoes' and 'We Love Spring Vegetables', and had supported Die Laughing a couple of times as a stand-up. He was a remarkable performer, could write plays and sketches, and had an unparalleled knowledge of the Marx Brothers and W.C. Fields.

Along with this was his talent for music. Where Dan and I had felt like equals, treading a similarly crooked route away from metal, Richard had popped out apparently fully formed, hip to The Red Crayola and the Third Ear Band from the age of thirteen. He'd never been through a Marillion phase. I felt overshadowed by his musical expertise and had now become apprehensive about my abilities.

Where in Plymouth I'd been a forthright and outspoken figure at the centre of a provincial scene, in London I was untethered and lonely and, for the first time, unable to write music that I felt had any worth. What I attempted sounded forced and self-conscious. I might write a verse or a riff that I quite liked, but I was incapable of completing much else.

Where had this 'bent path' led me, exactly? Listening back to Die Laughing now made me maudlin. I felt like a phoney and was haunted *by a recurring premonition of being sat around a table at a dinner party. Dressed in a sensible jumper, surrounded by similarly responsible taxpaying adults, I imagined the subject of music coming up. I could hear my future ex-wife saying, 'Oh, Kavus used to play in a band for a while, didn't you?' as I stared at my plate and shrugged dismissively.*

My dad had always hoped I'd follow him into medicine, but pop music had put paid to that before I'd even hit puberty. As a proud, hard-working Persian, my being on the dole was shameful. His parents were over on a rare trip to the UK and, when asked what I was doing in London, he translated into Farsi that I was studying at university to be a film-maker. A mere two years earlier, charged with energy and ideas, I could justify my lifestyle, but now, spurned and despondent, pop music had deserted me. I was thoroughly lost.

With no bonus income from weekly DJ sets or extra money from gigs, I had to sell my Roland Juno-6 synthesiser to pay a gas bill. I fell, not for the last time, into a disinterested, apathetic slump.

The tape in the post didn't help. Dan had formed a new band, Squid Squad. Sarah Measures was singing and playing flute, and the talented songwriter, our friend Nick Evens, had joined on guitar and vocals, too. In the accompanying letter, Dan wrote: 'Remember that ideal drummer we were always looking for? I've found him.'

I knew him, too. Jim Keddie was a ferociously proud Welshman who had been on the periphery of our gang for a while. His girlfriend, Briony, had moved to Plymouth to study metalwork and sculpture at the art college while Jim took a fine art degree in Newport. Surrounded by conceptual artists, he was the only painter on the course, which marked him out. He was as stubborn and opinionated as I was and in no doubt about his abilities. I'd seen his enormous reworking of Theodore Gericault's The Raft of the Medusa *painting in his chosen medium of bitumen and wax – it was dark and austere, resonating with an eerie gothic charge.*

It wasn't until we shared a van to the Forest of Dean festival in 1992 that we spoke to each another at any length. After enthusiastically selling Cardiacs to him, he told me that he thought Die Laughing were the only band of any interest in Plymouth before expounding about how good a drummer he was, going on to suggest I should get him in my band. I had no need for another drummer, particularly this likeable but brashly self-assured one, and just thought, yeah, yeah, mate.

As would often infuriatingly prove true, he was right. What I thought of as overconfidence turned out to be modesty. Jim Keddie was the best – the more complex and awkward the time signature, the more inspired he became – and in spite of the name, Squid Squad were fantastic. While I was stagnating, feeling sorry for myself, Dan had advanced our music into an intricate and perplexing new sphere, its hairy rock roots now barely visible.

Feeling estranged and lonesome, I returned to the south-west that summer to watch them play at Calstock Village Hall in Cornwall. Following the gig, with the tact of a Torabi, I blurted out to Dan and Sarah that I'd love to be in the band and would move back, if need be. Unbeknown to me, this declamation spelled their end.

Aboard the National Express coach that Christmas, guitar in the luggage compartment, I resolved first to see Dan and Sarah and announce I was moving back. I thought I'd rather be following the bent path in Plymouth than isolated in London. Inside his pad on Nelson Street, Dan and Sarah were animated and excited. Before I had the opportunity to say much, Dan announced, 'Well basically, Kavy, you were right. No one gets us – we're moving to London.'

The following day, the four of us played together for the first time. Dan's voice was now a confident croon, his poetic stream of consciousness lyrics, which veered between the beatific and the anxious, with Sarah's soaring and powerful harmonies, knocked me out. I never knew what a terrific musician and singer she was and, like Dan, a quick learner, essential for playing anything remotely rehearsal intensive without using sheet music. Having a wind instrument play or double our obtuse melodies gave the songs a strange authority. As we would come to realise, these non-rock instruments made our sound unique and divisive in equal measure.

To raise the money to buy his drums back in Wales, Jim Keddie had worked part-time in a funeral home. 'I bought this by washing the faces of the dead,' he explained, proudly waving a hand over his Pearl Export kit.

He'd used a Prince's Trust grant to buy his cymbals. On the premise that I needed it to start a career as a guitar teacher, I'd used the same method to get a new guitar – a bird's-eye maple Westone Rainbow semi – shortly before moving to London. That Sarah Measures was a volunteer at the Prince's Trust and approved both of our applications was entirely coincidental. I've never given a guitar lesson in my life.

Laurie Osborne, a beautiful, lanky freak, had played bass in Deluxe, a Plymouth shoegaze band. He was a thoughtful and sensitive guy with an eccentric dress sense. He looked good, had a broad knowledge of music and was funny, too. And he was a caner. Dan and I arranged to visit him the following day.

That afternoon, after getting high, we played 'Aladdin' and showed him what we thought the bass might do. It didn't take Laurie long to get it. Like the rest of us, he only had a cheap instrument, a Yamaha, but he played it like a bass player, not a guitarist who plays bass – he had an innate feel that grounded the tune. Many guitarists snootily think they can play the bass, that it's merely the first four strings of a guitar an octave lower, but it isn't – it requires a different practice. After the drummer, the bass is the next most important member of any rock group. The guitar is just the scribbling about on top.

That afternoon, stoned and elated, I heard our fantastical music brought further to life. Laurie understood 'the one', knew what and when to play, and felt no compulsion to muddy phrases with virtuosic runs, instead building a solid foundation over which Dan and I could construct our crazy, shifting architecture. Following the split of his old band, he'd wanted to do something that challenged him and wanted in.

But he was only eighteen and had just left home.

'Well, here's the thing,' said Dan. 'We're moving up to London with Kavus.'

Laurie let out an infectious laugh, thought about it for a few seconds and said, 'Come on, boys. Let's go.'

Years of playing metal had given me discipline and accuracy but now, using a cleaner tone, I'd abandoned the rigid down-picking of Die Laughing in favour of alternate picking that freed up my playing, incorporating open-stringed drones and unusual inversions that let the chords chime and ring out. Reunited with Dan, our guitar styles fused again, and two days later, in Laurie's spacious front room, the five of us played together for the first time.

As we played, twinkling dust particles blinked on and off, caught in a diagonal shaft of sunlight above the parquet floor.

This didn't feel like any band I'd been in before.

We needed a name. Unusually, I had nothing.

Following a string of (if you can believe it) even lumpier suggestions, Dan finally offered Monsoon Bassoon.

Jesus Christ.

'I don't think so,' I said.

'All right,' he persisted. 'How about The Monsoon Bassoon?'

In my THC-addled brain, adding the definite article somehow made the name sound more psychedelic, like The Pink Floyd, The Strawberry Alarm Clock or The Revolving Paint Dream, and I relented.

Lamenting our terrible name a couple of years later (something I did regularly), Dan suggested that it was the least of people's problems, arguing it served as a test: if you couldn't get past the name, you weren't ready for our music which was, he reasoned, 'basically telling you to fuck off anyway.'

The Monsoon Bassoon was more than a band. Up until then, I'd never played with people who got on so well. As five childlike misfits away from the provinces, being in the capital brought us closer and gave us a tenacious loyalty. While Dan and I wrote the music, in rehearsals the whole band would scrutinise every phrase or riff, trying different approaches until we were content each section was as absolute as we could make it. It wasn't uncommon for us to spend a couple of hours working on a two-bar phrase. If anything reminded us too much of something else, we'd alter or abandon it, and while we could argue fiercely about the music, outside rehearsals we lived, cooked, laughed and sort of grew up together.

It was the band I'd always wanted to be in, like being in The Monkees. The avant-rock Monkees. Having moved away from our families and friends, we were committed to making it work. In our solipsistic bubble, The Monsoon Bassoon was like being part of a cult – it was our entire *life which, unsurprisingly, proved to be detrimental to our personal relationships both outside and eventually inside the band.*

Our collective move to East London had coincided with the birth of drum and bass. Laurie, who was already totally into electronic and dance music, turned us on to labels like Moving Shadow, Rephlex and Warp, as well as sharing his love of British folk which, while at school, I considered to be worthy and boring, both of which were unforgivable. I'd felt the same about jazz, too, but then I used to listen to Kiss quite a lot back then.

Dan, Sarah and I brought our rock, avant and pop while Jim came with jazz, hip-hop and US hardcore. We listened to what we thought of as the best of everything and against a swirling, variegated soundtrack of minimalism and maximalism, we turned each other on, joining the dots between genres, countries, decades and styles.

Music is the purest expression of self, not confined by the limits of language, that raises us from the tawdry and mundane to the divine, the metaphysical. It takes us out of videotape and on to 70 mm technicolour film.

The very idea that any one genre had exclusive claim on the visionary seemed ridiculous. God Almighty, there are even some good fusion albums.

Away from band practice, Jim and Laurie were unlocking the intricacies of Photek's The Hidden Camera *EP and translating them onto their respective drums and bass. We thought of Cylob, Aphex Twin, Luke Vibert's Plug, and Squarepusher as fellow travellers, whose kinetic rhythms and labyrinthine arrangements were the logical continuation of Aksak Maboul, This Heat and Henry Cow. Like Yoshida Tatsuya's Ruins reimagined as electronica, this was the true prog of the nineties, fearless, strange, inventive and musical.*

Dan, Sarah and Laurie lived on one side of Leyton High Road in York Road, while Andrea and I had moved into Colville Road, behind the tube station on the other. Even in Plymouth we'd never lived so close. Adjacent to Colville Road was the entirely squatted Claremont Road, which was due to be flattened to make way for an extension to the M11 motorway.

MEDICAL GRADE MUSIC

Claremont Road was a major nerve centre in the growing anti-road protest movement of the early to mid-nineties. Full of live-in buses, it was home to large-scale art projects, poets, ramshackle sculptures and earnest singer-songwriters. It was a small attempt at utopia, similar in spirit to the recently outlawed free festivals. Sympathetic to the cause, we found ourselves on the fringe of a welcoming and idealistic community, a London we felt connected to. The stereo in the upstairs Jazz Cafe pumped out anything from John Coltrane to Here & Now. Aside from the vegetarian food, it was an easy and convenient place to buy weed, too, and it was here, using a borrowed backline, that The Monsoon Bassoon made our first public performance. There were only about twenty people in attendance, but one of them told us we reminded him of Captain Beefheart, which nobody had ever said about Die Laughing.

Despite the non-repetitive nature of our songs and use of irregular bar lengths, we were unable to prevent the arrival of the diggers and cranes and a few weeks later, Colville Road was filled with police vans and cordoned off at both ends. We were quizzed by suspicious officers any time we wanted to leave or enter our own road. We watched, angry and helpless, as the police enacted familiarly brutal tactics before finally evicting the most hardcore of protesters to make way for the dismantling of our neighbourhood and the dispersal of new friends.

Twenty years later, I would regularly use the M11 extension on my weekly drive from Hackney to Phoenix FM in Brentwood, Essex.

Chapter 23

more The Utopia Strong

Steve

Our first gig was a strange affair. In some ways it was one to forget, or rather one not to judge ourselves by. Elevator Sound in Bristol, one of only a handful (if that) of high-street shops in the UK specialising in modular synthesis, had decided to put on a trade show at a nightclub venue in Bristol called Motion. The event was named Machina Bristronica and, to complement the manufacturers' stands, there was a live-performance room planned as well as workshop and forum areas.

It was a wonderful concept for the expanding UK modular market to complement the likes of SuperBooth in Berlin. I was in the shop chatting to owner Marco Bernardi and, in a rush of blood to the brain, without asking either Mike or Kavus, I offered The Utopia Strong up for a slot during the afternoon. There's nothing like having a novelty act. Our album was nowhere near completion but, in a blind leap of faith by all concerned, we had our first gig. From our perspective, our debut performance turned into a mini nightmare. Absolutely nobody's fault . . . other than mine for suggesting it in the first place.

The performance area was one long bench table and about three feet of clearance behind that was a wall with a big screen attached for visuals. Perfect for a modular performer. Mike and I managed to plonk all of our synth stuff on the bench, but Kavus was struggling to work out where to put his harmonium, cymbal and guitar pedal board, as well as trying to avoid bashing his guitar into the screen. The three of us were effectively debuting in the aisle on a Ryanair flight. Mike barely had enough room to swing his bagpipes and I had a recurring vision of the scene in *Airplane!* with the guitar and the kid losing his drip. We were all squashed together and, at

any moment, I could have had an eye taken out by either a guitar
tuning key or a bagpipes bass drone.

One of the monitors that was on the bench was right in Kavus'
face and the pick-up mic on his harmonium was feeding back.
We did forty-five minutes of what we felt was a collage of pretty
insipid opening gambits without being able to hear well enough to
take them on any significant journey. We were deflated, although
we got a fair amount of praise for our lacklustre performance as,
regardless of our misgivings, it was still pretty psychedelic and
chilled out and a nice foil to the acts taking centre stage, who were
giving their modular synths a far more intense workout than mine
got. Not many acts have performed at a modular synth trade show
and got away with almost an hour of music that incorporated an
Indian harmonium and a set of Macedonian gaida pipes, but we
just about pulled it off.

Prior to our live performance I'd agreed to have a public chat
in the discussion forum area with Alex Theakston - aka the amazing modular synth artist Mylar Melodies - as my interviewer. It
attracted a fair turn-out, which was another nightmare for me.
Everyone in the room probably knew more about the subject
than I did and yet somehow, I had to bullshit my way through
thirty minutes of questions. All good experience, I suppose. The
whole event was a great first effort and even though in 2020 it was
a casualty of the Covid-19 pandemic, like pretty much everything
else, fingers crossed it returns bigger and better and I can visit in
a more relaxed frame of mind as just an enthusiast.

Glastonbury Festival 2019, in the welcoming Crow's Nest Bar,
was to be our first proper live show. This was a venue that in
previous muddy years had been impossible to climb up the hill
to and if you could have somehow arranged to be dropped off in
a helicopter, it would have been far easier descending to the rest
of the Park area in a bobsleigh. As the name suggests, the view of
the festival from the Crow's Nest is truly amazing, especially at
night, but in 2019 there wasn't a drop of mud to be found - Glasto
was sun-baked so hard that the drug dealers were making more

profit from knocking out Ambre Solaire than Scooby Snacks.

The Utopia Strong's first stage gig was on the Sunday evening but, unfortunately, it clashed with The Cure on the Pyramid Stage. There was nothing they could do about it. Our agent, Rick Morton, refused to budge. Usually by the Sunday a fair percentage of festival attendees have given up on the idea of washing and gone totally feral. This was not the case for us, because Mike – somewhat conveniently – lived less than two miles from the Worthy Farm site. While the Glasto throng burned to a crisp, we rehearsed during the day in Mike's cool stone house before venturing out at dusk to party like true vampires. Kavus and I also squeezed in another DJ set at the Spike Bar on the Friday evening. By now we'd become relatively experienced DJs and even though our album hadn't been released yet, we were regularly playing an unmastered version of 'Brainsurgeons 3' at our gigs.

With our first stage show looming, the prospect of a DJ set seemed far less traumatic. Three years earlier we'd been gibbering wrecks before our first ever Glastonbury appearance, but this felt like a walk in the park in comparison. All of our anxiety had migrated to group live performance. We'd already built up a head of steam in the packed venue by the time we dropped 'Brainsurgeons 3', when Mike – who had brought his pipes along – jumped up on a table and accompanied the piece. The place went ballistic.

The great thing about Glastonbury is that you hit upon a place where the music suits and then just bop along with like-minded people. Everyone is wasted in whatever way they choose to be and nobody gives a flying fuck. Regardless of the fact many people say it's not what it used to be, it's still just a happy place.

Sunday's hangover arrived far too quickly, but our minds were relatively focused and we proceeded to lug all of our gear to the car. This was a new experience for me. At one stage in the eighties I had someone carrying my snooker cue case just in case I had to sign an autograph or twenty. Now, here I was lugging my two synth cases with Kavus' harmonium stand under my arm. I kept telling myself we needed to start at the bottom and work up . . .

even though Glastonbury did happen to be our first conventional gig.

We've done the whole band thing arse about face. Historically, I suppose most bands got together, did a few local live gigs, recorded some music and eventually got signed up for a record deal. In Utopia, bands roll in the opposite direction. We got together and jammed for a bit of fun. Got drunk that night on 2 January 2018, listened back to our recordings and realised it was pretty *out there* stuff. We then made the quantum leap of faith to create an album and see what happened. It only seemed like a blip in time before we signed on the dotted line with Rocket Recordings and the wheels of industry started turning. I'd been excited about the album coming out, but when it was confirmed that Rocket really did want us to back it up by gigging, I couldn't envisage a proper tour. However, in the spirit of always saying yes because nothing ever happens if you say no, I found myself staring a new career in the face.

I've got to say, I can't remember a thing about the Glastonbury gig. Nothing traumatic happened and although the three of us were as nervous as kittens prior to going on, I was secretly relieved that there weren't that many people turning up for a band called The Utopia Strong who nobody knew and no mention of a novelty synth player had been spilled. The Crow's Nest are a class act!

At the Bristronica event, I'd felt like fleeing from the room halfway through the performance, but this wasn't that bad. We were pretty psychedelic, nothing too drum-oriented, and there were a few people lounging on the floor looking nicely blissed out. It could have been Kavus' choice of harmonium drone chords or possibly three days of a heatwave that had made the folk in there too exhausted to move, but it wasn't the worst experience in the world. We bowed and exited stage right, patted ourselves on the back and then hung around for the next act. Mike had met up with a few mates, so Kavus and I volunteered to attempt to get transport back to the car park with all the gear. Finally, after realising we hadn't exactly remembered where we'd parked the car, we returned back to the Crow's Nest ninety minutes later, gasping for a beer, only to witness Mike downing the last can of ale from our rider with no sign of a mixed mezze in sight.

I reckon The Utopia Strong, with a combined age of over a maximum break, have gone in relatively hard. We've caned the alcohol a bit since meeting up. We're all easily led - I think that's half the problem. It's not clever, I know, but we like craft ale. The first album was basically fuelled by 6 per cent IPA (5 per cent being quickly demoted to a breakfast beer).

There may have been harder-partying bands than The Utopia Strong, but I think we've done a pretty good job of keeping the sex, drugs and rock-and-roll lifestyle alive and kicking. Obviously, we don't do any of those three, but on the eve of our first tour, we weren't ruling any of them out - we didn't want to let the industry image down, after all.

Considering we all had partners, the sex bit had to be of the solo variety and preferably not onstage. The drugs thing was a tricky one. They just don't feel like drugs when they're sold in Sainsbury's. Alcohol must have been amazing back during the prohibition years when Elliot Ness was smashing up barrels of hooch left, right and centre in his trilby.

You've gotta love governments trying to control their peasants, haven't you? Having played a game most of my life, I'm partial to a set of rules, but it's frustrating when the goalposts keep moving. How amazing to think that MDMA was once legally prescribed by marriage guidance counsellors and 2C-B was dished out by German doctors to improve their patients' libido. Those activities obviously had to stop. I'd love to have been at the committee meeting when they discussed the rules for magic mushrooms.

Committee member A: OK, you can't buy or sell them.
Committee member B: Or pick them! We should stop them being picked.
A: What, they grow? But they're drugs!
B: Yeah, in the woods, everywhere! They're like mushrooms.
A: Fuck! Right, yeah, no picking, either.

B: Yeah, you can't possess them.

C: Are we saying you can't eat them?

A/B: . . .

C: What about if you get on your knees and just eat them from the ground?

A/B: . . . Ah, no! You're still possessing them by doing that.

C: What if you make a tea with them and then throw the mushrooms away?

A: Fuck off, Dave.

Obviously, I'd never knowingly condone taking illegal drugs, or, for that matter, sticking my cock in a dead pig's head, but I'm happy to be guided by my government. I assume it's a given that a pig's head isn't as illegal as a dead human being's head. The legality all seems to revolve around whether the head in question is alive or not.

The hash cake incident at Kavus' house was just unfortunate. Putting them so close to the biscuit tin was an accident waiting to happen. I mean, I doubt if you bought a space cake in a reputable shop in Amsterdam that it would have been anywhere near the premiership Ozric Tentacles-tinged monstrosity I allegedly accidentally nearly ate.

During the eighties, when the powers that be in the snooker world started having delusions that the game might eventually be an Olympic event, drug testing was introduced to show their commitment to the cause. Very few players ever fell foul of positively pissing in a bottle, even while a doctor observed in order to check they didn't have a pre-made sample stuffed in their underpants.

The World Professional Billiards and Snooker Association was far more lenient with us on the consumption of alcohol and coffee than the Olympiads, but all the usual chemical suspects were banned. The cuddly Canadian Bill Werbeniuk who had a hereditary nervous condition and also a dodgy heart had to retire owing to the fact that he couldn't continue to take beta blockers. Yeah, a couple of players tested positive for inhaling something approaching the length of the baulk line and a few were also exposed in the tabloids as 'drug cheats' for still having a residue of cannabis in their bloodstream, albeit weeks after they'd probably been passed a joint at a party. But that was it.

I haven't got a clue about making music or performing onstage under the 'influence', but my only real experience of stimulants while competing was realising that I couldn't cope with the light-headedness of drinking tea while the adrenaline was pumping through my veins. I drank gallons of the stuff during practice, but I was in a head spin if I had one cup prior to walking into the arena.

One year at the World Championship towards the end of my career (when I was struggling to settle down quickly enough in matches), I tried a stiff double whisky in the style of many thespians who had also trodden the boards of the Crucible Theatre. I can't say that it made any difference to my standard of play.

Now that I've retired, I suppose it would be an interesting experiment to see how different drugs affected the incredibly accurate margins needed to play a game like snooker. It would be a brilliant YouTube channel. Watch a six-times world champion attempt to make a century break on a variety of illegal substances. Maybe this could be extended to other sports. Boxing on Ecstasy (The Cuddle in the Jungle), acid archery (The in-and-out-of-Body Experience) . . . I'm not sure if I could manage to pot a ball into a pocket just as a pink elephant emerged out of it, but at some stage in the future, once my kids have chosen the care home I'm destined to experience the next pandemic in, I'm going to request that a snooker table is installed and start the trials.

Chapter 24

more Cardiacs

Kavus

We played a rehearsal tape to Sean and Marina from The Organ, *who agreed to put us first on the bill of a night they promoted at the Camden Monarch on Chalk Farm Road. The Monarch was a small downstairs dive that, until both were refurbished, ranked only a little higher than the Camden Falcon on the London toilet circuit. The headliners, Pop-A-Cat-A-Petal, would later – with a couple of line-up changes – find brief mainstream success as Ultrasound. I recognised their drummer, Stephen 'Stuffy' Gilchrist, from Cardiacs gigs we'd both attended. He'd been getting lessons from Dominic Luckman, Cardiacs' drummer, and it showed. He was fantastic.*

In April 1995, The Monsoon Bassoon went into Cazimi Studios to record our debut EP, Redoubtable. *Cazimi was situated on the top floor of a railway arch by Bakers Arms station in Leyton. Post-rock band Disco Inferno had recently recorded there. When the owner/engineer, Charlie Macintosh, mentioned it was where Iron Maiden had rehearsed in the late seventies, we knew the hand of fate was working in our favour.*

The Organ *offered to 'release'* Redoubtable *as a cassette EP on their label, Org Music, and Sean told us that if he could sell all 150 copies, he'd put us in the studio with Tim Smith to record a 7-inch single.*

A 7-inch single? With Tim Smith? Imagine!

Following a couple of gigs at the Bull and Gate in Kentish Town, we returned to The Monarch, this time supporting ex-Cardiacs keyboard player William D. Drake's Lake of Puppies, a band that also featured Craig Fortnam and Sharron Saddington.

Sarah used to play a rare single-barrel clarinet, which she'd bought for £12 at a flea market in the Plymouth Guildhall. It sounded warm and rich but was slightly flatter than concert pitch, so before we played, we'd have to tune our guitars to it, eliminating the option of a dramatic entrance. I'd been jittery enough meeting Drake after the Lake of Puppies soundcheck, but now, as we took to the stage to enact the necessary 'single-barrel rigmarole', I looked up to see Tim Smith and his girlfriend, Dawn Staple, walk in.

I'd first met Tim in 1990, at Drake and guitarist Bic Hayes' final Cardiacs gig at the Co-op hall in Oxford. Spying him talking to fans across the street that afternoon, Richard Larcombe and I waited until they'd gone before crossing over and nervously gushing that we'd come from Plymouth to see his band. Quite at odds with his onstage persona, Tim was engaging and friendly, and he chatted with us for what must have been ten minutes. Before we let him get on his way, Richard produced a tiny light bulb from his pocket and gave it to him.

Inspired by Fugazi, I'd been on a six-month straight-edge tip but, unable to contain my excitement at actually meeting the maestro, I downed two pints of Guinness in quick succession in a nearby Irish bar immediately after. We were delighted when that night, between songs, Tim held it up and announced to the audience, 'I got given a bulb today.'

Knowing it was Bic's last gig and that they'd need a new guitarist, I sent a copy of 'Artificial Playground' to Tim, via the Alphabet Business Concern (Cardiacs' shadowy label) postal address along with a florid letter offering my services. I never heard anything back.

I'd met Tim briefly a few more times since and, now living in London, would see him out at gigs with Dawn, Bic and other faces I'd half recognise. I'd attempt to engage him in conversation, planning something interesting and enigmatic to say beforehand, but usually excused myself shortly afterwards, uncertain as to whether or not my interesting and enigmatic conversation was making me sound like a wanker.

I knew our friend Sean Kitching had given him a copy of Redoubtable, but I had no idea if he'd listened to it. As thrilled as I was by the thought of him owning a copy, it also made me apprehensive. What if he didn't like it? We later heard from Claire Lemmon, singer and guitarist of Sidi Bou Said, who had recorded with Tim and toured with Cardiacs, that after hearing the tape, he'd told her he was unable to decide whether we were brilliant or terrible – a common reaction, it *would transpire– which was why he'd got down to The Monarch at 8.30 p.m. for the start of our set.*

Roles reversed, I eyed him nervously from the stage. I was now shorn of my dreadlocks, using clippers to go 'devoid of grade', while Tim's grey hair had grown into a messy bob with ratty dreads poking out at the back. No longer the skinny, Joker-like figure of the 'classic' line-up, at six foot, Tim was portly but graceful, wearing a pair of hole-ridden, too-short-in-the-ankle blue canvas trousers, tatty Dunlop 'Green Flash' plimsolls and a T-shirt of Dennis the Menace flipping the bird, with a speech bubble that read 'Up Yours!'

As we played, he stood in front of the small stage, arms folded across his chest, head tilted back with eyes closed and that enormous smile across his face.

We ended the set with Redoubtable *highlight 'Tokhmeh'. During the coda I'd play a chiming, cyclical, fourteen-beat Lydian riff over an open A, counted as a bar of six and a bar of eight. Meanwhile Dan switched between playing the same part in unison and then in harmony, over which Sarah blew a pretty, repetitive Reich-esque sequence on the flute. The bass and drums held down a laid-back but staccato phrase in 7/8. After a few rounds, while otherwise keeping their parts intact, Dan and Sarah started phasing, both dropping a beat to modify their cycle as 13/8. Jim and Laurie remained with me. Now, the band had split into two separate orbits, the idea being that the listener, unable to follow both parts simultaneously, would feel like they were on drugs. Once the two cycles reconnected, heralded by a seventeen-beat, choked-cymbal phrase, Dan and Sarah returned to their previous seven-beat pattern and the whole band played together again, the drums picking up a jaunty shuffle for the next eight rounds. Finally, Dan and I hit our distortion pedals for a no-fixed-length rock out, which would be ended by an 'eye contact' cue, slowing into a final crashing chord.*

As we were packing up our gear at the side of the stage, Tim approached me.

'Bloody hell!' he said, his blue eyes widening into an intense stare. 'What are you lot thinking?'

I looked at him uncertainly before he burst into laughter.

'Forgive me, but how the fuck did you guys just do that?'

He loved the gig and told me he'd been intrigued by our tape, convinced that the section we just played was the result of studio trickery. He expressed genuine amazement that we were able to pull it off live. Then, lifting his right arm up and shaking his hand in a gesture that would become so familiar over the following decade, he nodded towards the bar and asked, 'Jar?'

Andrea and I had moved into a little flat on Cricketfield Road in Clapton, overlooking Hackney Downs. Following a two-week Restart scheme, I'd started attending South Thames College in Wandsworth, studying part-time for a diploma in music technology and sound engineering. I'd opted for an additional module in guitar making and was fortunate to be taught by Russell Fong, guitarist in Moose and guitar tech to a few bands on the 4AD label.

It didn't take long for us to establish our mutual love of Stray Cats and XTC. Russell thought he was the only other person into both bands. I pumped him for stories about touring while he taught me the essentials of being a guitar tech; where to snip the end of a guitar string before winding it on and how to curl a guitar cable properly.

Keen to explore our new Hackney locale, Andrea and I went for a drink in the Samuel Pepys, a punk rock bar underneath the Hackney Empire. It was run by a guy out of Head On A Stick, a local crusty punk band who we'd seen play at a squat party in Claremont Road the previous year. Hackney still had a punk rock vibe in the mid-nineties that has since all but disappeared. There's still a stink of it in Deptford, but even there it's receding.

I recognised a solemn figure sat reading alone. 'That guy works for Cardiacs,' I told Andrea. I'd seen him onstage, as part of the crew for the last couple of years. I felt too shy to talk to him that night, but we spoke a month later after a Cardiacs gig at the Army &Navy in Chelmsford. His name was Captain Jon. He'd just moved into a shared flat by Hackney Downs station. He didn't know too many people locally, so we arranged to meet up in the Samuel Pepys the following week.

Once there, I grilled him with questions about his involvement with Cardiacs. He'd come to them from working with Levitation, an acutely

239

psychedelic band fronted by ex-House of Love guitarist Terry Bickers. They'd released two brilliant EPs on Ultimate Records before putting out their Tim Smith-produced debut, Need for Not, *on Rough Trade.*

I'd seen them a few times, twice supporting Cardiacs, and they were always devastatingly good. Captain had seen them in Chelmsford a couple of years earlier and was so mesmerised by Bic's performance that he caught a coach up to watch them in Wolverhampton, knowing he'd miss his return and have to sleep rough if he watched the entire gig. When he spoke to the band afterwards, drummer Dave Francolini invited him onto the van, as they had a spare room at a Travelodge. The following morning, they asked him if he fancied helping out sell- ing T-shirts and by the time the tour was over, he was living in their windowless lock-up in West London, where they referred to him as 'The Caretaker', before recently moving to Hackney.

Inevitably, like a gateway drug, Levitation had led to Cardiacs.

After a few drinks, and inspired by the technical lessons Russell Fong had taught me, I blurted out, 'Well, if Cardiacs ever need a guitar tech, you've got my number.'

A couple of weeks later, I returned home from college to hear Andrea say, 'You're not going to believe this . . . Tim Smith rang you this afternoon. Here's his number. He said to give him ring him back.'

I rang the following day and Tim picked up. Cardiacs had been offered a tour with Chumbawamba, which was starting in a fortnight. Was I up for guitar tech-ing?

He invited me down to a rehearsal at the Sunday School in Elephant and Castle the day before the tour started. This was like no rehearsal space I'd ever been in before: a large room with stage, lights and a proper PA, it was better equipped than most of the venues we were playing. I met the team. Jim, the bassist, was Tim's older brother and had been in the band from the start. Jim's girlfriend, Jane, ran the merch stall, John Daniel was tour manager, Captain Jon was operating the tapes and Dave Murder was doing the front-of-house sound.

When Bic joined Levitation, he'd been replaced by Jon Poole, who I already knew a little, and I'd hitched up to Nottingham from Plymouth to watch his first Cardiacs show in 1991. The newest member was drummer Bob Leith, who joined the previous year. Bob had replaced Dominic Luckman, who was sick of the deafening click track required to play with tapes. Later, in the 2000s, Cardiacs would go digital, but back then they used a reel-to-reel eight-track tape machine. Each tape could only fit backing tracks for three songs, so there were gaps factored in for Tim to talk to 'the kidz with a zed' – as Cardiacs' zealous following were fondly dubbed – while Captain Jon changed the tapes, wound them on and signalled to Bob to start.

This was a fairly tight operation, but the process wasn't without mishaps. Once, during 'Stoneage Dinosaurs', the tape mysteriously slowed down, making the whole band sound out of tune. Affordable digital technology was still a few years away and the only way to counter this was for the band to descend into a thrumming wall of noise, as if it were deliberate. The tape machine and Captain Jon were hidden behind a tatty sky-blue 'Iron Maiden Drums' flight case on which Tim's Marshall speaker cabinet and amp stood. Tim never used pedals – his entire sound came from an ancient, grimy HH transistor amp, the gain knob of which had long since snapped off and was set permanently at full. This, he 'slaved' into his cab, which weighed more than any other Marshall I'd ever carried. Naturally, only one speaker actually worked. His whole precarious rig was in a sorry state, but when he rolled up the volume on his green Washburn semi and started picking the guitar intro to 'Icing On The World', it sounded righteous.

Chumbawamba and Cardiacs were an unlikely pairing, although one unifying factor was the equal contempt in which both bands were held by the music press. One review for the tour in the NME asked: 'Why did Chumbawamba and Cardiacs play together? So the music press would only need one bomb to get rid of both bands.'

Cardiacs and crew travelled and slept in a fairly run-down but big Nightliner tour bus, along with a couple of caterers, and a lighting and monitor tech from Chumbawamba's crew. Being used to travelling in the back of a transit van with the backline, this was luxury – a lounge with a TV, hi-fi and my own bunk! I was instantly welcomed into the Cardiacs family and have, happily, been part of it since.

'Johnson! Where's my tea?' Jim would bellow. I was initially so eager to please that he and Jane named me as if I were their butler. It was one of the happiest fortnights of my life. On completion of the tour, Jim presented me with a gold Maglite torch for services rendered. Returning to London, I never went back to college to complete my course. None of that mattered now.

Later that year, while recording a session for Mark Radcliffe in Manchester, Cardiacs' manager, Mark Walmsley, showed up with a box containing Sing to God, the forthcoming double album, to give copies to everyone. I was credited as 'Kavus Johnson'.

It wasn't so much that I understood Cardiacs' music, but rather that it understood me. And once I got on the bus – both figuratively and literally – with Tim Smith, I found myself in the presence of someone who got me completely, who loved me absolutely and non-judgmentally for everything I was, in spite of all of my faults. It was as if the effect his music had on me back in Plymouth was an enchantment to facilitate our later friendship.

Whether in a half-empty pub, shopping in Budgens, in the back of the bus, watching a gig or just in his living room, wherever Tim was seemed like the most fun place to be in the world. He saw the magic in the mundane. Warmth, love and friendship poured out of him.

You never heard stories from anyone who had worked with Tim who found him anything less than charming. Of course, as I'd find out, Tim was never more charming than when he wanted you to do something for him, but I didn't care. I don't think any of us around him did, because I've never laughed so much as when I was with Tim – and by extension, I've never been as funny, either. Tim, for whatever reason, found pretty much everything I said uproarious.

We quickly became very close and over the next decade were like partners in crime. I'd come to act as Tim's off-switch. Once we'd squeezed as much fun out of any situation as there was to be had, I'd always be the one to suggest we called a cab before things became too dangerously messy.

The Monsoon Bassoon had outgrown playing downstairs at The Monarch and were confident we were ready for the Dublin Castle, up the road on Camden Parkway – first on, of course. A rather terse *conversation with Sean Worrall in the Wetherspoons on Chalk Farm Road made it clear he felt differently. Despite having sold the whole run of* Redoubtable, *his offer of recording a single with Tim Smith wasn't forthcoming and whatever loose arrangement The Monsoon Bassoon and* The Organ *had ended there.*

We'd seen John Fowers around hawking his fanzine, Earzone, *at the same gigs we went to and had struck up a friendship after he interviewed us, contributing our track 'Digger' to his fundraising compilation,* They Call This Justice. *Despite the jagged chorus in 13/8, the Criminal Justice Bill remained stubbornly unrevoked.*

John Fowers sure liked to talk. For hours. We called him John 'Talks' Fowers. Talksy was hard to dislike, a rare treasure, who would engage in affable conversation with anyone he spoke to. He loved our band and an initial offer to help out quickly escalated into something more.

His first job as manager was to get another couple of hundred copies of Redoubtable *made – using an actual manufacturer – and some T-shirts to sell at the gigs. He took care of booking the gigs, hiring the van, sorting out drivers and collecting money from the promoters at the end of the night – all in his chatty, personable way. Talksy wasn't one for 'The Peter Grant Approach'. While it's a necessary rigmarole, the admin role always makes me stressy. Having it taken out of our hands meant we could concentrate on the music, leaving Talksy to become the public face of the group.*

Together, we moved in to Smalley Close, a shabby red brick town-house on Smalley Road Estate, behind Stoke Newington High Street. Stoke Newington had yet to become the gentrified extension of Islington it is now and was still full of artists, film-makers, musicians and writers of all stripes, living in large, run-down shared properties or warehouses and congregating in the many pubs, alluringly seedy late-night bars, Turkish pool halls and rehearsal spaces – notably Zen Arcade Studios where we rehearsed. I imagined this was what downtown New York felt like in the late seventies.

We played wherever we could in 1996, beginning a run of a year and a half at the Dublin Castle, which felt like a residency. We started out first on the bill on a weekday until we were selling the place out as a Saturday-night headliner and had to move on. It was an electric time, with strange late nights of insanity and synchronicity, of finding other artists, heading for something new, untried and exciting. I've never been interested in cool. Cool seemed to be about detachment. I wanted attachment, and among a raft of new bands and friends, we played gigs with Nub, Sidi Bou Said, Guapo, Shrubbies, Rothko and later Lapsus Linguae, Geiger Counter, Ursa, Nøught, Camp Blackfoot, Chicago's Sweep the Leg Johnny and American Heritage.

Because Talksy was so well liked among promoters, we could generally get on the guest list for most gigs, whether Miranda Sex Garden, Melvins, Foetus, Add N to (X) or Evil Superstars. Tim Smith would always want to extend the festivities further and seemed to know someone at every late-night bar or club in Camden, jumping us ahead of the queue as we were waved in like royalty. Yet, it was never nasty, never sordid and nothing ever went weird. Inside, we'd find a quiet spot to continue our preposterous conversations. We'd be joined by more beautiful heads and lunatics while beers magically materialised in front of us before piling back to Efes, the all-night Turkish pool bar in Stoke Newington, where the revelry continued among small-time gangsters and drug dealers.

Having stopped at an all-night offy, we'd finally return to Smalley Close at sunrise with various cackling stragglers in tow, to smoke, drink and talk love, music and magic. But mainly just to repeat the same infantile phrases again and again as new meanings emerged and they became funnier and funnier. We'd drift off gently to Bert Jansch, White Noise, Global Communication or Talk Talk until the Rochester Castle – the flagship Wetherspoons on Stoke Newington High Street – opened its doors at 10 a.m. and we could start anew, drinking Bloody Marys like medicine.

Tim would grab my wrist and look into my eyes, enunciating slowly to make his point. 'We are the luckiest cunts in the world, you know.' And we were. This was the life unimagined. Hedonism without the consequences. London in the nineties was like a school playground with no prefects on duty.

Chapter 25

Spacemen 3

Steve

Our Teeth of the Sea connection kept on giving when we were booked to support them at Oslo in Hackney on 5 September 2019. It was to be our first London gig - our fifth ever - and it felt like the stakes had been raised. While we'd survived our previous outings relatively unscathed, I think all three of us still felt like we hadn't really found our groove yet.

This was also (sort of) our album launch gig. We had our CD on sale and even though the vinyl was still cooling down at the pressing plant, the machinery had already been grinding as far as interviews for the music press were concerned. For us, if ever a gig was going to have the 'legendary' sticker applied to it, then it became apparent that fate had chosen this one. The place was packed and many of our friends from the music world and radio show had turned out to show support - mixed, no doubt, with a healthy dose of curiosity.

I'm writing this during the months of lockdown in the middle of the Covid-19 pandemic and like every other band and performer, nothing is happening for The Utopia Strong. It all seems like a distant memory now. There might be another analogy here with learning to swim in terms of finally doing your first length in a pool but then not being able to get back in the water for a year. As a consequence of what's occurred in the interim, it feels like this Oslo gig may never have actually really happened and I'm also struggling to believe I survived it. Maybe the whole thing was a strange sci-fi dream and the pandemic is the culmination of that nightmare. Perhaps when I wake up I'll be back in the Romford Snooker Club hitting the cue ball up and down the spots in preparation for the 1982 Lada Classic. But wait! While I haven't got solid evidence of the Lada car I won for making the first televised 147 break, I have got proof that the Oslo gig happened: 'Dreamsweeper'.

Musically, nothing was planned. Improvisation is our chosen path. We did our soundcheck and things appeared under control. I messed around with one of my sequencers and found a riff that felt good and then I just left those settings where they were. Soon after, the sound engineer gave the thumbs up and we vacated the stage for the Teeth of the Sea lads to do their soundcheck.

Oslo was the first gig where I decided to sit facing partially inwards and with my back slightly to the crowd. This was a game changer! My shyness about being onstage was and still is there, but having Kavus and Mike directly in my eyeline felt far better. In my anxious state before our previous gigs, I'd overseen myself getting nervous. The same verbal diarrhoea started to pour out of my mouth as it was getting closer to going onstage. I kept asking Mike and Kavus to tell me it was just going to be like a jam session in one of our living rooms. But they weren't obliging, as unbeknown to me, they were also shitting themselves in their own unique ways. However, if we could only achieve that collective act of self-delusion, then possibly magic might happen. Just before our stage call, I walked into the Teeth of the Sea lads' band room backstage. In a fit of nervous tension (with a slight tongue in cheek), I confronted Mike Bourne and told him that this was all his fault. He laughed, which didn't make me feel any better.

We walked onstage to a wonderful reception and the room hushed as I reached forwards and introduced the opening bars of what was to be our equivalent of what happened on 19 August 1988 at the Watermans Arts Centre, Brentford. OK, so Spacemen 3 are a legendary band, and I'm not even attempting to put 'Dreamsweeper' into the same category or league as their album *Dreamweapon*. For a start, all of our amps were switched on.

I'm not that well read in the autobiographical music department, but if you've never read *Playing the Bass with Three Left Hands* by Will Carruthers, formerly of Spacemen 3, then that situation needs to be rectified. After reading the book, I'd even go as far as to say they partied fractionally harder than us . . . but then Will might have been partial to exaggeration. I should say at this point that the similarity in the titles of *Dreamweapon* and 'Dreamsweeper' is completely coincidental.

A guy named John Alfred has a rather wonderful hobby. He gives artists origami gifts, presumably as an appreciation of the pleasure the artists have given him. He'd approached us prior to the Oslo gig and gave the three of us a piece of origami each in a little plastic box. We all still have them as good luck charms. The gig went so well and because we had a great sound-desk recording, we decided it was worthy of releasing as a private pressing (the second in our *Alphabet of the Magi* series) in between working on our second studio album and amid the logistical problems of meeting up during the lockdown. The pieces of origami had been christened 'Dreamsweeper' by their architect, so there was only ever going to be one name for the track.

In my limited experience, as a general rule, it appears nigh on impossible to judge how good something is while you're onstage. This could be down to not being able to hear it properly or even that you are in a different mode of your brain, but it might also relate to the level of familiarity? I suppose if you're playing a rehearsed piece onstage, you can get a feeling for how well it went in comparison to previous shows. But with an improvised piece, you're so caught up in the moment, it's probably hard to 'oversee' the situation. Regardless, it stands to reason that because you've never 'heard' the music before, how on earth could you possibly evaluate it?

However, on this occasion, we all felt like something special had happened. Our set was over in a split second of eternity and then we were able to breathe, hang out with our mates, watch the amazing Teeth of the Sea perform and then also sign some of our CDs. This was another surreal experience for me. Yeah, I've signed items aplenty over the years, including cues, books, balls, programmes, photos, breasts, arse cheeks, inner thighs and one spare prosthetic leg, but signing our CDs was honestly up there with the inner-thigh moment, and that was pretty up there from memory.

Our self-titled album *The Utopia Strong* was released not long after the Oslo gig and the response was amazing. It would probably be fair to say we got a healthy dose of publicity based on 'The Thing', but I honestly don't think we got a bad review.

It wasn't easy to predict the response to my involvement in a band from the serious music press. I assume that the initial contact from Rocket's press agent would have caused a fair amount of interest, but it would have been understandable had that not also been received with a dollop of scepticism. In our favour was our label's track record of excellence, and obviously the CV's of Kavus and Mike weren't to be sniffed at, either. Had their names been Ken Doherty and Mark Williams, things could have been trickier, especially as Ken's snooker walk-on music is The Pogues doing 'The Irish Rover' with The Dubliners and Mark's is Tom Jones' 'Delilah'.

Regardless, we were pretty confident that if we could get people to listen to the music it would become obvious that it was 'credible'. At the same time, hopefully, the very implausibility of such a band might guarantee some column inches. The next thing that happened was really cool. A smattering of BBC Radio 6 Music DJs (including Gideon Coe and Stuart Maconie) liked what they heard and started playing a number of the tracks.

We were off to a flying start and with pre-sales into record shops, The Utopia Strong featured in the Official Independent Album Charts on 20 September 2019 at number thirty-one. Ahead of Thom Yorke, Adele and the Arctic Monkeys.

This wasn't my first experience of that novelty. The week in May 1986 when 'Snooker Loopy' by Chas and Dave & the Matchroom Mob peaked at number six in the singles chart, we were above Whitney Houston, Madonna and Kate Bush. I can just picture Whitney studying the *Billboard* charts and saying, 'What the fuck's snooker!?' Apparently, in the distant past, ex-pro Tony Meo went to the same school as Kate Bush. I reckon it would have come as quite a shock to her that while she'd possibly leapfrogged him in the playground as a kid, he'd subsequently jumped above her in the singles charts. Kate tried to rally round and toured again in 2014, but her heart wasn't in it after that. The Utopia Strong, on the other hand, were ready to rumble.

Preparing yourself for a situation in which your brief is to improvise is a tough one. My main concern was that I felt under-cooked. I hadn't put myself on the clock during my steep modular synth-learning curve, but I felt I was woefully short of the 10,000 hours identified as the bare minimum for excellence set out in Malcolm Gladwell's practice-makes-perfect theory.

However, Kavus and Mike assured me that they'd played with loads of musicians, who had done plenty more time than that, and they were still rubbish! It transpires that when it comes to improvisation, it's not what you play but what you don't play that can be the defining factor. Maybe the 10,000 hours I'd spent listening to music might just come to my rescue.

As someone with so little experience of performing live, going on tour felt like an overawing expedition. I had to admire Kavus and Mike's willingness to risk their reputations onstage with some-one who was still a novice. But I understood enough not to get out of line by experimenting too much onstage. I tried to postulate a football-based analogy about me as the central defender, giving Mike and Kavus both free rein to be Lionel Messi-esque, but given that Mike isn't remotely interested in football or sport in general, the impeccable credentials of Barcelona's finest and his roving role fell on stony ground. Mike's fingers have been far too busy covering the holes of woodwind instruments to feel the pulse of the Champions League.

So it panned out like this: I'd be doing rhythm, bass and drums, but not too many drums. Plus, our music isn't bass dependent anyway and any rhythm as such doesn't have to be set in stone to make sense in a 4/4 way (whatever that was!). Effectively, I wasn't going to do anything. Correction. I knew I was going to do something, but it wasn't obvious what. Considering that when we'd listened back to our *The Utopia Strong* album, none of us could identify, with any confidence, what sounds were made by which of the three of us, maybe I shouldn't have worried too much.

Our first ever recorded piece of music and the opening album track 'Emerald Tablet' was 'unclocked'. That is to say that Mike's and my synths weren't connected by a patch cable and therefore not marking the same BPM. The shape of our live sets seemed to be panning out in a similar way, but not necessarily with any specific set list. I'm sure we could have planned a whole gig based around our album, but it probably wouldn't have worked out as such onstage and seriously, where was the fun in using laptops and software merely to help replicate the album? The improvised route appealed to all of us much more. It was a slight concern to me that we weren't going to attempt to play our banger 'Brainsurgeons 3', but there were enough other challenges to be dealt with to keep me distracted.

The modular synth is a strange beast. The best thing to do is let it run around a bit onstage and find a comfortable footing before attempting to corral it into any particular musical paddock. The best we could plan for was a general shape to the way a gig was going to pan out. Each of our early shows had just been one long piece of music, but we decided to be braver on our first full tour and do more pieces. That was a nightmare scenario for me. It takes time to re-patch a modular synth extensively. Fortunately, ignorance is bliss and also, improvising, when there are three people in a band, is certainly easier than attempting consecutive modular solo pieces. Less is more is generally a good ethos and we'd had rehearsals where all three of us felt we hadn't done much, but the sum was far greater than the parts.

Creating different pieces meant I knew I was potentially going to look like a Stasi switchboard operator on the stage, but I was as ready as I'd ever be. The idea of calling myself a musician still seemed entirely bonkers, but I'd just have to ride the wave.

Chapter 26

Mercury Rev

Kavus

Talksy ended up blowing a sizeable part of his meagre redundancy on The Monsoon Bassoon, starting in 1997 with a recording session with Tim producing for mates' rates. We recorded the drums with Cardiacs engineer Dave Murder during downtime at The Fortress Studios, starting at midnight.

Rocksteady Keddie never took more than two takes to nail his parts. Murder and Tim had expected an all-nighter, but we were out of there by 3 a.m. The session continued a few days later at Apollo 8, Tim's studio in the garage at the bottom of his mum Eileen's garden in the Chessington house he and Jim had grown up in. Small and cosy, it housed Tim's 24-channel mixing desk, racks of outboard gear, his little Atari computer and a 2-inch multitrack tape machine. In contrast to Tim's stage equipment, everything was in impeccable condition. In the centre of one of the windows, otherwise coated in impenetrable black paint, was the famous little plastic daisy used on the cover of A Little Man and a House and the Whole World Window *that has adorned countless T-shirts ever since.*

Each morning we'd catch the train from Waterloo to Chessington, talking excitedly as we walked from the station. We'd make two cups of tea, one for Eileen and one for Cleo, Jim's enormous German Shepherd, which we'd pour– with two sugars– into her bowl. She'd lap it up noisily as we made our way out of the back door and down the path, avoiding the dog shit and snails, to that lovely warm womb of Apollo 8. Here Tim, illuminated by the twinkling lights from the racks, dials and V/U meters on the desk, would turn around and beam 'Wotcher!'

Inside, in knee-length shorts and socks and faded Cardiacs T-shirt, he was like a little boy in his element. Although we'd been friends for a couple of years, I'd never been in the studio with him before. We'd never been produced by anyone before, either. Tim knew our music as well as we did. Plus he was a visionary, so we had every faith in him. Almost everything I know about recording, engineering and production, I learned from those sessions.

We thought the results were staggering. Whatever we'd imagined we sounded like, Tim had pushed the sound somewhere further again. He'd given the parts space. Talksy fruitlessly set about trying to land us that all-elusive record real we'd been dreaming about since we were kids. Despite our lack of choruses, unorthodox instrumentation, awkward bar lengths, unconventional song structures and terrible name, we genuinely believed we were going to be massive. Somehow, we were going to be the weirdo band that got big.

Meanwhile, Sarah Measures had been on at me for ages to listen to Mercury Rev's See You on the Other Side, *but I had yet to bite. They'd already released two fantastic albums of unbalanced and freewheeling psychedelia,* Yerself Is Steam *and* Boces, *before parting ways with volatile singer David Baker. I had still to hear this new post-Baker effort, imagining it was probably not as good.*

On a gorgeous sunny morning, Sarah and Dan came over to Smalley Close to drop acid with us. The household was already fully immersed when, at 11 a.m., Sarah produced the CD, saying, 'It's time to listen to this.' She pressed Play on the opening track 'Empire State (Son House in Excelsis)'.

A single insistent piano chord, pulsing and unchanging, and a yoyo-ing electric jug immediately reconstructed my drab front room as an exotic, verdant Shangri-La before the soothing tones of Jonathan Donohue called out a hypnotic two-note melody across the flora. Each parable of wonder terminated with 'Life in the Empire State, life in the Empire State.'

I knew he was addressing us and that he knew we were wide, wide open to receive his message.

After an acoustic guitar laid down an Indian-inspired melody, another verse heralded the drums and introduced Suzanne Thorpe's soothing flutes. Hold on, flutes in rock 'n' roll? Each verse was punctuated by a bigger, more unhinged release. Pulsating and expanding, adding flocks of flapping birds – an entire menagerie – and wildlife and spiralling inwards and upwards, just building and building into an orgasm of demented woodwinds that detonated into a joyous melody of all life going faster. Faster into a supernova's explosion that spelled out in golden hieroglyphics that this whole unpredictable life was raining gemstones of meaning, each one the best and all of them truly momentous. And inside and around the notes, the words were beaming out as coded information and galloping forwards, each moment announcing new facets of itself. I kept turning to a now hysterically laughing Sarah to point at the speakers and ask, 'Does it really go like this?'

We couldn't believe music like this existed and was being made by our contemporaries, but what struck me most, with its multiple vocals, wild, delirious rock-outs, extended structures, clarinets, saxophone, flutes and angular riffing was that it kind of sounded like our band. Our band but more fully realised.

See You on the Other Side *absolutely floored me. It became essential listening for the next few years, but what we all understood that day was that we just hadn't been aiming high enough.*

Must. Try. Harder.

After the album finished, I excused myself and went upstairs to my room, where I picked up my guitar and immediately happened upon a choppy circular riff in 7/8 time. The sun, now streaming in through the windows, bathed both me and my room in an opalescent glow, confirming that every note I played was charged with divinity. As electrons orbited the nucleus of atoms and planets around the sun, everything we are was tied to a mad spiralling rotation. All atoms of my being, which in turn was all beings, furthermore all creations and beyond that, all matter, were vibrating with endless possibility. There was only this moment. Everything that had ever happened and would happen condensed into this singular now: this riff. Everything was happening all at once and always had been. Forever.

I descended from the Chamber of Pure Healing Light to join the others. Christ only knows what they'd been through during my lifetime upstairs, but Dan and Andrea were now communicating via photographs of fish in a large book, language now being an alien concept.

'Guys,' I said, face aching from smiling, 'you have to come up and see this.'

Hesitant with awe and reverence, we ascended the staircase from the dark hallway outside the living room until we arrived at the top floor, now blossoming in a dazzling brilliance. I ushered them into my brightly lit room, all objects humming with an intense luminosity. Untethered from the anxiety of self-doubt, synapses crackling with potential, I took a deep breath before announcing, 'Check it out. This is heaven.'

Talksy advanced to the window, cast his eye upon the broken bottles, discarded drinks cans and takeaway cartons littering the feldspar roof of the garages at the front of our house, and added, 'If this is heaven, I don't think much of the view.'

I returned to my room at sunset, now so disassociated from my ego that I couldn't for the life of me remember if I was a boy or a girl. 'I'm a boy,' I'd say to myself before giving it more thought and concluding, 'No, I'm a girl . . . hang on, that can't be right. I'm a boy, surely.' Putting a hand between my legs would have given a definitive answer, but the thought never crossed my mind. The brief few minutes of ambiguity were most liberating.

These were beauteous, lysergic days of implausible brainstorming, where ideas and music just tumbled out. 'Pyramid' and 'Kosh Boy' were recorded during a fevered 24-hour recording session in a North London studio we'd been given free access to, with Tim at the helm. Sarah Cutts, Tim Smith's ex-wife, popped down with Dawn to hang out and listen for a couple of hours. Something was happening between Sarah and me, because I found it hard to concentrate on the recording while she was there.

Tim had already told me a lot about her. He was convinced we'd get along famously and he was right. I'd known her as Sarah Smith, sax player in the classic Cardiacs line-up throughout the eighties. She'd left in 1989, just after On Land and in the Sea, to be replaced by Bic on guitar. We'd met a few months before at a big party at Jim and Jane's pad, out in the sticks at Horsham. She was one of the wisest, most enlightened and enchanted people I'd ever met – an artist and witch who leaves light and a trail of fairy dust behind her wherever she goes.

Dawn later told me that after the party, Sarah had gone back to the house to conduct a magic love spell to get me. This evidently worked, because shortly after the recording session, we started courting.

She'd recently started playing sax and singing a bit in Shrubbies, the band started by Craig Fortnam and Sharron Saddington, with ex-Cardiac Dominic Luckman on drums. I'd never been out with a musician before; our bands played together a few times, too.

Andrea, on the other hand, would never go out with a musician again. Who could blame her? We broke up fairly amicably and she moved out of Smalley Close, followed by Talksy. Once Jim Keddie and Captain Jon moved in, it became more of a party house. It would soon serve as the refuge of the recently split up, that shabby first-floor living room doubling as a makeshift bedroom for jilted friends, or anyone from out of town who happened to be visiting. 'Heartbreak Hotel' was the last pad I'd ever lived in where people would drop by uninvited at all hours.

More often than not, the entire Cardiacs backline lived on our ground floor. The Monsoon Bassoon were now gigging on a weekly basis and in return for the storage, we were welcome to borrow what we liked. We'd use the drum riser, smoke machine and industrial-sized fans for bigger gigs, while Jim Smith's punchy Trace Elliot meant that Laurie finally had a decent bass rig. It wasn't the done thing to ask a support band to borrow gear and by now, we were increasingly headlining.

Surprisingly, the arrival of a Labour government in 1997 made the blissful doss of dole life much less tenable. In their drive to reduce unemployment figures, Unemployment Benefit was rebranded as 'Jobseeker's Allowance'. Every fortnightly signing-on required a Jobseeker's Diary to be presented, detailing each day's effort to find a job. Any day left blank could result in loss of benefits. At £30 a gig, guitar tech for Cardiacs was neither regular nor well paid enough to qualify as work. Despite including every gig I attended in the diary as 'research', I soon found myself on another Restart course.

Restarts were a drag, like having to go back to school for a couple of weeks every year. This one was different – it required mandatory attendance from 9 a.m. to 1 p.m. every weekday to apply for work. With no end. You were there until you got a job. I found myself among the *thoroughly unemployed and unemployable. Men and women for whom life hadn't thrown up the kind of opportunities I had, and who weren't on the dole as a lifestyle choice. Desperate people who would never be able to hold down any kind of responsible or even irresponsible work, but were nonetheless humiliatingly forced to attend and apply for jobs it was clear they'd never get. These were the broken, knocked over and luckless blighted by ill weather or the consequences of bad decisions – shuffling attendants who had been kicked over so many times they could no longer get up. These were not the luckiest cunts in the world and for them, London was anything but a playground.*

I felt like a fraud. I was able-bodied and of reasonable intelligence and while Unemployment Benefit had facilitated my being a full-time musician, the game was up. Sarah Measures had already started working at the Ticketmaster call centre in Leicester Square, which was flexible enough that she was still able to do the band. Following a miserable month of sending my anaemic CV to every music and record shop in the capital, Jim Keddie and I both signed up to work at Ticketmaster, too, and I never signed on again.

This came as something of a relief to the other Sarah, my girlfriend, having spent her entire twenties largely penniless, playing and touring with Cardiacs. She left the band at the end of the eighties, when she and Tim split up, and started a new life away from the madness, with relatively little to show for it other than some amazing albums and funny stories. Although the ten-year age gap between us was never an obstacle to our relationship, my commitment to Monsoons, being generally skint and wanting to party constantly, was too much like the life she'd left behind. I think she was grateful we could now at least go out for dinner together without her always having to pick up the bill.

Romantically, 1997 was a turbulent year in our bohemian bubble. Couples were breaking up all over the place, not only Sarah and me, but also Tim and Dawn. Dawn spent a week in the front room of Heartbreak Hotel before disappearing from the scene to become a lawyer. For the next two years I would hardly see her.

I managed less than a year at Ticketmaster. There had been almost nothing good about it, so I joined Dan working for the crew company

Showstars. This involved emptying trucks and setting up equipment and stages for anything from three-hour shifts at small corporate events in the function rooms of central London hotels, to five-day builds at enormous festivals. Apart from the macho, competitive atmosphere on the bigger jobs, I didn't mind the work so much. I could show up stoned and think about riffs and spaceships while I hauled steel-deck, rolled flight cases, uncurled cables and assembled lighting trusses. The job made me fitter, too, like being paid to go to the gym.

Once Dan and I completed the arrangement of the song I'd started in the bedroom-cum-Temple of Incandescent Light, we worked on the parts with Sarah and Laurie before we all reconvened at Zen Arcade to complete it together.

As with most of our songs, the title – 'Wise Guy' – referred to the actual music rather than alluding to anything in the lyrics. Although only three short verses, which were over within the first minute, following that flash of clarity in that Room of Divine Illumination, I'd finally found my voice. It wasn't much of a voice, but it was the first song on which I sang lead. 'Wise Guy' coming together is my most enduring memory of The Monsoon Bassoon. The molecules in the air vibrated with a new strangeness as we played it over and over, bursting into laughter each time we finished. Like a collective sculpture that, suddenly made animate, opens its eyes and starts walking around, we couldn't quite comprehend what exactly this song was and how we'd harnessed it. Over those four hours we became a different band. We'd moved up to the next plateau. Once he'd heard us debut it, at TJ's in Woolwich, a brightly lit venue that felt more like a swimming pool canteen, Talksy decided we should abandon our futile attempts to 'get signed', record it immediately and release it ourselves as a single. Now it was happening.

Talksy and I drew up a detailed one-year plan – three singles, an album, corresponding gigs. We made a calendar, marking exactly when things would need to happen, and over the following year we stuck to it We rarely deviated by anything more than a week here or there, crossing off each successful event as it happened.

We returned to The Fortress and then Apollo 8 again with Tim at the helm to record 'Wise Guy'. The last couple of minutes of the song *were already fairly wild, but at Tim's suggestion, we overdubbed more woodwind, squealing horns, handclaps and multiple guitars. It sounded immense. We were aiming high enough now, all right.*

'Rock This Town' by Stray Cats was my first single, bought with my own pocket money from the Music Box in Tavistock in 1981. As a kid, singles were great, not requiring the financial commitment of a full album. I'd only buy albums of artists I was really into, but with singles . . . if I liked the song, I'd buy it. Consequently, my 45s from the early eighties are far more eclectic than my albums from the same period. To be releasing a proper 7-inch vinyl single felt like validation.

'Wise Guy' was on our own Weird Neighbourhood label, released as a double A-side in June 1998 with '28 Days in Rocket Ship' (recorded during the same session – a complex and knotty mindfuck) on the other side. With a distribution deal from Shellshock, it was available at independent record shops as well as the likes of HMV and Virgin. Oh boy. I'd waited so long for this to happen. It had been ten long years since I'd dropped out of school and now, finally, we were in the game.

In September 1997, Xfm Radio had just been given a license to broadcast full-time in the Greater London area. An independent radio station that ostensibly championed 'indie' music, the evening shows, particularly those presented by Keith Cameron and John Kennedy, tended towards a more experimental, outré and obscure selection.

We'd diligently sent our single out to all the appropriate journalists and DJs, and Talksy followed up with phone calls. Because of his evident sincerity, genuine enthusiasm and belief in what we were doing, he was well liked, and within days of receiving it, John Kennedy made 'Wise Guy' his 'Monster Midnight Mover', playing it every night for a week. The whole band circled around the hi-fi in Smalley Close to hear our song subjected to lovely radio compression, shivering with excitement as he announced our name. Hearing someone on the radio actually saying the words 'Wise Guy' was too much, hence Laurie's incredulous laughter as he pointed at the stereo and danced from one foot to the other.

The NME *got in touch; Martyn Goodacre photographed us sat on that glass-strewn garage roof at the front of Smalley Close before journalist Jim Wirth came to Stoke Newington to interview us in the beer garden of the Magpie & Stump on Church Street. It was for an 'On' piece, a half-page feature dedicated to up-and-coming bands.*

He enthused: 'Imagine King Crimson being stamped into the ground by deranged peasant farmers and then propelled up to the moon on Sun Ra's rocket ship. Amazingly enough, you're still miles away, because "Wise Guy" is so weird it defies language.'

We couldn't argue with that.

The next headline gig we played at the Water Rats in Kings Cross was rammed. After we'd finished, people bought us drinks and asked us to sign records. It was happening. It was really fucking happening – and on our own terms, too. Another 7-inch single was part of the plan. In August 1998, full of confidence and chutzpah, we 'went large' and released 'In the Iceman's Back Garden', our ominous set closer. At seven minutes, it was too long to play at 45rpm, so it was pressed at 33rpm.

The new NME *hit all the newsagents nationally every Wednesday, but the street vendors in central London usually stocked it from late Tuesday afternoon. Knowing the single would be reviewed, Talksy jumped on the number 73 into town to pick up a copy, while the rest of us waited eagerly at Smalley Close.*

He returned unable to contain himself.

'We've only got single of the fucking week!'

As if that wasn't enough, writing for the Melody Maker, *Stevie Chick declared 'Iceman's' that week's absolute stinker, calling it 'Dead-hearted music made by fools who value the mind above the soul (and are, crucially, scared of gurlz!)' before claiming, 'This is a hollow laugh at your expense. Treat it as the insult it is.'*

Given that the Melody Maker *was the publication that had championed Romo, after all, we took this pasting as a further triumph. Now we had haters.*

We had arrived, all right.

Chapter 27

yet more The Utopia Strong

Steve

Sometimes you've just got to listen to the voice of experience. It was the first day of our debut tour and as the veteran of many a round-Britain jaunt with such popular beat combos as Coil and Current 93, Mike York's plan for how best to prepare ourselves for the journey from Essex to the wonderful Hare & Hounds music venue in King's Heath, Birmingham, was to raid my fridge for any remaining beer and make a craft ale morning cocktail.

While Kavus and I waded through some breakfast cereal and waited for our tour driver to arrive, two jugs of 5-and 10-percenters were sacrilegiously blended together by the ever-inventive bagpipe maker. With a full stomach of muesli, blueberries, IPA and oat milk, we loaded our newly acquired roof rack full of equipment and merchandise and set sail for Spaghetti Junction. By South Mimms services, I was busting for my first piss.

The roofrack was an attempt to tour on a budget. I bought what I thought was a big enough one, but it turns out you can never have enough space. The fucking equipment is a nightmare and it's not like a supermarket, where after you meticulously select your veg and once you get to the checkout, you just ram it all in the bags. Instruments are fragile. Guitar necks can snap at any given moment, so Mike told me. And then when you get to the venue you've got to find somewhere to park that's not illegal, carry the stuff in and bloody set it up, as well as lug all the merchandise in. Then you spend another hour doing a soundcheck, do the show (which constitutes seemingly 1 per cent of the whole day), and then repeat the process in reverse.

Fuck knows what it's going to be like when we decide to break America! Then we'll have all the airline restrictions and flight cases to add to the palaver. Snooker was easy by comparison – one cue case and that was it. It used to be even easier, because you could take your cue on as hand luggage. Then 9/11 happened, airport security started getting as tight as Stephen Hendry on a night out with John Higgins and cues were no longer allowed into the cabin.

I recall the first time I was knocked back on making this previously uncontroversial request. When the girl at check-in responded to my inquiry as to why, with the statement that my cue was a security risk, I remember blurting out, 'What am I going to do with it! Burst into the cockpit and threaten to roll the captain up behind the yellow!?' Fucking hell! Guitars are more dangerous and they're allowed on board. Take your top E off and you can garrotte the asshole in front of you as punishment for reclining too far back in his seat. Anyway, there's no room to swing a cue on board. The worst you could manage would be to take someone's eye out with it accidentally while you were chalking up . . . but surely not at pro level?

One bit of baggage we didn't need was a laptop. For me, Kavus' 'no laptops onstage' philosophy has got to be a future consideration for the vast majority of live music. Yes, I'm aware that there are a ton of groove boxes out there that are evermore sophisticated and the boundaries are getting blurred, but I'd rather someone cocked up than just stare at a screen and hit Play. I know, there's still skilful stuff at hand, but it's tougher to relate to when you can't be certain that the whole thing isn't just being sucked off a USB stick.

OK, I lied about the laptop. We did have one, but only for visuals. Our debut album was unanimously well received, but even if you didn't like the style of music in the grooves, one area there was no doubt about was the quality of the packaging. Rocket Recordings went to town on our record cover. It's a work of art – a holographic foil masterpiece that when caught in the right light becomes incandescent. Johnny O'Carroll, take a bow!

We also got off to a flyer when 'Brainsurgeons 3' was unleashed onto YouTube by Rocket with an accompanying psychedelic video.

We were all set to take this short visual piece on tour with us and whack it on a loop during the show . . . but then things got stupid.

On a night out in Bristol, I bumped into some friends of friends, Neil Harris and Tom Hodgkinson, who informed me they owned a design studio company called SHOP.

'Ah, lovely!' I said to Neil. 'Have you done anything I'd know?'

'Not sure,' Neil lied. 'It would be fun to do some visuals for your tour.'

Obviously, I wasn't stupid enough to fall for that load of old bollocks, so I changed the subject and sloped off to the bar to get some beers in.

Anyway, it transpired that over the years SHOP have done visuals for Stormzy, Ed Sheeran, Katy Perry, The Rolling Stones, Rita Ora, Sam Smith, Coldplay, One Direction, Robbie Williams, Olly Murs, 5SOS, The Libertines, Queens of the Stone Age, Taylor Swift, Cheryl, Helene Fischer, Little Mix, Leona Lewis, Demi Lovato, Hunter Hayes, Redlight, Miguel Campbell, Boston, *Lord of the Dance*, *Big Brother*, RHS Chelsea Flower Show, MTV European Music Awards, National Television Awards, Radio 1's Big Weekend, *The X Factor*, *Britain's Got Talent*, *America's Got Talent*, Audi, Red Bull, American Music Awards, Capital's Summertime Ball, BBC, ITV, Channel 5 and the Emmys. So it stood to reason that The Utopia Strong were their logical next step.

The second leg of our tour was in Bristol at The Cube. And for the fun of it, Neil and Tom had decided to do our visuals. I haven't got a clue what they'd charged the guy on the Pyramid Stage who was jumping around, sort of nearly singing the monstrosity 'Big for Your Boots' the previous summer, but good on them. They did ours that night out of the goodness of their hearts on the pretence that they wanted to learn new VJ'ing hardware. After recording their perfectly crafted psychedelic visuals that night onto a USB stick, they gave us their blessing to use it for the rest of our tour.

Over these first couple of gigs I confirmed my favoured onstage position. Standing up is obviously an option in the style of the late great Florian Keller, but so far I have done my best work (unlike my previous career) in a sitting position. It definitely feels more like a home set-up and one that we've previously jammed in, even though after the gig at the Hare & Hounds a friend told me that once my leg started tapping to the beat, it looked like I was operating a Singer sewing machine.

It's also a question of how you present the instrument to the audience. In the same way the laptop is a massive visual barrier as well as a psychological one, playing a modular synth and facing the audience means they don't have a clue what's in the box. For all they know, it could contain a rabbit and a lady cut in half. OK, even if you showed them, they might not fully understand or even care, but at least give them the option.

The pre-show nerves are something else, though. I thought that the day I retired from competitive snooker was the day I was free forever of the angst in my pants, but no, the subconscious adrenaline junkie in me had other ideas. I joined a band and agreed to a tour to promote our debut album. What sort of fucking idiot would do that in retirement, instead of taking up gardening?! That was what had been going through my mind ever since our first gig, but it seemed like the stakes had been raised now we were properly on tour.

For some reason, the butterflies were particularly flappy on the third leg of the tour at The Cluny in Newcastle. Prior to going onstage, Kavus and Mike had wandered out of our band room and gone to the bar in what looked to me to be in a relaxed and confident state - leaving me to pace the floor anxiously and deal with the torment alone. In the course of this long, dark early evening of the soul, I found myself breaking the key unwritten rule of band life on the road.

I'd already been made aware of this rule but didn't think it would apply under these circumstances. Kavus had spoken to me about it, as obviously, due to copyright restrictions, there was no other way to find out. No shitting on the tour bus. (There. I've said it!) That's it, written down. Fuck knows what will happen as a consequence.

What I wasn't aware of was that in the imaginary small print, it stated that the 'tour bus' was an umbrella term that included the band dressing room at venues, as well. I didn't know if Kavus was winding me up, but as a tour virgin, I couldn't argue. If he'd sent me out to get a sky hook for his guitar amp, I'd have known, owing to my teenage Saturday job in the butcher's department of a supermarket, but this was new territory.

The 'no laptops onstage' rule (except for visuals), I was definitely down with, as I've explained. In fact, I'd say it's an essential stipulation, especially for an improvisational ensemble. I was also coming to terms with the 'no white four-gang power blocks on the stage' rule; although at short notice, Kavus had to concede that one, owing to not being able to find a Maplin's that was open anywhere. But at the risk of crossing the same 'too much information' boundary that makes Mötley Crüe's *The Dirt* a book it's not advisable to read aloud in mixed company, let's just say that had Kavus and Mike not been aware of how nervous I was prior to vacating the band room, I reckon the speed at which they vacated it again when they returned was testament to the stratospheric level of my pre-gig apprehensiveness.

In all my time as a snooker player, the love-hate relationship with competitive play was always there, mainly because of this ghastly pre-event turmoil. We've all experienced it in some form, but imagine a cocktail of your first date, driving test, school exam, visit to the dentist and job interview. Now drink that fucker just before you go off to work every day! The dressing room thirty minutes before a match at the Crucible was a horrible place to be. I once witnessed a player throwing up before his debut appearance. But once the match got underway and you started to concentrate on the job in hand, the nerves usually evaporated. I'm happy to say the same rule applies in The Utopia Strong.

So what have I learned from my first ever series of gigs? First, that I still have a bloody long way to go to earn my stripes, but regardless, it's a fantastic buzz. I've also realised how amazing Kavus and Mike are as musicians. I'd like to think that I was keeping up my end of the bargain and responding to the musical twists and turns during the show, but understandably, I got the feeling that the pair of them were much more on the money in that regard.

And shit! Nobody told me about the sound onstage. It doesn't resemble anything the crowd are listening to. You know when the artist starts pointing to the monitor and gesturing? I can now confirm that's for a reason. It was all new to me, though. The first time I got asked by a sound guy what I wanted in my monitor, I responded by saying, 'Er . . . the show?'

But it turns out it's more fucking complicated than that. I'm still not totally sure what I want in my monitor. At The Cluny, I'd have been better off with Radio 2 than what I heard, but I just about got away with it. I've definitely learned that it's a good idea to keep the sound guy in the loop with what you're intending to do, volume-wise. We did the soundcheck and I turned my modular synth mixer up to what I assumed would be my maximum levels. But because I neglected to explain properly that I might only reach these levels occasionally (if at all) during the show, when we started the gig he quite understandably assumed I was too low and subsequently compensated on his desk. Then when I went to turn my volume up, we went into that nasty feedback thing . . . I always wondered why that happened and now I bloody know at least one of the reasons!

For the rest of that show I had zero room for manoeuvre with my internal volumes. I hadn't read the signs, but the omens for this happening had manifested themselves in the shower at the hotel earlier that evening, where I'd needed the skill of a safe-cracker to achieve a happy temperature balance between Antarctica and the Death Valley desert. But regardless of my own personal aural nightmare at The Cluny, Kavus and Mike were on better terms with the sound guy and we ended up recording 'The Keeper' that night, so that's a clue for future gigs. If I can't hear anything and subsequently don't play anything, we do great music.

We also need to talk about VCOs . . . the modules in a system that generate the core sound. The digital ones are as solid as a rock as far as staying in tune is concerned, but some of the analogue variety are not as stable, especially over time, and are also susceptible to temperature change. This isn't a huge problem, because you can always retune the little fuckers if they get too out of hand, even on the fly, but make sure you've checked the batteries in your tuner beforehand. I mean, that would be sensible, wouldn't it?

So there I was, struggling to hear my own synth onstage, wondering what ungodly dissonant sounds it was spewing out and leaning far over to my right to get my ear down close enough to the monitor to hear it. This led one person to suggest afterwards that I looked like I was directing my attention into the cellar to call for another barrel of beer to be brought up. Not a bad idea in itself, but not exactly showbiz gold for our debut tour.

Luckily, I'm not without the ability to hear when something is out of whack, but hopefully I've learned my lesson with monitors. However, while being able to hear yourself onstage is obviously important, there are other potential problems staring you in the face . . . Or not, as the case may be. There's also the possibility that you won't be able to see anything, either. So here's another piece of advice for the budding modular synth performer: bring a clip-on light with you, otherwise you might as well put a blindfold on.

The road that The Utopia Strong's live sets will be going down in the future is firmly established now. The musical cement will be wet every night. Every gig is guaranteed to be different. We'll be going onstage without a safety net (and fingers crossed, not wearing masks) and hopefully, this will prove to be a braver and better way to progress rather than a foolish one.

For me, as far as performing in the future goes, I'm with David Bowie when he said, 'If you feel safe in the area you're working in, you're not working in the right area. Always go a little further into the water than you feel you're capable of being in. Go a little bit out of your depth.'

On balance, I think Kavus and Mike are enjoying the freedom of being onstage with no rehearsed plan, even though they're possibly feeling a little more apprehension because of it. There was one track that we'd loosely rehearsed that Mike York came up with. It was a sort of Steve Reichy pipes piece. I think for a first tour it was probably a good idea to have something to fall back on just in case things went completely tits-up. It was superb, but listening back, I think we all feel that it was the other moments (good or sometimes even bad) that seemed to be where the magic originated from.

It might appear a massive leap of faith for me to jump straight in the deep end and play improvised music from a standing start, but I think that's easier for someone coming from a non-musician's background. While repeating a piece of music night after night must have its own rewards and is incredibly skilful, perhaps the thrill of the unknown is more akin to sport than the repetition that usually happens on a stage or in a theatre.

Are the nerves worse when you're improvising? I don't know, but I think Kavus and Mike felt that was the case for them. One thing is certain, at least in one way – it's harder to disappoint a crowd if they don't know what's coming next. The conundrum, I suppose, is the possibility of leaving people feeling short-changed should they come along expecting to hear a certain track from previously recorded material. In this respect, I'm hoping that we can please most of the people most of the time, rather than some of the people some of the time. The longer I've been on the planet and going to gigs, I've realised I'm starting to appreciate the experience of a journey into the unknown as opposed to revelling in a track I've already heard at home. I know I must be in the minority and obviously I'm not saying I don't enjoy watching, say, the current Gong line-up performing 'You Can't Kill Me', but now I'd love to hear a band like Magma do an improvised gig. That could be mind-blowing.

I've got to say – not blowing smoke up my own arse *too* much – that I'm pretty proud of myself for the fact that I haven't as yet totally fucked up onstage. Obviously, it will happen at some point, and I suppose where the 10,000 hours comes into its own is having the experience to dig yourself out of the hole. The thing I'm most proud of is having put myself in a potentially vulnerable situation by saying 'yes' to gigging. It wasn't something I needed to do, and it would have been understandable had I just said 'too scary' and The Utopia Strong had become a studio project only. But I'm glad I didn't shy away from the challenge. Whatever the reasons for making this decision - either blissful ignorance of what it entailed, or just not wanting to bottle it and let the side down, or possibly just the subconscious adrenaline junkie in me taking charge - I'm glad I made it.

Chapter 28

XTC

Kavus

Although we had almost an album's worth of material already stockpiled, The Monsoon Bassoon were improving exponentially. Our debut album would have to reflect where we were right now, rather than where we were previously, so we went into overdrive writing new songs.

I documented the romantic estrangements of the previous year in 'The Very Best of BadLuck '97', a song that had become yet more germane now that Dan and Sarah had broken up, too. Thankfully, they'd both decided that the band was more important and we carried on, becoming closer as a result. Having struggled to battle against the increasing volume, Sarah had ditched her clarinet in favour of a beautiful alto sax. We'd all but stopped writing for flute, too - something Tim told us he missed. I'd like to say it was for a better reason than being sick of getting lazily compared to Jethro Tull, but it wasn't.

On 'Volcano', a sedately psychedelic ballad of the apocalypse, I recorded my first foray into gliss guitar, a technique developed by Gong's Daevid Allen after watching Syd Barrett use a Zippo lighter on his Telecaster. The strings are bowed by a not entirely smooth metal object – a screwdriver will do or, if you're Steve Hillage, a gynaecological tool. Adding a little delay and overdrive transforms the guitar into a choir of weeping angels. When Sonic Youth played at The Forum on the Washing Machine tour, I'd seen Thurston Moore use a drumstick instead of a metal rod, giving a thicker, more unpredictable sound. It looked more dramatic, too, as the wooden stick required more movement to get the desired sound, so I opted for that method.

The album recording followed the now established path of drums at The Fortress then down to Chessington. Given the recent dissolution of their romantic union, I thought Dan and Sarah's positive attitude was particularly grown up. But, clearly, they were both uncomfortable *spending days together in close proximity in the tiny Apollo 8 studio, especially during 'The Constrictor', which was pointedly about their break-up. It was almost like being in Fleetwood Mac. The avant-rock Fleetwood Mac; although, unless she was keeping it unusually quiet, no one was administering cocaine via Sarah's asshole.*

We'd been opening our set with 'The King of Evil' since we wrote it. We all agreed it should be the next single.

Talksy returned once again from his trek into central London. 'The King of Evil' was Single of the Week in the NME. We'd done it again. For the second time in a row.

This was cause for a celebration at the Rochester Castle – a round of drinks, at least. We emptied our pockets. Despite the Rochy being the cheapest pub in the world, on that Tuesday afternoon, we could barely even scrape enough for a pint of Stella between us. This called for desperate measures. I retrieved my shrapnel jar from upstairs and emptied it onto the carpet. From coppers to five, ten and twenty-pence pieces, we counted out £7. At £1.20 a pint, that would buy a round for six. Although legal tender, we anticipated some resistance and took along the NME by way of explanation.

In the late seventies, the Rochester Castle had been a venue. The Jam played a couple of times and XTC once had a residency there, which elevated its status even higher. Stoke Newington had plenty of lovely pubs, particularly on Church Street, but aside from the affordability of the beer, The Rochy was winningly non-judgmental and had been our go-to pub ever since we'd moved there. In this haven of the career drinker, regardless of the state we arrived or left in, we were never asked to leave.

With no music and no TV sports, it was furnished, dampening the ambience, and the veggie burger and beer offer was a winner. The large central table permanently seated a vocal clique of middle-aged Socialist Workers drinking about politics, one of whom I recognised from my final Restart course, perpetually slamming the table to emphasise important points. I slept easier knowing their daytime dipsomania would eventually bring about the end of capitalism.

The prime spot was a booth that would cosily accommodate The

Monsoon Bassoon and manager, preferably not the one adjacent to the men's lavatory. Here, we could merrily slam the table to emphasise the finer points of rehearsal-intensive music, knowing it would soon collapse the corporate music structure, with us leading the charge. Now, with NME *in hand and one step closer to that goal, we approached the familiar barman we'd nicknamed 'Mole Man'. I announced, 'Six pints of Stella, please,' before sheepishly emptying the large pile of change from a carrier bag onto the bar and mumbling, 'Er, yeah, sorry about . . . this.'*

The bartender didn't bat an eyelid as he counted it into the till. Ah! the Rochy. Clearly, this manner of transaction was standard.

We dubbed the launch party for 'The King of Evil' The Good Friday Agreement. Max Tundra and Rothko supported, with XFM's John Kennedy DJ'ing 'Upstairs At The Garage' in Highbury.

The night before the gig, Rothko's Crawford Blair rang me up. 'What are you doing before soundcheck tomorrow?'

'Um . . . nothing?'

'Wanna go into town and meet XTC?'

XTC had just released the pastoral Apple Venus, *which, because of a contractual dispute with Virgin, was their first album since 1992's* Nonsuch. *Andy Partridge was one of my favourite songwriters and guitarists. XTC were a top five band for me. Every album, from their angular, scratchy post-punk beginnings to their lush, widescreen later works and their psychedelic offshoot band, The Dukes of Stratosphear, was wonderful.* Apple Venus *was no exception. Because of Partridge's stage fright, they'd stopped touring in 1982 and I never expected to meet them. Partridge and Moulding were guesting on Phil Jupitus' GLR radio show to promote the new album and Crawford, a massive XTC fan himself, was friends with the producer, so he asked if we could tag along.*

We arrived at GLR mid-afternoon and after being introduced to Phil Jupitus, who seemed pleasant enough, we sat nervously in the green room until the producer popped his head round the door and asked, 'Do you wanna let them in? They're at the back door.'

Behind the frosted, meshed glass I saw two blurry but familiar shapes. What should I say to them? As I tentatively swung open the door to

Swindon's finest. Partridge immediately asked, 'Where's the crapper? I'm dying for a shit.'

They both graciously chatted with Crawford and me for about half an hour. Partridge, wisecracking throughout, was just as I hoped he'd be and, there in the flesh, I truly understood why Moulding had been dubbed the handsomest man in Swindon. We invited them to the gig, but they told us they needed to leave for Swindon at six. I had to get to soundcheck, so couldn't stay for the interview, although before I left, I presented them both with the three Monsoons singles.

'What label's this on?' Partridge asked. I told him Weird Neighbourhood, our own. 'Ah! Good move. If I'd been smart enough to do that back in the day, we might actually have some fucking money now.'

The launch party sold out before the doors opened and we were told that 'the guitarist out of The Verve' had attempted to gain entry but was refused. Right on. At 1 a.m., about thirty of us retreated to Smalley Close to continue. I rigged up one of Cardiacs' enormous industrial fans and a smoke machine at the bottom hallway in front of the kitchen, opened my bedroom window at the top and sent plumes of fog up the stairwell while rinsing Slayer's non-stop party classic, Reign in Blood, at battle volume from the living room. We didn't get on especially well with our neighbours.

Our debut album, I Dig Your Voodoo, was released in June 1999. It received good reviews across the board and even managed to enter the indie album charts at number 21. Following the release, we spent the next year gigging, playing a couple of shows with Cardiacs and touring wherever we could in the UK, including a ten-date jaunt with Max Tundra (whose debut album Some Best Friend You Turned Out to Be had just been released on Domino) in which we alternated headline spots. XFM broadcast an entire gig, our return to The Monarch, a much larger venue since it had moved upstairs. Following the show, an A&R man from Polydor told Talksy we were the best band he'd seen in twenty years. 'Get your wallet out, then,' Talksy joked, to be told that if he tried to sign us, he'd lose his job.

Finishing a gig at The Borderline, someone asked, 'How do remember all that?' To which Dan replied, 'How do you remember your way *home?' And throughout a set at The Lift in Brighton, Pere Ubu's David Thomas stood at the front, arms folded, scrutinising us in a most discombobulating way after we played with his band, David Thomas and Two Pale Boys. Following the gig, he asked if he could buy a CD, saying we reminded him of seeing the MC5. That was an improvement on Jethro Tull.*

In the meantime, tiring of the unpredictable nature of the work at Showstars, Jim Keddie and I started labouring for our friend Martin Hawkes. Martin was formerly Marty Tuff from the seminal Ipswich hardcore band, The Stupids. After leaving The Stupids, he moved into a career as a recording engineer. But having received no credits for engineering the Stereo MCs Connected *album or Galliano's debut, he'd become disillusioned with the business and opted for building instead. Understandable.*

'The posh builder', as he was known around Stoke Newington, wasn't especially posh but was certainly polite and well mannered. He'd helped to build Zen Arcade, where we got to know him, and he offered Jim, another Plymothian musician pal, Tom Clues and myself, all Plymouth expats, work digging trenches for £50 cash a day. We'd start at 7 a.m., be all done by 2 p.m. and in the Rochy by three. It was a wonderful job; not wholly unenjoyable physical exertion, working among friends with a mellow boss. How hard a taskmaster was the guitarist of The Stupids going to be? Labouring also proved to be a gateway to painting and decorating, which became my main source of income for the following two decades.

Decorating was flexible enough to fit round the commitments of a so-called music career. After training under meticulous Australian perfectionist Simon Mofitt who I'd met on one of Martin's jobs for £80 a day, I took on my own jobs. Here, I was free to set my own hours, my own daily rate and work at my own pace. It would transpire that many, many musicians were hip to the same idea.

While Dan and I worked on writing album number two, tentatively titled I Am The Master And You Are Coming With Me To Hell, *we decided that what was needed to keep up our 'profile' was a series of collaborative split 7-inch singles we called 'Wall of Suss'. The first Wall of Suss was with Rothko, the three-bass instrumental band. The A-side was our reworking of their 'Seventy-seven A', which we named 'N73' (the night bus from central London to Stoke Newington), while they reimagined our 'Fuck You Fuck Your Telescope' as 'Fuck You Fuck Your Endoscope' on the B-side. Unsurprisingly, it was Single of the Week in the NME. That was three in a row. 'Not even The Jam or The Smiths managed that,' noted Talksy.*

Despite reaching this improbable landmark, we'd hit a ceiling, popularity-wise. There would be no sports cars made out of vaginas or swimming pools hewn from cocaine for The Monsoon Bassoon. Once our version of Max Tundra's 'Life in a Lift Shaft' was recorded for Wall of Suss #2, our insistence on the title 'I've Seen Shit Smeared Around the Inside of a Lift (Baby)' proved the final straw for Talksy. We actually had an argument about it and everything, even doubling down on our choice before eventually relenting, settling on 'North Prospect'. But, having generously haemorrhaged all of his savings on us, Talksy bade us farewell. Wall of Suss #2, released in 2000, failed to garner any sort of review from the NME, despite Max Tundra's uncannily forensic reworking of 'Commando', one of our densest tunes. If only we'd kept the original title.

Although Laurie and I lived together, we didn't see much of each other by this time, and while Dan and I continued to write together regularly, rehearsals were becoming largely joyless affairs, now fitting around the various band members' other commitments and our work schedules.

The song 'God Bless The Monsoon Bassoon', from what turned out to be our final three-track EP, is one of my favourite songs we wrote. Sadly, its valedictory tone was right on the money. Our final show was headlining The Garage, one of my favourite music venues in London, where I'd seen so many brilliant gigs. Although we'd been first or second on many bills over the previous few years, now we were a 'headline at The Garage'-level band! 'We'll be back with a new album,' I announced as we left the stage. I hope no one was holding their breath.

Jim had become a father, moved to South London and now had a proper job. Whenever I asked him what he did, I'd get bored and stop listening before he finished explaining. I'm still not sure what it is. It was only a matter of time before he left the band. He'd done this a few times before, but now I didn't have the energy to try to talk him back. It was disappointing, but I couldn't blame him - it had stopped being fun. Laurie had also been unhappy during the last year, sick of being perpetually skint, and sick of London, I suppose. He'd show up late for rehearsal and spend most of the time avoiding eye contact with anyone.

We didn't feel like the same band that had created 'Wise Guy' three years earlier. The Monsoon Bassoon had always been about the five of us. I liked it best when we all lived together and only cared about our band. I didn't want to try out another drummer. Dan and I met up - we'd been here before on the Aladdin trip - and decided to split the band and start a new one. We wrote the songs, anyway, we had a whole album of demos. We could finally ditch that dreadful fucking name and call ourselves Miss Helsinki. Our audience would follow us anyway.

They didn't, though. Not really.

Chapter 29

The Gasman

Steve

During lockdown in the spring of 2020 – in between watching *The Prisoner*, series three of *Twin Peaks*, *The Singing Detective*, *The Wire* and then rewatching episode 8 of *Twin Peaks* a dozen times – I spent a great deal of time watching modular synth demos and video blogs on YouTube. Their advice has been invaluable and since playing live, I've found myself much better able to relate to a lot of the experience and guidance on offer.

For the budding modular synth explorer, I'd recommend the videos on YouTube by Molten Music Technology (Robin Vincent) and his series enticingly titled 'Molten Modular – Getting into Eurorack Synthesis'. There's also a great explanation of how modular synths work by Modular Landing in his series 'Exploring Modular Synths – Beginner's Mind'. Beyond those excellent resources, you'll be totally inspired by Mylar Melodies and once you've reached a highly proficient level, DivKid (aka Ben Wilson) provides an extensive deep dive into the world of synthesis. And if you're looking for printed matter on the subject, then look no further than the excellent book *Patch & Tweak* by Kim Bjørn and Chris Meyer.

So here I am, a few years on from my introduction to learning a musical instrument and what do I know about the modular synth that I didn't know before? Well, it's like no other instrument on the planet and while it doesn't require the same skillset as the vast majority of instruments, it's still far removed from creating music just on your computer.

At some stage in the not-too-distant past while listening to Kavus playing The Gasman (aka Christopher Reeves) on our radio show, I was astonished by the complexity of his music. When Kavus told me he made it all 'in the box', I was inspired to try this route. Creating music on a computer, in a piece of software called a DAW (Digital Audio Workstation), seemed to be something I could achieve. However, when I started my first steps on this path, I quickly realised that it wasn't for me. There was a process of composition that felt like a hurdle that I was never going to overcome. Currently, it seems like many people have turned their backs on creating music in software and revisited the hardware format. I think I have more admiration for The Gasman now than previously, knowing how creative his mind must be in order to produce music for as astonishing an album as *Hiding Place* all within the box. He's like a modern-day Conlon Nancarrow!

The modular synth has a learning curve that's not dexterity-based. It's knowledge-driven. But, wonderfully, it rewards even the newbie with unexpected magical moments. Regardless of your level of understanding, these entrancing events seemingly never stop. If you seek out any one of the growing number of synth outlets (either bricks and mortar or online) and ask to buy a complete modular system, any seller worth their salt will first ask you what style of music you intend to make.

Unlike buying an electronic keyboard, where to a large degree the signal path is already hardwired, with the modular synth you decide and, more importantly, you get to choose what modules you acquire. This gives you a vast range of musical possibilities and new directions ultimately limited only by your imagination. In many ways, it's the most flexible and astonishing instrument out there.

As far as the skill levels of learning a modular synth are concerned further down the line, knowing your instrument and harnessing its capabilities become highly valued attributes. The knowledge levels are akin to an onion. Not only in their potential to drive you to tears, but also in the fact that you might think you have learned about how your modules interact with each other, and then someone shows you (or you stumble upon) another layer beneath.

Plenty of people get into the hobby side of modular synthesis. They might make music, but purely for their own enjoyment.

There are a growing number of modular meets around the globe where like-minded people can get together and have a jam or just discuss stuff as well as get involved in DIY projects. I think I would have happily done only that, as I can easily just mess around at home and lose myself for the whole night in what's commonly known as a 'patch', but I've been stupidly lucky enough to have been involved in a project that's effectively gone supernova compared to what could have unfolded.

That changes the equation for what's required from a modular synth (and from me), especially when it's being played in a band environment. Regardless of whether you're playing solo or not, I'm on my way to understanding the requirements in regard to improvisation.

In one of his wonderful online demos, Mylar Melodies was discussing the skill required to play a modular as opposed to other more traditional instruments and said words to this effect:

> While there is no dexterity required, there is a skill in deciding when what you are playing is right or not. The skill is knowing when to keep something happening and when to change things. Ultimately, it is your musical taste which can be defined as both a skill and something that is unique to you. Philosophically, there is no difference between writing a melody or waiting until you feel the melody is right.

Bang on the money, in my opinion (even though some traditional musicians might disagree). But the more you understand your set-up, the more you can harness its power and flexibility and aspire one day to control it rather than it controlling you. Regardless, it'll always produce astonishing results and, with the right levels of acumen, you can still then take the accolades!

There are synth modules, similar to groove boxes, where you could totally pre-program what's going to be churned out. All the drums and melodies could be preset and the only real thing you'd need to do would be to bring up the faders and occasionally twiddle a filter. That's an option as a safety net for a live performance, but for me, the holy grail would be the polar opposite. I'm by no stretch of my imagination there yet, but that's the plan.

The career of a pro snooker player has changed over the years. The current breed of players generate the vast majority of their earnings from competitive play, but back in the seventies, when I was coming through the ranks as a young amateur, the pros would make the bulk of their wages from exhibitions. At the end of a show that often involved massacring the local club team, the pro would do a bunch of trick shots. This was a chance to entertain the crowd, not only visually, but also verbally.

These exhibition evenings had nothing to do with competitive sport but everything to do with being an entertainer. From the age of about twenty, I started doing these shows and subsequently learned my trade in both disciplines. As the years went by I started to do more and more public speaking, with my cue never leaving its case. Regardless of how you go about speaking, the job spec is to entertain and what you're doing is really no different to the comedian who may follow you on the bill to wrap things up.

Material that you know is good, and accidental ad-libbing that gets a laugh, gets kept in and the more you do of this, the more a mental script formulates. The amazing thing is that once you become word-perfect at this, you become able to 'oversee' yourself – another part of your brain can then start monitoring what you're saying, how you're delivering the lines and how the audience are responding to your delivery. You start to be able to judge your own performance irrespective of how it's being received by the crowd. I suppose that's what happens when you play the same piece of music night after night on tour.

Improvising feels different, but I guess the more you do it, the more there's a possibility that some kind of script or learned behaviour can develop. The same is true as a listener. A lot of people get stuck in a rut of one kind or another.

Sometimes that can mean listening to our favourite albums too much when we could be challenging ourselves with something less familiar. How many times should we listen to an established classic at the possible expense of a new revelation? I guess that's an issue of time management. Time being a commodity in ever shorter supply for all of us – even Peter Pan wannabes like myself.

Another of those possible ruts is the sordid world of hi-fi. It's an awful vortex to get sucked into, with its potentially no less destructive sub-vortex of vinyl purism culminating in only listening to audiophile recordings. Of course, if you believe the hype, vinyl is and has always been better than digital – an analogue signal is far 'more natural' than a 1s and 0s signal, regardless of the bit rate. Even if digital sounds sharper with less background noise, the vinyl purists will tell you that it's too clinical and nowhere near as warm as vinyl, especially when a valve amplifier is in the hi-fi chain.

Yet, I get the sense musicians aren't generally in agreement. Their insider knowledge tells them that the music we all listen to has for many decades been digitally manipulated far more than the enthusiast would ever realise. Today's 'analogue' vinyl LP is just an illusion. Yeah, go back to the mono jazz recordings on, say, the Blue Note label and maybe you've got a point, but not any more. If you want to be cured of ever going down the hi-fi rabbit hole, then pick up a book called *Perfecting Sound Forever* by Greg Milner.

To be honest, I don't think I can spot the difference, other than a bad digital reissue that's been compressed to the ceiling. The vinyl purist would say I haven't got the correct set-up, but my enjoyment of music doesn't depend solely on whether I have silver speaker wire or not. OK, I certainly don't want to listen via a pair of crappy earbuds, but the musical experience is, for me, more about the context rather than the 'nth degree' quality.

A live gig is obviously the ultimate experience, regardless of the precision or muddiness of the sound. It's also more of an event if you're at a gig with like-minded friends. But when it comes to listening to a record on my own, my own preference – especially for a first audition – is not to listen too intently . . . or rather, not to be positioned at the exact midpoint between two high-end speakers. Not because I can't hear the benefits of such deluxe listening environments, but because especially on a first listen, I just want the experience to be about the impact of the music itself, rather than the precise details of how I'm listening to it.

That's probably why two of my favourite places to listen to music are in the bath and in the car. In both cases, the sound quality isn't perfect, but it's probably more to do with what part of my brain I'm listening with. I reckon my subconscious ear is better suited to listening than my analytical brain, especially when it comes to new music. Even with a record I know inside out like Gong's amazing album *You*, my favourite memory of listening to it was while playing online poker and winning a nice few quid as Daevid Allen's pixies wove their hidden magic on my opponents and the pot was pushed in my direction.

Recently, Kavus and I were chatting away and I said that it's funny how if you asked everyone if they liked music, they'd pretty much all say yes. But there are a significant minority of people - scientists estimate between 3 and 5 per cent - who suffer from 'musical anhedonia', which is an inability to feel any kind of pleasure from music.

On the other side of the coin, the fact that you're still reading our book at this late stage indicates a strong likelihood that you're hyperhedonic as far as music is concerned (and I envy you if you have the synaesthesia gene as a bonus ball). The stronger a musical hyperhedonic you are, I suppose the better the auditory and reward parts of your brain are linked. You're more likely to hear music in your head and feel chills and goosebumps stimulated by particular sounds or songs. You're more likely to be a musician, want to go to concerts and to listen to a wider range of music than is considered 'normal'. Welcome to the fucking club . . . as if you didn't already know you were in it!

From my own carefully monitored and entirely reliable study of my previous job, assuming the scientists are correct, 3 to 5 per cent of snooker players should be musically illiterate. To be honest, I reckon that's a conservative estimate. Perhaps the hedonistic snooker player gets his or her serotonin from a different pool. I must admit, when I was in competition mode, I naturally suppressed my musical intake and certainly didn't listen to music when I practised or in preparation for a match. So could it be that sports competitors are more inclined to musical anhedonia than the average Joe? I've certainly heard a few musical recommendations from premiership footballers that have suggested as much.

The idea that I might be the exception that proves the rule isn't one that I've ever had a problem with. The probable truth of this proposition was never more firmly underlined than a decade ago, when a new promoter and entrepreneur took over at snooker's helm. My mate Barry Hearn is a borderline musical anhedonist (don't worry, he'll never get this far through the book!), but he knows about TV and entertainment and proceeded to ask players in the World Championship to choose their walk-on music.

I've already mentioned what Ken Doherty and Mark Williams subjected us to, and most of the other players' choices were also just the obvious routine inspirational stuff you'd expect: the *Rocky* and *Superman* theme tunes, 'Simply the Best', 'Don't Stop Me Now' . . . you get the general idea. I was still playing at the time and while I'd always thought that idea of walking out to 'euphoric' music, dressed in a waistcoat and bow tie, and then proceeding to just rearrange balls on a table was something to be discouraged, I had to choose something . . . otherwise the officials were going to pick a U2 track for me! I briefly considered Stealers Wheel's 'Stuck in the Middle with You' for its very apt lyrics before finally settling on 'Anaphase II' from Art Zoyd's album *Nosferatu*.

Admittedly, this isn't the catchiest of numbers. The first time I heard it I thought it was music meant to be listened to lying on a sofa having a cry wank with a bottle of sleeping pills in the other hand, and that's speaking as a fan (of Art Zoyd, not the other activities). But given snooker's all-ages demographic, I thought there might still be a couple of people in the crowd who had watched the first ever vampire film directed by F.W. Murnau when it originally came out in 1922.

Surely they'd appreciate Art Zoyd's 1990 soundtrack interpretation of this silent film, especially as 'Anaphase II' is the scary part (or was back then) where Max Schreck appears at the bedroom window of his bride-to-be. It was only a brief twenty-second clip of the track, but in 2010, I walked down the stairs into the Crucible arena to play the defending world champion John Higgins, with the massive synth bass of Patricia Dallio shaking the table legs, totally psyched up to play the role of the undead and hopefully sink my teeth into John's jugular. John wasn't on top form that day (having had to walk 500 miles to the table), and in the best and most rewarding performance of my career, I won the match. Back in my dressing room, after I'd calmed down, Barry Hearn turned to me and said, 'Davis! What the fuck was that walk-on shit!? Can't you choose something better for the next round?'

Sadly, my vampire powers didn't last. After two sessions of the best of twenty-five quarter finals, I re-emerged for the start of the third session 12–4 behind, effectively walking out for Neil Robertson to ease a pointed wooden stake into my heart. 'Anaphase II' didn't seem quite so menacing and the crowd clapped more in condolence than enthusiasm. Backstage, prior to walking on, I'd asked if I could switch to the *Steptoe and Son* theme tune, but to no avail, as the Wi-Fi wasn't that great back in 2010.

Chapter 30

Leonard Cohen

Kavus

Throughout my twenties, I didn't feel any different from when I'd just left home, but turning thirty seemed daunting. What exactly did I have to show for being a grown-up? A string of bands and relationships I'd formed over the previous decade that hadn't amounted to much. I wanted to get into my thirties without any of the baggage I'd been carrying.

From the age of seventeen, I'd always had a girlfriend, jumping from one relationship every few years to another. Now, at twenty-nine, free from the commitment of bands or a partner, I absorbed myself in writing and recording. I'd been given a digital eight-track machine and inspired by a song called 'Blue Junction' in the dog days of Monsoons – the first song I'd ever written that I could perform by myself, just voice and guitar – I planned on a self-produced, self-recorded solo album.

I managed about three months of being single before I got in touch with Dawn and arranged to meet up. Throughout the time we'd known each other, we'd say, 'We're going to end up together, aren't we?' There was no one else I'd rather spend the rest of my life with and I didn't want to wait until we were forty. We went out for a drink and shortly afterwards, ended up together.

When I wasn't working or seeing Dawn, all I wanted to do was write and record in my room. I was running a cracked copy of Cubase on an Atari that was synched up to my digital eight-track. Even with this relatively modest set-up, there was so much to learn. It was a liberation from being in a band. I could record anything I thought up and have it go as I heard it in my head.

Heartbreak Hotel was falling to bits, though. The roof leaked and we were so behind on the rent that the letting agents had no pressing incentive to get it fixed. One time when Dawn stayed over, she had her rollerblades and leather jacket nicked from the boot of her car. I was also getting tired of having my recording work interrupted by the regular influx of friends knocking on the door at all hours on the way to or from Zen Arcade or the Rochy. Laurie bailed first. Captain and I considered getting someone else in, but there wasn't too much appealing about the old place now. The nineties were over and I didn't want to live in a dilapidated party house any more. Dawn's suggestion was, 'I think you move in with me now.' So I said goodbye to Stoke Newington and we moved into a small two-bedroom basement flat in Clapton, only a few roads away from where Iron Maiden's Dave Murray and Adrian Smith had grown up.

I set up my studio in the back room and renamed it 'The Cop's Dream'. From here on in, whenever Tim was in London we'd drag the futon into The Cop's Dream and it would become his London base.

Tim's girlfriend, Jo Spratley, had found them a large bungalow in Coombe Bissett, near Salisbury, on a beautiful piece of wooded farmland with plenty of room to set up Apollo 8 and run the Cardiacs shop. 'Treat this place like your own,' Tim would say whenever we were over. There were plenty of spare rooms, and Jo and Tim had made the place look eccentrically homely. It would be our country retreat from London. Their rent was considerably cheaper than our flat in Clapton, too.

Now Dawn was back on the scene, the fantastic dynamic that was Tim, Dawn and me had returned. It made no difference that Dawn and I were a couple now.

After enduring horrifying turbulence on the plane on our way to Crete for a holiday, I white-knuckled the hand rest and vowed that if I made it alive out of this bucking metal death-tube, I'd ask Dawn to marry me. The following morning, after a couple of shots of raki, the Cretan spirit, I popped the question. My thinking was that we'd have a further ten days to change our minds without anyone other than us being any the wiser.

Dawn and I were wed in the treehouse of Tim's garden in July 2003. Dan Chudley was my best man. There were no long speeches. Dan's was merely, 'In fifteen years of knowing this bloke, this is the first time I've been able to get a word in edgeways. Live long, die young and don't fear the prog.' While Dawn's dad managed: 'I feel like I'm not so much gaining a son as a full head of hair.'

On return from our honeymoon in Madeira, Tim asked me if I wanted to play guitar in Cardiacs. Between 1977 and 1983, Cardiacs had recorded three cassette albums, The Obvious Identity, Toy World *and* The Seaside, *which had only been available at gigs. He'd never been especially happy with the recordings or the performance on the original three cassettes and wanted Cardiacs to play all the songs, thirty-three in total, over the course of three nights at The Garage that October. The plan was to record all three performances for release as two live albums. Including encores (one classic from elsewhere in their repertoire each night), that meant learning thirty-six songs – thirty-six Cardiacs songs.*

Setting his musical stall out from the very beginning, Tim Smith started Cardiacs as Cardiac Arrest when he was sixteen. Although still just a teenager, all the ideas that would grow into the later eighties albums were present in his early work, albeit in a much more frantic, post-punk form. Tim had invented his own harmonic language. He'd taught himself to read music while still at school by following the score to The Who's Quadrophenia. *From that point onwards, until he started working exclusively on computer in the mid-nineties, Tim scored every piece of music he ever wrote, to the point of even including a separate stave for the aerosol can part on 'A Little Man and a House'.*

While I'd learned to read and write music a little at school, I was never fluent and, having never used this skill since, had almost completely forgotten it by this point. Apart from the odd cover version and a short-lived stint of playing Pogues' songs with Spider Stacey's band The Vendettas *(but that's another story), I'd never sat down and worked on anyone else's music before. I'd always seen the guitar primarily as a tool for making up my own tunes.*

Once the concerts were announced, all three nights sold out quickly (Cardiacs usually headlined The Astoria in Charing Cross Rd, so The Garage at 600 was a relatively small gig). The gigs were booked for the middle of October – it was now August. By day, I was working as part of a team renovating and decorating an opulent flat in Knightsbridge. Evenings were dedicated to learning the material.

The first song I looked at was 'As Cold as Can Be in an English Sea' -one of my favourite early Cardiacs tunes. As Cold as Can Be was an early indication of what the band would become. It was relatively epic, with a number of sections, so was as good a place to start as any. I learned the entire tune chord by chord, riff by riff. The Pause and Cue button of my CD player had never enjoyed so much use.

Tim wrote using major and minors almost exclusively - he used to joke about the 'snazzy chords' in my songs - so if I thought something sounded like a ninth or a seventh, it was probably another instrument making it seem that way, which made identifying ambiguous chords easier. Once I'd worked out the parts, I spent the rest of the evening running the song over and over. The following morning, before leaving for work, I ran the tune a couple of times just to make sure it had gone in.

That night, I attempted 'Hope Day', a fairly complex song from The Seaside. *I'd had a few ideas, particularly playing the fast keyboard melody before the breakdown on guitar. I rang Tim and asked him if that would be OK: 'Fucking hell . . . if you can manage it.' It would require a bit of practice, but it wasn't beyond the realms of possibility. By 10 p.m., I had the whole song nailed. I had no idea I could play like that.*

The following night I added another, then on Thursday I learned three relatively more straightforward tunes, the proto-Voivod 'Scratching Crawling Scrawling', 'Icky Qualms' and the first Cardiac Arrest *single 'A Bus for a Bus on the Bus'.*

Each Saturday Jim, Bob and I would convene at Tim's place and spend the weekend perfecting the songs as a band. My guitar playing improved no end during those two intense months and I discovered a lot about myself, specifically my capacity to retain musical information, and about the nature of short-term memory, too. Learning by ear, I was surprised at the tricks my mind unconsciously invented.

One of the hardest parts to master was a long string of notes played high up the neck over a continuous chord cycle during the instrumental break of 'Hello Mr Minnow', an unreleased song I'd never heard before. There was a point midway where I kept hitting the wrong note. In order to train myself to get it right, I'd have to start the entire section from the beginning. Whenever I passed the sticky point correctly, uninvited, the chef's hat from the Peek Freans biscuits logo would appear in my mind. Always. Similarly, after a string of chords in 'Gina Lollabrigida' (her name was spelled wrong but no-one seemed to notice) a particular C major would trigger the word 'LION'.

To get the best possible versions for the live recording, we'd play all the material over the first two nights and anything we weren't completely happy with we'd play again on night three. All three gigs would feature a different classic Cardiacs track as an encore. 'Big Ship' would be the first – one of the band's most well-known and beloved tunes with an anthemic, hymn-like singalong at the end. On night two, we'd finish with 'Dirty Boy'.

When Cardiacs released Sing To God in 1996 and I first heard 'Dirty Boy', which opened disc two, it was the song I'd always wanted Led Zeppelin's 'Stairway to Heaven' to be. 'Dirty Boy' was a rocket to eternity – if not the indisputable proof of a god, then at the very least clear evidence of another dimension. It isn't necessarily my favourite Tim Smith composition – they're all my favourites – but in terms of sheer scale, power, magnificence, bombast and total gloriousness, it's unbeatable.

It may or may not be a song about wanking, but it definitely is a hymn to eternity and besides, aren't they the same thing? If everything is happening all at once and of equal significance, if the sacred and divine are present in every single moment, in every atom of our being, if both the big bang and sitting on a wet park bench are of the same importance, as I truly believe they are, then surely by extension, a song about masturbation can also be the most profoundly cosmic slab of ecclesiastic, slow-motion clairvoyant rock so far imagined.

With an opening riff that borrows from Alice Cooper's 'I'm Eighteen', the two long verses that follow are a refracting prism of key changes and modulations over which a star-etched melody shoots ever upwards. A terrifying and exhilarating bridge ascending and expanding, growing more luminous, now bursting with light, until the final, desperate words, increased in fervour for being doubled an octave above by the *remarkably inhuman voice of Claire Lemmon. 'Hold his mouth and stop him breathing. Over and out' finally explodes into the most hallowed three-chord coda of the ages. The word 'out' hits a high E stretched over two and a half minutes – take that, Bill Withers – made out of voices, twenty stacked tremolo'd acoustic guitars and oscillating with the first, last and everything you truly dig. The absolute numinous spark of all creation and all destruction; Kali, Anubis, Allah, Thor, Jehovah, Zeus, J.R. 'Bob' Dobbs, the atom bomb and LSD all condensed into a single vibrating frequency, under which an E major, A♭ minor and C♯ major riff cycled to infinity. All of life – the terror and joy, fear and heartbreak, the unspeakable beauty and crushing sadness of the world had been crammed into the codas of 'The Whole World Window' and 'The Everso Closely Guarded Line' – before, but with 'Dirty Boy' Tim Smith took on the universe, the very nature of existence itself. It was devastating.*

Over and out.

'This is the one song we can't fuck up,' said Tim, to himself as much as Jim, Bob and me. 'I mean the others, if we fluff a chord or make a mistake, so what? It's punk rock, innit. But this, we have to get right.'

Although he claimed not to be, Tim was the most superstitious person I've ever known. I'd heard about the piss test, it was a Cardiacs ritual dating back years, based on one of Tim's many half-cocked theories. The idea was to get as drunk as humanly possible, absolutely fucking arseholed, then attempt to play the set. This wasn't a 'let's see if we can still remember everything after a few drinks' run-through – Bob wouldn't touch a drop before gigs – it was getting completely, borderline hallucinations, paralytic. The psychology behind the piss test was that it doesn't matter how badly you do, once you've done the piss test, it 'glues' the songs into your brain. Of course it does.

We began drinking from midday during rehearsal, heading to the Fox & Goose late afternoon, where we continued hammering it until closing time, at which point we took a cab back to Tim's place. Guitars were dropped, microphone stands knocked over, cables pulled out, but although the songs were unplayably fast and the entire repertoire was over in an ear-ringing blur, we got through it.

The following morning, with crippling hangovers, we played the set perfectly. As conversation turned to what this new line-up might wear, Tim announced that he saw me in a kilt. 'Look!' he said, opening his laptop hopefully. 'There's one I've seen on eBay already.' But no amount of his flattery and charm could sway me. I'd take a bullet for that prick, but I drew the line at a kilt. When the big night at The Garage finally came, Jim and I wore a black suit and trousers with magisterial red sashes and thin black ties made from curtain cord, while Tim, as always in his massive Crombie that didn't even belong to him, looked like the headmaster.

The piss test had worked splendidly. All three shows were insane, including the all-important second-night encore of 'Dirty Boy', with Claire Lemmon and Melanie Woods from Sidi Bou Said joining us for additional vocals. The Cardiacs' Special Garage Concerts *were released as two albums in October 2005 and thankfully, extremely well received by 'the kidz with a zed'. That November, we headed off on a jaunt across England in preparation for a final date at The Astoria, which was being filmed by a large eight-camera crew for a later DVD release.*

Since being demoted from crew member to full-time Cardiac (the band were paid less than the crew!), I bought my dream guitar – a Gretsch White Falcon. I'd wanted one ever since I saw Matthew Ashman play his on Top of the Pops *with Bow Wow Wow. I'd play the Falcon exclusively for the next fifteen years. It would go into Cardiacs lore as my 'expensive guitar'.*

With the addition of Cathy Harabaras and Melanie Woods, both on vocals and percussion, this expanded line-up, stately presentation and emphasis on the more ostentatious material inaugurated a new era for the band – different again from the classic six-piece of the eighties that had drawn me in and the thrashier, stripped-down nineties quartet that I watched from the side of the stage. The millennial Cardiacs had their own identity: bold and imperious, lofty and confident – this was a fresh chapter and I felt honoured to be a part of it.

The 'Ditzy Scene' EP was released in 2007, ahead of an eleven-date UK tour. Without discussing it with the band, Tim had blown the entire budget on hiring a top-of-the-range tour bus. Excited as I was by the prospect of travelling in a vehicle previously used by Steps, the bombshell at the final rehearsal that the band would be paid £15 per gig came as something of a surprise. With no savings, I was living hand to mouth on the proceeds of decorating. I was incredulous.

'Jesus, Tim, you've got to be fucking joking. This won't even cover my rent!'

'Oh, come on, Kavy. It's a holiday, innit.'

Holiday, my eye. Not wanting to embark on a tour with a bad atmosphere, I let it lie but was taken aback by Tim's apparent lack of consideration, although to be fair, the tour bus was amazing.

As we played the first show in Brighton, there was a sense that a change was in the air. After years of being lambasted or just plain ignored by the British music press, ahead of the tour, the NME called us 'indie legends'. The crowds were large and responsive. Jim said, 'In thirty years of being in this band, it never felt like this.' Something had definitely changed. Maybe Cardiacs' time was finally coming.

As Cardiacs entered their fourth decade, Tim told me he wanted us to start writing together. I had twenty years' experience of collaborating with Dan, of stretching or retracting ideas, and the thought of now doing it with Tim made me giddy. Look where the bent path had led me! I was playing in my favourite band, with one of my closest friends, someone I regarded as a rare genius, and we were going to write music together. We'd spend long evenings talking up great plans. The album we were having such a great time making was just the beginning. We'd make a film – half fake documentary and half dream – and an album of Neil Young-ish songs, or at least our version of Neil Young-ish songs, and we'd release an album that just contained one long, gradually evolving epic piece called simply 'The Alphabet Business Concern'.

Every time we had a new idea, Tim would get out his big yellow folder and write notes. Each night over the dining table, the folder would come out and continued to expand with musical excerpts, drawings and storyboards, interesting turns of phrases and detailed descriptions of ideas for songs.

To get the ball rolling on the forthcoming album, Tim had given me three CDs of music, in excess of thirty tunes. Mainly, they consisted of keyboard chords over a basic programmed drum track with occasional

guitar and him singing the melodies as 'Blah, blah, blah, blah . . .
On-the-ground. Blah, blah, blah, blah, Ivy-dog' in lieu of words. I
listened a few times, picked my favourites, which became the basis for
the next record. Bob put down the drums and, in late spring, I returned
to the Apollo 8 studios I'd recently helped renovate and expand for a
joyful few weeks of recording the guitars.

On 23 June 2008, Cardiacs headed up to BBC Manchester to play for
Marc Riley at BBC Radio 6 Music, the third session since I'd been in the
band. After the performance, Tim, Jim, Jane and I decided to hit the pub
and hang out with Marc. We didn't leave Manchester until after closing
time. Tim and I sat in the back seat of Jim's car and continued to drink
wine throughout the journey back to Salisbury. We were both horribly
drunk and I remember almost nothing about the conversation – except
I finally let him have it about the situation with band wages, which
had been bothering me since the tour. 'I will always want to play in
this band,' I told him, 'and you know I'm not a fucking breadhead, but
£15 a gig? If we're selling out The Astoria, you've at least got to cover
my rent, man.'

Tim and I had never so much as disagreed before. I wish I'd never
brought it up – not then, anyway. Never talk about serious stuff when
drunk. I can't remember how we resolved it, but I know the journey
ended with us cuddling and kissing. I'm sure Jane and Jim – sober in
the front – remember the whole embarrassing incident, but I'm glad to
have forgotten it.

The following morning, I woke with the kind of nauseously churning
hangover that could only be caused by the unholy triptych of beer,
whiskey and wine. Naturally, Tim was still fast-a-bloody-sleep and I
didn't bother waking him to say goodbye. Suzy, his then girlfriend,
offered to drive me to Salisbury station. As we left the house, two sets
of colourful hand bells arrived that Tim had ordered to feature on the
new album.

It's not so much the physical pain of a hangover that I find so hard
now than the mean, dark spectre of guilt, regret and self-loathing,
poisoning every memory of the previous night. The train journey was
hellish – flashes of the argument kept returning to detonate bombs of

remorse. Once at home, I lay on the sofa hoping Tim had forgotten most of the conversation, too.

That afternoon, he sent me a text: 'I'm on the train – you coming to MBV, then?'

My Bloody Valentine had just reformed and were playing the last of a four-night run at the Roundhouse in Camden. Loveless was a favourite album and I'd never seen them live before. What's more, Bic was now Kevin Shields' guitar tech. Although he told us he could only get one of us on the guest list, I could have come along to the pub beforehand at least, and I'm sure I could have blagged my way in, especially with Tim onside. As it was, there was no way I was even getting up to go to the kitchen.

I texted back: 'After last night? You're joking, aren't you?'

Where would he be staying? Oh well, he's a grown-up, I'm sure he'll have something planned.

At around 4 a.m. the following morning, the landline in our bedroom rang.

'Hey, Kavy. Can I come over? I think I'm going to get into trouble.'
I knew it. I didn't mind. What kind of trouble, though?
'Yeah, of course. I'll see you in a bit.'
And that was that.
From the bed, Dawn asked, 'Who was it?'
I rolled my eyes. 'Fucking Tim, of course.'

I dragged the futon from the living room into my studio, put on a clean sheet and quilt, turned my mobile on and went back to bed.

At that time of night, a car from Camden shouldn't take more than half an hour.

By half five, there was no sign of him. I imagined him sat up by Clapton Pond at the top of our road, probably having a blub about how lovely the sunlight on the water looked or something. Then my phone rang – it was Suzy. Why would she be ringing me at this hour? She sounded completely spun out. She'd received a call from Tim's phone – and it wasn't Tim. She didn't know what was going on. Something was wrong.

I rang Tim and a stranger answered. He sounded sketchy. Tim was *round at his place, had fallen asleep and couldn't be woken. He wanted him out. 'Give me your address,' I told him, 'and we'll come and get him.' But the guy was totally freaking out and I struggled to make sense of what he was saying. Now I was panicking, too. I managed to establish that they were in Somers Town, near Camden, but little else. Then he hung up.*

Hearing the commotion at the other end of the flat, Dawn was awake and out of bed.

I rang back a few times before he answered again. He sounded even more desperate.

'Your mate's going into cardiac! He's going into cardiac!'

Jesus-fucking-Christ!

'Call an ambulance. Please, just call an ambulance!'

'I have, I have. I don't know what's happening! He's going blue.'

Then he hung up again.

I kept ringing back but now got nothing.

There were three hospitals near Camden. Time was moving in slow motion as I searched for the numbers online. With trembling hands and heart pounding like the fucking clappers, I tried the Royal Free in Hampstead first.

Next, I rang the UCH in Euston.

'Has a man been admitted? He's forty-six years old, about sixteen stone, with messy grey hair and a bit of a beard. He'll be wearing combat trousers, brown leather hiking boots, probably a grey T-shirt that says "Cardiacs" and a plaid shirt over that.'

'Yes, he's here.'

'Is he alive or dead?'

'He's alive.'

I grabbed my helmet, jumped on the back of Dawn's Vespa and we took off.

Tim was a force of nature. A beautiful, benign presence who would float into any room and light it up. You'd happily walk over a mile of broken glass for that persuasive smile. A man who had been central to my life before we'd ever met, before I'd even kissed a girl. A magician who enchanted me into his orbit from 200 miles away, who gifted me, as he had with all his friends, the adventure of a lifetime.

At the entrance to UCH, he was waiting for me. Surrounded by hospital staff, he looked so fragile, so mortal. I'd never been more terrified.

Oh, Tim.

Laid out, horizontal and lifeless.

I looked down upon sixteen stone of useless flesh.

I wanted to say, 'Do something! Don't you know who that is?'

But they knew. He was Alan Smith. It said so on the clipboard at the foot of his stretcher.

And then a blur of cigarettes and frantic phone calls.

'Is he going to be all right?'

'I don't know. I don't know what's going on.'

Jim and Jane arrived next, as did Suzy. At some point, Mark Cawthra (a childhood friend of Tim's and one of the original Cardiacs line-up) joined us, too. My memories of the next few days are pretty nebulous.

I went in to see him and he was packed in ice to keep his temperature down, I remember that.

And I remember Jim saying, 'When he comes round, we'll form an orderly queue to punch his lights out.'

The next time we were allowed in, he had a ventilator breathing for him. He'd pull through, though. He always did. Tim was blessed.

By the following day he was breathing for himself and his registrar, Lars, came to speak to us. He'd had a heart attack. Or a stroke. Or both. He'd effectively died for a couple of minutes but had been revived.

'He's been very lucky,' he told us.

But then we knew that – Tim was the luckiest cunt in the world.

As he explained Tim's miraculous recovery, I could feel relief like sunlight breaking through the dark clouds of dread. Of course, this is all part of Tim's crazy story. I saw us again in the back lounge of the bus, in a booth at the Rochy or sat behind the mixing desk in Apollo 8. 'Hey, Tim. That time you died, though. Jesus, man, you had us all so scared, you fucking idiot.'

Lars wasn't done, though.

'But as to whether Tim will ever be able to get out of bed and get himself a can of lager from the fridge . . . well, we just don't know.'

Katharine Blake and I had first met properly in 2001 after we were both hired as 'performing extras' (her violin, me guitar) for a marriage scene on a horrible ITV kids programme called Gypsy Girl. *We've been close friends ever since. I knew her from Miranda Sex Garden and later, I'd go on to tour and record for a few years in her ensemble, The Mediaeval Baebes, until I got too busy with Gong to do anything else. In 2008, though, I was playing guitar and cuatro in the brief live outing of her solo project. We'd been booked to play at the last day of Glastonbury Festival, Sunday, 29 June.*

After five days at UCH, and being assured there was nothing I could do, I honoured my commitment – I never blow out gigs – and got in the van heading to Somerset that morning, grateful to be around a different set of friends; although they knew Tim anyway. Everyone knew Tim. Once we'd sorted out our accreditation, we headed to the Pyramid Stage. Dawn had turned me on to Leonard Cohen when we first got together and he was due to play that afternoon. His set was the only thing I wanted to watch. The sun was out and we seated ourselves halfway down the hill in front of the stage as he opened with 'Dance Me to the End of Love'.

He played 'Bird on a Wire' followed by 'Everybody Knows' – this was one hell of a set. The sound was clear, the arrangements magnificent and the band terrific. From 'Tower of Song' to my favourite, 'Suzanne', the timbre of his 73-year-old baritone was much richer than on the original recordings, which gave me hope for what the NME *once described as my 'spooked bark'.*

And then he started 'Hallelujah'. A lovely song, granted, but from the Jeff Buckley version to the countless lesser ones, I'd heard it enough. Or so I thought. Before he'd reached the first chorus, I felt it coming. Not now, you stupid fucker. But it advanced closer anyway. Come on, though, on this song? Surrounded by all these people? It was so corny, I thought, but like trying to hold back an orgasm, or vomiting, I was powerless to stop. It was irreversible and inevitable.

He hit the chorus and I bawled my stupid fucking short-sighted eyes out.

The impossible fact that we could all be there, then – beneath this setting Avalonian sun, spellbound under the power of a music so beautiful – was just too sad and miraculous. A sea of people, a mass of consciousness, each one of us the lead in our own weird film. Today a tragedy, tomorrow a comedy or a romance. Sometimes, subtitled, slow-moving and beautifully shot, pregnant with pathos and sentiment, or else a garish, brightly lit porn film on videotape, each day a different script or genre but all with the same central character playing out the action, loss, redemption and mortality – at times the wisecracker, but periodically the tongue-tied stooge.

This was the heroic part in Leonard's film, where he comes out of retirement and sings his best-known song during a career-defining concert at Glastonbury; the pitiful moment in mine, where I blub like a helpless child for the fate of my dear friend to the soundtrack of 'Hallelujah'; and the visual punchline of the scene, where the random guy watching Leonard Cohen looks over to see a hokey emotional twat weeping his eyes out.

Each of us falling in love or falling to pieces, fucking up and then fucking up again. All the mean, selfish things I'd ever done and would continue to do, all the hurtful things I'd said that could never be unsaid, the times where I'd brought happiness and joy that I wished could have been more frequent. Each one of us living through a carnival of tragedy and ecstasy, of guilt, regret and laughter until the day when we don't any more. Regardless of what you think of the view, this was heaven. It had always been heaven and back in London, one of its angels, whose gentle voice I would only hear again in my dreams, lay crippled on a hospital bed he would never really leave.

Afterwords

(Kavus and Steve)

Kavus

From the UCH in London, Tim was moved to Salisbury Hospital, where his condition seemed to worsen. Eventually, he moved to Glenside, a residential hospital for the rehabilitation of patients with neurological conditions and brain injury, but we all felt his dystonia was too great for what the place had to offer. Tim's mind was very much intact, just the same as ever, but he was unable to speak. Instead, he communicated via a laminated alphabet attached to a cushion. I used to call it his Ouija board. Trapped in his broken body and communicating slowly, the determination and effort on Tim's part to try to improve his condition was extraordinary. 'My hands are cunts,' he once finally spelled out after a particularly difficult session.

On a good day, his muscles would relax, the spasms would lessen and he was able to fly around the Ouija board deftly. When spelling things out, he never used abbreviations or shortcuts. He'd pepper his conversations with expletives, qualifications ('sort of thing' and 'I suppose what I'm trying to say is') and poetic turns of phrase that, while adding a further five minutes to the time it took him to tell you something, really felt like having a conversation with the old Tim. And he'd still shake with laughter over any infantile observation about his condition I might make.

On a bad day, it was so hard to see him struggling and be powerless to help. It might take him a frustrating hour, punctuated by constant spasms and seizures, just to explain that he needed his arm to be moved, or his chair to be adjusted. It was even harder to leave him behind when we had to go. Although I was always glad to spend time with him, visits were often difficult. Sometimes I'd be grateful when he fell asleep so I didn't have to face the desperate look of disappointment that came with an 'I've got to get back to London, man,' announcement.

Although it was obvious he'd never walk, sing or play the guitar again, he'd always wanted to return home and continue working on music, assisted and surrounded by his friends. Sales from Cardiacs albums and merchandise continued to pay the rent, which meant Tim could still come home for a few hours. He'd invite the whole gang for parties, or we'd put on special gigs for him in his front room.

While it was always lovely to be hanging out with him back at the old house again, these were melancholy-soaked times. Tim's condition had cast such a long shadow over all of us and our lives, which had been orbiting his extraordinary existence, were different now. By this time Dawn and I were parents - our daughter, Sima, was born in October 2009. I have musician friends who relegated playing and writing back to a hobby once they had children, deciding the responsibility called for a proper job, but it had the opposite effect on me. I wanted her to grow up and know her father as someone who was committed to his art, not just a decorator who mucked about with some funny chords in his spare time.

As a result, since her birth, I've been more prolific writing, recording and touring with various groups or on my own than at any time before. Not that it was always easy - I was haunted by the spectre of depression while making The Unravelling, Knifeworld's second album, during 2012. I'd holed myself up in my little studio, now in a shed in the garden renamed 'Skyhenge', overwhelmed by the enormity of the record I was trying to make. Against a backdrop of my new role as a father, generating very little income, I struggled to complete it. The worry of what the future held for Tim didn't help, either. Because of the weekly radio show with Steve, Monday evening became a highlight. As well as giving me respite from this seemingly unscalable mountain I'd given myself to climb, it was also because of the show that Daevid Allen asked me to join Gong.

Perhaps it was validation from the charming old wizard, but almost immediately, things started to look up. My ever more unwieldy octet Knifeworld finally got that elusive record deal. I saw this less as me becoming more successful than a dying music industry meeting me on *its way down – but still, our difficult second album was finally released in 2014, to a five-star review in* The Guardian, *whatever that's worth. Shortly afterwards, we were touring Europe. DJ'ing with Steve at festivals and venues across the UK, regularly sorting out the heads from the haircuts, coupled with extensive international touring with Gong, meant that I was finally able to put my decorator's overalls back under the bed. And then, born out of that marvellous day of happenstance in January 2018, The Utopia Strong occurred.*

Steve

During the period of time that Kavus was unravelling, I wasn't exactly having a ball myself. I was still a professional snooker player and while I was continuing to turn in the odd uplifting performance, generally the balls were hitting far too many cushions and not enough holes for my liking. My father's health was deteriorating and, in hindsight, I was only playing to give him some enjoyment on the odd occasion I made it to the TV stages of an event. If circumstances had been different, I might well have retired a few years earlier than I did. The radio show was such an important thing for both of us. It was our little fantasy world. I don't think either of us were totally aware of each other's situations when we rolled up each week for the show. We had a shedload of fun and the two hours used to fly by. We were happy to forget any of our problems outside the studio, even though they were of the First World variety.

I've always seen Kavus as such an uplifting force. His exuberance for music and whatever he's immersed in is infectious. The only other person I've ever known who possesses that aura swirling around them is my great friend Barry Hearn.

Once we started venue and festival DJ'ing, it felt like a new lease of life and enthusiasm had been bestowed upon me. However, The Utopia Strong was another league above that. I won six World Snooker Championships, but no bullshit, being involved in the band with Kavus and Mike York and what we've achieved has made me as proud and as happy as anything I've ever done as a snooker player.

Kavus

From the first time we met at that Magma gig in Paris in 2005, music was all Steve wanted to talk about, and once I'd introduced him to my circle of hedonistic nerds, they took to each other completely. His notoriety and success at his other job never really came into it. Being with Steve was always like being with another musician. He may not have dressed like one, but he thought and spoke like one, so the transition into him becoming one has been far less of a surprise to me than it has been to him.

He's always had that same easy-going, laid-back attitude to everything other than music, on which subject he's opinionated, brash and cocksure. Quite right. I never envisaged we'd be making music together but then, I never envisaged much of what this crazy life has thrown up.

Steve

Having now experienced performing music on a stage (albeit to a small degree), as well as playing competitive sport, I suppose I'm quite well placed to see connections and contrasts between these two activities. One thing common to both is that you're putting on a performance.

In a world final, you psych yourself up for the superhuman battle that's about to commence, convince yourself you're Rocky Balboa and often surprise yourself at how well you withstand the pressure of the Crucible heat. I was usually at my best when I'd generated a healthy amount of intensity prior to walking out, channelling the nerves into resolve and focus. Bizarrely, there was nothing worse than not being nervous. Occasionally, when a match wasn't in the highest-profile tournament on the calendar, I was able to induce this mental state by some form of self-hypnosis, akin to how a stage actor gets into the role prior to walking out.

Gigs feel the same and I think what's apparent is that regardless of your personality offstage, whether you're competing in a sport or playing music in front of an audience, a certain part of your psyche comes to the forefront. It's not exactly an act, but you tap into the hero or extrovert inside you, even if you didn't think you had that in your armoury. During the performance, you're usually flying by the seat of your pants, living in the moment, and I suppose tapping into a huge part of your subconscious brain as your natural instincts come to the fore.

After you come offstage, there are obvious similarities. You're hopefully buzzing from the thrill of the moment and even if you've lost, or had a nightmare gig, that adrenaline is still surging around your body. It takes a good while to come back down to earth.

When you're waiting behind the curtains, perhaps the musician (at least one who isn't improvising to any degree) has more of the mentality of an actor in a stage play, in terms of having a score or a script that they need to have learned. Whereas the sports person is walking out with no real idea what's ahead – ready to improvise – even if they did have some sort of pre-match game plan. This might be why, for me at least, improvising as a musician seems to be less of a stretch.

Because even with a 'still ball' game like snooker, the player has to be very much 'in that moment'. There's no benefit in stewing on what's already happened and it's an absolute no-no to project any further ahead. Even though the 'still ball' games are considered a slightly different mental challenge to the 'reaction' games like tennis or football, the golfer Arnold Palmer nailed it for all sports when he announced that: 'Golf is a game of inches. The most important are the six between your ears.'

Kavus

That's a great point, and one that applies to both improvised and rehearsed music. You have to move on from a mistake, not let it spoil the rest of the gig, which it really can.

I suppose the difference is that in improvised music, no one knows it's a mistake and sometimes it can be better than what you intended to play anyway. Miles Davis said: 'Do not fear mistakes. There are none.' Or, as Eddie Van Halen's father told him, 'If you make a mistake, do it twice and smile.'

Steve

I suspect having time to think can be a potential hindrance in both sport and music. What I do know for certain, though, is that in both disciplines, my brain has felt totally wired. And I bet if you were able to monitor my cerebral activity visually at the time, it would be lit up like a Christmas tree.

I don't have the experience to know if repeating rehearsed music onstage taps into a slightly different part of the brain. I did once read an article proclaiming that for music to be truly improvised, the musician should have no 'learned behaviour' on an instrument. That's getting deep, but if true would mean that The Utopia Strong would involve me blowing bagpipes, Kavus patching a modular synth and, because he's a clever multi-instrumentalist bastard, Mike York would have to be onstage knocking balls around on a table with my cue.

Kavus

Whether solo or part of an ensemble, through-composed or entirely improvised, as the sergeant major giving the orders or as a foot soldier happy to serve, if I'm making music that I think is interesting and worthwhile, then I'm treading the righteous path and obeying the will of the universe.

I love our DJ'ing and evangelising together on the radio shows. But most of all, I'm so grateful that this friendship with Steve has led to a situation in which the three of us, as The Utopia Strong, are able to make music which, I feel, has a real importance. Even after doing this for over thirty years, it still genuinely surprises and rewards me with that most rare and treasured sensation of 'Did we really make this?' when listening back. There are things we've done, especially since recording the first album, that I think get closer to the bullseye - that brief supernatural feeling I first got from that Stray Cats tune - than anything I've done before.

Left to my own devices, I'd never have come up with a unit like The Utopia Strong. But the sheer unlikeliness that this elusive, otherworldly and psychedelic realm could be accessed as a result of working with a household name whose previous foray into music was 'Snooker Loopy' is even more absurd than my joining Cardiacs or fronting Gong and yet completely fitting somehow, too. After a lifetime of writing rehearsal-intensive music, it's been so liberating to compose in real time with two like-minded alchemists. To still have the feeling that your best stuff is yet to come, rather than wallowing in nostalgia for the highs of yesteryear, is the greatest thing you can hope for.

Steve

One of the biggest problems for retired sports people is finding something to fill the void. By the time I'd stopped competing in 2016, I was well past my sell-by date as a force within the game. To announce my retirement, I walked out into the Crucible Theatre with a tear in my eye and the trophy I'd won six times in my career held aloft and received a truly heart-warming standing ovation. My father, who was my wingman throughout my career, had just passed away and it felt like the right time to end that particular journey.

I never knew Tim Smith, but Kavus assures me I'd have loved him. In the lyrics of probably Kavus' most emotional composition – 'This Empty Room Once Was Alive' from the Knifeworld album *The Unravelling* – Kavus calls Tim 'my sweet captain', and rightly so. During his time on the planet, Tim was an amazing pilot of the big ship Cardiacs. The legacy he leaves behind is immense.

I suppose if you were looking at Kavus' and my friendship from the outside, you might point out that we both lost our respective captains around the time that we embarked on this new musical adventure, and that this shaped things. But I wouldn't make too much of that. After all, it would be strange to get to our advanced ages without losing someone dear to us. A more accurate analysis might be that everything is determined by timing and chance, whether it be in business, music or sport. We were drawn together by circumstances (only some of which were out of our control), and Kavus and I proceeded to have another roll of the dice. And guess what? We only went and threw a fucking double six!

Kavus

Steve and Tim are similar in some ways – they're both total anarchists. Despite my disregard for authority, I'm actually pretty uptight and always felt I was something of a goody-goody, worried about getting into trouble or what other people might think.

Like Tim, Steve doesn't give a fuck. Whenever we're together, regardless of what we're doing, everything is just more fun. Because he's so non-judgemental, I've always felt completely relaxed around him. His whole philosophy is 'I just go with the flow', which is infectious. He just has this breezy attitude and never overthinks situations and, like a contact high, that loosens me up too. He really loves getting up to mischief, nothing morally reprehensible of course, but often I'll suggest something naughty or ludicrous that I'd never normally have the balls to see through and the next minute we'll be doing it.

Steve

If your hobby becomes your profession, then you're halfway to paradise. Considering that two of my hobbies have ended up this way, I feel like a very fortunate traveller indeed. The sequence of events that have led to me becoming a musician are unlikely in the extreme, but maybe somehow we determine our own fate, or at the very least encourage a path to evolve.

One thing is for certain – meeting up with Kavus has been an absolute blast. We've had so much fun on the road DJ'ing together and when it seemed like things couldn't get any more enjoyable, we bumped into the beautiful human being that is Mike York and the laughter moved into overdrive. The journey the three of us have been on has been incredible and I'm not only delighted to have been on board, but I'm also thankful that I've made two amazing friends.

Kavus

In October 2018, Tim Smith received the honorary degree of Doctor of Music from the Royal Conservatoire of Scotland. He died following a heart attack on the evening of 21 July 2020 having listened to mixes of the unfinished Cardiacs album earlier that day.

Dr Tim Smith had been due to return home permanently a fortnight later. Before the Covid-19 outbreak of 2020, he and his girlfriend, Emily Jones, were planning a 'Summer Symposium' in the village hall in nearby Coombe Bissett, for all his favourite bands to play. He had asked for The Utopia Strong to be Sunday night headliners.

Appendices

i.

Glastonbury Set List

The Stonebridge Bar, Thursday, 23 June 2016

Weidorje: 'Vilna' (*Weidorje*)

Camberwell Now: 'Speculative Fiction' (*The Ghost Trade*)

Robert Fripp, The League of Gentlemen: 'Inductive Resonance' (*God Save the King*)

Charming Hostess: 'Aish Ye Kdish' (*Punch*)

Captain Beefheart and the Magic Band: 'Tropical Hot Dog Night' (*Shiny Beast [Bat Chain Puller]*)

Battles: 'Non-Violence' (*La Di Da Di*)

The Beatles: 'Tomorrow Never Knows' (*Revolver*)

Mikrokosmos: 'Dark:Warm' (*The Seven Stars*)

Polymorphie: 'Suite N.C. Part 3' (*Voix*)

Squarepusher: 'Baltang Arg' (*Damogen Furies*)

Ozric Tentacles: 'Kick Muck' (*Pungent Effulgent*)

The Gasman: 'Trip' (*Aeriform*)

Véronique Vincent & Aksak Maboul with The Honeymoon Killers: 'Afflux De Luxe' (*Ex-Futur Album*)

Deerhoof: 'Fête D'Adieu' (*Breakup Song*)

OLD: 'Underglass' (*Formula*)

Magma: 'De Futura' (*Üdü Ẁüdü*)

Steve Reich: 'The Four Sections – IV. Full Orchestra' (*The Four Sections / Music for Mallet Instruments, Voices and Organ*)

ii.

Medical Grade Music
an album a week by Kavus Torabi

Aksak Maboul: *Figures*
Beck: *Mutations*
Black Sabbath: *Sabotage*
Bunty Chunks: *Brain EP*
Captain Beefheart and The Magic Band: *Doc at the Radar Station*
Cheer-Accident: *Fear Draws Misfortune*
Valentin Clastrier: *Hérésie*
Alice Coltrane: *Journey in Satchidananda*
Danielson: *Best of Gloucester County*
Don Caballero: *American Don*
Deerhoof: *Offend Maggie*
Bob Drake: *The Skull Mailbox (and Other Horrors)*
Evil Superstars: *Love Is OK*
eX-Girl: *Revenge of Kero Kero*
Foetus: *Hide*
4tRECk: *Je Me Promenade*
Fred Frith: *Speechless*
Gorguts: *Pleiades' Dust*
John Greaves, Peter Blegvad, Lisa Herman: *Kew. Rhone.*
Roy Harper: *Stormcock*
Hatfield and the North: *Hatfield and the North*
Mark Hollis: *Mark Hollis*
Robyn Hitchcock: *I Often Dream of Trains*
Kōenji Hyakkei: *Angherr Shisspa*

MEDICAL GRADE MUSIC

Lost Crowns: *Every Night Something Happens*
Madness: *Keep Moving*
Albert Marcoeur: *Celui Où Y'A Joseph*
Max Tundra: *Parallax Error Beheads You*
Melvins: *Gluey Porch Treatments*
Joni Mitchell: *Hejira*
Moondog: *The German Years 1977-1999*
Naked City: *Torture Garden*
The Necks: *Aether*
News From Babel: *Letters Home*
Nico: *The Marble Index*
Nomeansno: *0+2=1*
North Sea Radio Orchestra: *I a Moon*
OLD: *Formula*
Other Men: *Wake Up Swimming*
Andrew Poppy: *The Beating of Wings*
Prefuse 73: *The Only She Chapters*
The Sea Nymphs: *The Sea Nymphs*
Stars In Battledress: *Secrets and Signals*
Steve Reich: *Octet*
Shudder to Think: *Pony Express Record*
Sun Ra: *Lanquidity*
These New Puritans: *Field of Reeds*
Thumpermonkey: *Sleep Furiously*
Tipographica: *God Says I Can't Dance*
White Noise: *An Electric Storm*
XTC: *Black Sea*
Frank Zappa: *The Yellow Shark*

Medical Grade Music
an album a week by Steve Davis

Please note: on some occasions, the label information points to the best version to obtain when the CD reissue may include extra tracks. In many cases, these are not the original labels.

5UU's: *Hunger's Teeth* (ReR Megacorp)
Ahvak: *Ahvak* (Cuneiform)
Aksak Maboul: *Onze Danses Pour Combattre la Migraine* (Crammed)
Aquaserge: *À L'Amitié* (Chambre404)
Art Zoyd: *Berlin* (In-Possible)
Caterina Barbieri: *Patterns of Consciousness* (Important)
Biosphere & Higher Intelligence Agency: *Polar Sequences* (Biophon)
Biota: *Cape Flyaway* (ReR Megacorp)
Broadcast and The Focus Group: *Investigate Witch Cults of the Radio Age* (Warp)
Dirk 'Mont' Campbell: *Music from a Round Tower* (Resurgence)
Charming Hostess: *Punch* (ReR Megacorp/Ad Hoc)
Guigou Chenevier: *Les Rumeurs de la Ville* (Cuneiform)
Chris Cutler and Lutz Glandien: *Domestic Stories* (ReR Megacorp)
Patricia Dallio: *D'ou vient l'eau des puits?* (MSI)
Datashock: *Kräuter der Provinz* (Bureau B)
Dün: *Eros* (Soleil Zeuhl 33)
Dunaj: *Rosol* (Indies)
Egg: *The Civil Surface* (Caroline)
Fondation: *Les Cassettes 1980-1983* (Bureau B)

Robert Fripp/The League of Gentlemen: *God Save the King* (Editions EG)

Fred Frith/François-Michel Pesenti: *Helter Skelter* (RecRec Music)

Harmonia: *Musik Von Harmonia* (Brain)

Tim Hecker: *Ravedeath 1972* (Kranky)

Heldon: *It's Always Rock 'n' Roll/Electronique Guerilla* (Cuneiform)*

Jack O' The Clock: *How Are We Doing and Who Will Tell Us?* (self-released)

James Holden & The Animal Spirits: *The Animal Spirits* (Border Community)

Hugh Hopper & Alan Gowen: *Two Rainbows Daily* (Cuneiform Rune 77)

Looping Home Orchestra: *Vendeltid* (Krax)

Albert Marcoeur: *Plusieurs Cas de Figure* (Label Frères)

Matching Mole: *March* (Cuneiform)

Piero Milesi: *Modi* (Cuneiform)

Mother Mallard's Portable Masterpiece Co.: *Like a Duck to Water* (Cuneiform)

Nunbient One: *Just Another Dark Age* (Burning Shed)

Palm: *Rock Island* (Carpark)

Pienza Ethnorkestra: *Indiens d'Europe* (Soleil Zeuhl)

James Plotkin: *The Joy of Disease* (Avant)

Prescott: *One Did* (Slowfoot)

Present: *Triskaïdékaphobie* (Cuneiform)

Alec K. Redfearn: *The Quiet Room* (Cuneiform)

Secede: *Vega Libra* (Sending Orbs

Secret Chiefs 3/Ishraqiyun: *Perichoresis* (Web of Mimicry)

Skeletons: *Money* (Tomlab)

Tim Smith: *Tim Smith's Extra Special OceanLandWorld* (The Alphabet Business Concern)

Songs Between Cities and Waterholes: *Songs Between Cities and Waterholes* (Bauta BAR 1001)**

Michael Stearns: *Planetary Unfolding* (Continuum Montage/Sonic Atmospheres)

J.G. Thirlwell & Simon Steensland: *Oscillospira* (Ipecac)
Univers Zero: *Ceux du Dehors* (Cuneiform)
Urban Sax: *Inside* (Urban Noisy)
Vanishing Twin: *The Age Of Immunology* (Fire)
Von Zamla: *1983* (Cuneiform)
David Willey: *Songs from the Hamster Theatre* (Prolific)
Susumu Yokota: *Sakura* (Leaf/Skintone)

* These are Heldon's first and third albums combined as one release via Cuneiform
** This is the expanded version.

iv.

Kavus Torabi Selected Discography

Admirals Hard: *Upon a Painted Ocean* (Believers Roast, 2016)
Believers Roast Presents: *The Exquisite Corpse Game* (Believers Roast, 2013)
Gong: *I See You* (Madfish, 2014)
Gong: *Rejoice! I'm Dead!* (Madfish, 2016)
Gong: *The Universe Also Collapses* (Kscope, 2019)
Guapo: *History of the Visitation* (Cuneiform, 2013)
Guapo: *Obscure Knowledge* (Cuneiform, 2015)
The Holy Family: *The Holy Family* (Rocket Recordings, 2021)
Knifeworld: *Buried Alone (Tales of Crushing Defeat)* (Believers Roast, 2009)
Knifeworld: *The Unravelling* (InsideOut, 2014)
Knifeworld: *Home of the Newly Departed* (Believers Roast, 2015)
Knifeworld: *Bottled out of Eden* (InsideOut, 2016)
The Monsoon Bassoon: *I Dig Your Voodoo* (Weird Neighbourhood, 1999)
Kavus Torabi: *Hip To The Jag* (Believers Roast, 2020)
The Utopia Strong: *The Utopia Strong* (Rocket Recordings, 2019)
The Utopia Strong: *Alphabet of the Magi* (Self-released, 2020)
The Utopia Strong: *Dreamsweeper* (Self-released, 2020)
The Utopia Strong: *Ninth Art* (Self-released, 2021)

V.

Steve's Rig Rundown

This configuration of Eurorack modules was used by me during the Utopia Strong tour in December 2019:

Studio Electronics - Tonestar 2600 (combined VCO, VCF, ADSR and VCA)
Detroit Underground - DU-SEQ (CV and gate sequencer)
2 x Korg - SQ-1 (standalone CV and gate step sequencer)
2 x Intellijel - Dixie II+ (VCO)
WMD/SSF - Pole Zero (Filter and VCA)
Frequency Central - System X Envelope (ADSR)
Qu-Bit Electronix - Chord v2 (Polyphonic VCO)
Abstract Data - Octocontroller (modulation, pattern and clock distributor)
Strymon - Magneto (tape delay)
Mutable Instruments - Ripples (filter and VCA)
Joranalogue Audio Design - *TX2* (stereo balanced line outputs)
Expert Sleepers - Disting Mk 4 (utility module used in quantiser mode)
Intellijel - Mixup (mixer)
Arturia - DrumBrute Impact (standalone drum machine)

Other modules used since first recording in 2018:

Malekko Heavy Industry - Mix 4 (mixer)
2 x Erica Synths/Pico - Drums (drum sampler)
Erica Synths - Black Hole DSP (effects)

MEDICAL GRADE MUSIC

Klavis - Twin Waves (dual digital VCO)
Winter Modular - Eloquencer (CV and gate sequencer)
Noise Engineering - Loquelic Iteritas Percido (combined digital
   VCO and envelope)

vi.

The Top 50

1) Project Null: A Friend Of the People
2) Deforestations: Grapple Of Life
3) Zamvod Décharné: Girl Collapse 1
4) Capricorn Bloodweird: Hand, Hoof & Claw
5) The Nomad Boss: Goin' Modular
6) Bronze Alphabet: Hard Rock Friendship
7) Strobe Talbot: I Bought You a Rifle
8) Quilt: Pierrot Trott
9) Richard Hoodlum: I Tried My Best (To Mentor You)
10) Screams Are His Music: Castle Made out of Pharmaceuticals
11) Clive Salter: Givin' It My Best Shot
12) The Crospic Vainglor: I, Metaphysic
13) Dead and Exactly the Same: Our Alembic Summer
14) Antichrists: She's the Metronome
15) Mass Fatima: Memorial Unfortunate
16) Iron Growl: Annihilate the Druid
17) Roofers: Girl Astronaut
18) Ace Fowler: Mama's Waitin'
19) Bloath Respeculate: Growing Hoarse
20) Cormorant: Bludgeon Me
21) Frankie Crunfe: Drab Establishment (We Attended a)
22) Snout: Battle of Gravity
23) Biro Day: Rehash Majestic
24) Dominique Maze: There's a Male in Here
25) Grope Daguerreotype: I'm Fell Asleep

26) Istanbul: Baghdad
27) Earth Dancer: Guided by Gaia (Live)
28) Guitar Solo: The Infant Still Controls Us
29) Midas: I Fuck You
30) Forgotten Blast Beat: In Sickness I Found Sanctuary
31) Darwin Camelot: Calligraphies of the Unwell
32) The Tonite: Pointless Serenade
33) Duke Vinegar: My Party Sucks
34) Mantivule's Blacklist: Yes, We Know All About Your Bass Player
35) Have Haven't and The Have Nots: Crash My Samson (Tonight)
36) T.H.R.U.S.T.E.R: Dystopian Lust
37) Gregg Reggae: Greggae
38) Men of Granite: Why Is Tomorrow?
39) Roderick Penn: Have a Go on Roderick Penn
40) Val Fisher and Gordon Blackshaw: The Price of Love
41) Tribal Diversity: Who Stole My Teepee?
42) Synthesiser Duel: Dichotomy of Matey
43) Ashlee Tulk: Die Mesmerica
44) Lane 308: Lord, Wyoming
45) Warslave: Soon I Will Be Going to a War
46) Relay Relay: Here Comes Funeral Hornsby
47) Maxamillion Sterbile: BB: 212/F9356T
48) Syndicates feat. Global Rasmussen: The Zealot
49) The Odious Spansule: I Loved You as Instructed
50) The Grant Incantation: Incant Me

Acknowledgements

Steve thanks:

My mother, Jean, for putting up with The Utopia Strong racket. Lee Brackstone for having faith in this book when we'd lost it. Ben for an incredible job piecing this jigsaw together. Tim Young for our first DJ booking. Rick Morton for the brown M&M's and Nick Teale for his valiant efforts prior to that. Amy Miveld, Simon Crosse, Mike Holt and Chris Peacock Martinez for exposing us to the world! Paul Golder for his unrelenting efforts at Phoenix FM. Johnny O'Carroll and Chris Reeder for having the balls to believe in our album. Lauren Barley and Al Overdrive for press and image brilliance, Garreth Hughes for visual wizardry. Matttech Modular for a great first rig. Dawn Torabi for 'sorting the heads from the haircuts' - the best quote ever! Kavus and Mike for the rollercoaster ride, and beautiful Katie for just being you, and also for our wonderful cover photo. x

Kavus thanks:

To my many friends, musicians or otherwise, who were edited out, marginalised or I just couldn't fit in. Thank you for your continued love and support: David Barclay, Melanie Woods, Ben Hardy, Katharine Blake, Christian Hayes, Jo Spratley, Karen Thrussell, Ben Jacobs, Michael Chapman, Sharron Fortnam, James Larcombe, Rick Morton, Bob Drake, Maggie Thomas, Shona Davidson, Tom Clues, Jane Pannell, Laura Biggs, Jonny Karma, Andy Carne, Spider Stacy, Jon Poole, Matthew Cutts, Jesse Cutts, Malcom 'Scruff' Lewty, Katie Davies, Khyam Allami, Emmett Elvin, Chlöe Herington, Craig Fortnam, Ben Woollacott, Josh Perl, Charlie Cawood, Olly Selwood, Freddy Palmer, Dave Sturt, Fabio

Golfetti, Ian East, Cheb Nettles, Steve Hillage, Miquette Giraudy, Jonny Greene, Jasper Johns, Colin Hill, David J Smith, James Sedwards, Daniel O'Sullivan, Sam Warren, Rob Crow, Rhodri Marsden, Jimmy Martin, Mike Vennart, Joe Lazarus, Mike Hammer, Peter Ward Edwards, Steve Feigenbaum, Kris Smith, the entire Cardiacs family and the entire Torabi, Nevet, Shand and Staple family.

My schoolfriends: Carter Anderson, Matt Tiller, Ash the Destroyer, Tony Hodgetts, Alan McArthur, Nigel Rundle and Andy Wilson.

Steve Davis, Ben Thompson and Lee Brackstone for this ludicrous trip.

Most of all, Dawn and Sima Torabi, who are, miraculously, still talking to me.

Ben thanks:

Steve and Kavus for being more diligent and meticulous than even they probably thought possible; Dan Papps and Rick Morton for their sterling work on early versions of this project; Lee Brackstone for taking us down his White Rabbit hole and for timely injections of enthusiasm and publishing acumen throughout; the Orion A-team, Sarah Fortune, Ellie Freedman, Elizabeth Allen, Natalie Dawkins, Nicole Abel and Helen Ewing, for their professionalism and positive energy; Leila Arab and Graham Massey for knowing this book was a good idea before we'd even started it; Wesley Stace, Richard King, Jon Savage and Matt Thorne for helpful comments along the way; and Vicki Duffey of Bullet Coffee House, Hastings, for splendid on-site catering at the August Bank Holiday DJ Soundclash, for her intuitive grasp of the foibles of humanity and for making an old man very happy.